The Majority Press

IN NOBODY'S BACKYARD: The Grenada Revolution in its Own Words.
Volume II: Facing the World

TONY MARTIN is professor of Black Studies at Wellesley College, Massachusetts. He did his M.A. and Ph.D. in history at Michigan State University and the B.Sc. in economics at the University of Hull, England. In 1965 he qualified as a barrister-at-law at Gray's Inn, London. He has taught at the University of Michigan–Flint, the Cipriani Labor College (Trinidad) and St. Mary's College (Trinidad). He has been visiting professor at the University of Minnesota, Brandeis University and Colorado College. He has authored and edited several books, including *Literary Garveyism: Garvey, Black Arts and the Harlem Renaissance*, *The Pan-African Connection*, *Marcus Garvey, Hero* and *Race First: The Ideological and Organizational Struggles of Marcus Garvey and the Universal Negro Improvement Association.*

DESSIMA WILLIAMS is a Grenadian of tremendous and deep commitment to the cause of her country's rights and those of her people. In the 1970s she was one of the few Grenadians in the United States courageous enough to join the New Jewel Movement and play a leading role in the anti-Gairy struggle. In March 1979 she was appointed ambassador/permanent representative to the Organization of American States. This was followed some months later by a concurrent appointment as deputy governor for Grenada to the World Bank. She travelled widely and frequently as an able and trusted representative of party and government, engaging in bilateral and multilateral diplomacy. Today, still doing the people's work, she heads up the Grenada Foundation, Inc. in New York.

ON GRENADA

No. 1 In Nobody's Backyard: The Grenada Revolution in its Own Words. Vol I: the Revolution at Home

No. 2 In Nobody's Backyard: The Grenada Revolution in its Own Words. Vol. II: Facing the World

No. 3 The Invasion of Grenada: Caribbean and World Responses

In Nobody's Backyard

The Grenada Revolution in its Own Words

Volume II: Facing the World

Edited by
TONY MARTIN

With the assistance of DESSIMA WILLIAMS

On Grenada, No. 2

TM PRESS THE MAJORITY PRESS
Dover, Massachusetts

Library of Congress Cataloging in Publication Data

Main entry under title:

In nobody's backyard.

(On Grenada; no. 1–2)

Contents: v. 1. The revolution at home–v. 2. Facing the world.
1. Grenada–Politics and government–1974– –Addresses, essays, lectures. I. Martin, Tony, 1942–. II. Williams, Dessima. III. Series.
F2056.8.I56 1984 972.98′45 84-23536
ISBN 0-912469-12-9 (v. 1)
ISBN 0-912469-16-1 (v. 2)
ISBN 0-912469-13-7 (pbk. : v. 1)
ISBN 0-912469-17-X (pbk. : v. 2)

First published in 1985, simultaneously in hardbound and paperback volumes.

The Majority Press
P.O. Box 538
Dover, Massachusetts 02030

Printed in the United States of America

To Maurice Bishop, Unison Whiteman, Jacqueline Creft, Norris Bain, Fitzroy Bain, Vincent Noel and all the heroes and martyrs of October 19, 1983.

Poor rags and all tatters
My portion might be,
And yet robbed in Manhood
No slave dwells in me;
The world's dearest mantle
Is true liberty!
—T.A. Marryshow

OTHER BOOKS BY TONY MARTIN

Race First: The Ideological and Organizational Struggles of Marcus Garvey and the Universal Negro Improvement Association

Rare Afro-Americana: A Reconstruction of the Adger Library. (With Wendy Ball)

The Pan-African Connection: From Slavery to Garvey and Beyond

Literary Garveyism: Garvey, Black Arts and the Harlem Renaissance

The Poetical Works of Marcus Garvey

Marcus Garvey, Hero

In Nobody's Backyard: The Grenada Revolution in its Own Words. Volume I: The Revolution at Home. (With the assistance of Dessima Williams)

The Invasion of Grenada: Caribbean and World Responses

Table of Contents

Volume II — Facing the World

PART V – FOREIGN RELATIONS

Volume I — the Revolution at Home

VOLUME II
FACING THE WORLD

PART V

Foreign Relations

Left to right: Arnaldo Tamayo of Cuba, first Black person in space; Prime Minister Maurice Bishop; President Fidel Castro.

Free West Indian

16
General Principles

Introduction

The new direction of the revolution could perhaps be most clearly seen in its foreign policy. Built-in constraints to rapid change perhaps seemed less formidable than in the case of domestic relations. The threat of mercenary attack or United States invasion provided an added impetus for the diplomatic offensive launched by the new government.

Grenada's foreign policy was marked by a fierce independence. The PRG joined the Non-Aligned Movement (headquartered in Cuba in 1979), almost immediately. Despite close and growing friendship with Cuba and the Communist world, the PRG somehow managed to maintain membership in the Socialist International. Whether this was a deliberate reflection of its non-alignment, a simple transitional feature of a changing organization or a tell-tale sign of ideological differences within the movement, can only be the subject of speculation at this time.

Nowhere is the independence of Grenada's foreign policy better demonstrated than in its defiance of the United States. Against Uncle Sam's warnings and threats, revolutionary Grenada mobilized its people, built its army and militia, stockpiled arms, embarked on a diplomatic offensive and engaged the Colossus of the North in a war of words. "No, we are not in anybody's backyard," said Prime Minister Bishop. "The Caribbean is not an American lake," echoed an editorial in the Free West Indian; *"We will decide our own destiny."*

The PRG's foreign policy was also marked by deep solidarity with liberation movements around the world, including the struggles of Black peoples in metropolitan countries.

These new emphases were not developed, however, at the expense of traditional groupings. Grenada retained its membership in the British Commonwealth, the Organization of American States (OAS), the Caribbean Community (Caricom) and the Organization of Eastern Caribbean States (OECS), among others. Caribbean integration remained a dominant foreign policy objective.

THE FOREIGN POLICY OF GRENADA– Statement by the Ministry of External Affairs, May 1981

Principles

Grenada's Foreign Policy is guided by four basic principles.

1) Anti-Imperialism and Non-Alignment
2) Creation of a New International Economic Order.
3) Pursuit of Regional Cooperation and Integration.
4) Promotion of World Peace and Cooperation.

Anti-Imperialism and Non-Alignment

One of the fundamental principles of Grenada's foreign policy was first formulated in 1973 in the Manifesto of the New Jewel Movement, and it is in this context that a major aspect of the People's Revolutionary Government's policy is that of anti-imperialism and non-alignment.

Grenada's firm commitment to the principles of non-alignment informs its policy of resolute opposition to colonialism, neo-colonialism, apartheid, racism (including Zionism), fascism and imperialism; full support for peaceful co-existence and the principles and aims of détente. Prime Minister and Minister of External Affairs Maurice Bishop in addressing the 34th U.N. General Assembly categorically stated that:

> "Non-alignment does not imply for us that we must be neutral in the sterile and negative sense, nor does it imply that our country must regard itself as a political eunuch in the conduct of our international affairs. Our non-aligned policy will certainly not lead us to surrender our independence of judgment in world affairs, or to retreat from our right and duty to fully participate in international forums and discussions concerned with issues vital to our interests, concerns and principles. On the contrary, non-alignment for us is a positive concept characterising a vigorous and principled approach to international issues. It is an affirmation of that fundamental attribute of all peoples and states to sovereignty, independence and the right to freely determine their own domestic and foreign policies."

Furthermore, Grenada's policy of non-alignment and anti-imperialism is manifested by our determination to freely choose our own political and economic system free from all forms of domination and to establish control over our natural and national resources. These remain the foremost objectives of our foreign policy.

New International Economic Order

Grenada regards the present distribution of world economic power as manifestly unjust, especially since the accumulation of such power derives from the long history of imperialist expansion and control of the Third World. The small-island developing countries are especially disadvantaged in this situation, and we regard it as our special responsibility to work for the creation of a New International Economic Order (NIEO).

In clarifying Grenada's conception of this New International Economic Order, Prime Minister Maurice Bishop in his address to the 34th Session of the U.N. General Assembly stated,

> "By the New International Economic Order, we mean the assertion of national sovereignty over the ownership and control of our economic resources. Further, we mean the establishment of the freedom to determine the disposition and use of our resources in whatever ways our people wish, in furtherance of their own aspirations for economic development. We mean the creation of an equitable system of international trade based on just prices for our exports. We mean the opening up of markets internationally, in particular in the wealthy countries to facilitate the growth of exports in the Third World. We mean the establishment of an international agreement on the exploitation of the resources of the sea which would secure a just share of the resources and the wealth generated therefrom for the developing countries.... We desire a new system of international inter-dependence, based on mutual respect for sovereignty and a collective will to put an end to imperialist machinations designed to disrupt our unity and purpose."

Grenada's economy is based on four pillars, namely, agriculture, agro-industries, tourism and fisheries. As a result, the solution to the problems of limited markets, limited resources, lack of skilled manpower resources, underdeveloped money markets and infrastructure are critical to the development of our nation. It is in this context that we resolutely support the North-South Dialogue and continue to work vigorously for the development of economic cooperation among developing countries.

Regional Cooperation and Integration

Because of geographical location and shared historical and cultural experiences, Grenada is naturally linked to the Caribbean and the broader Latin American region. We are therefore firmly committed to strengthening the existing ties in this region.

For us the Caribbean includes not only the English-speaking islands, but in fact all those islands washed by the Caribbean Sea, including the Dutch, French and Spanish-speaking islands together with Belize, Guyana, Suriname and Cayenne.

We are convinced that the Caribbean as herein defined has a natural and close connection with the Continental Caribbean and also the rest of the Latin American region.

This Caribbean and Latin American perspective therefore accounts for our consistent efforts over the past two years to maintain and develop principled and good neighbourly relations with the entire region.

As an expression of our commitment towards deepening and strengthening integration in the region, we have continued to work towards further developing the Caribbean Community (CARICOM),a regional grouping of thirteen English-speaking Caribbean countries.

Our commitment towards sub-regional cooperation was clearly demonstrated in the Declaration of St. George's signed in July 1979. Through this Declaration, the Governments of Grenada, Dominica and St. Lucia undertook to further strengthen the ties of friendship and cooperation between the people and Governments of these three nations.

This commitment had also influenced our position towards the creation of the Organisation of Eastern Caribbean States (OECS), a sub-regional grouping of seven of the smaller islands of the English-speaking Eastern Caribbean, which will be formally inaugurated on July 4, 1981. We believe that this new organisation will be a positive force in strengthening the regional integration movement.

Grenada insists on legal equality for all nation states, mutual respect for sovereignty, territorial integrity, ideological pluralism, non-interference in the internal affairs of other states and the right of every country to develop its own process in its own way free from all forms of outside dictation and pressure.

Peace and Cooperation

World peace and cooperation is an important aspect of Grenada's foreign policy. This derives from Grenada's realisation that without peace and cooperation there can be no progressive development. When tension prevails, it means that a tremendous amount of resources is diverted to unproductive and often dangerous and destructive military purposes.

These enormous resources can be much more gainfully employed in the provision of material goods and services for the upliftment of society and the improvement of living conditions of the people of this world.

Since the New Jewel Movement and the People's Revolutionary Government are firmly committed to the improvement of the material conditions of the people, it is logical that our policy be rooted in the principles of peace and cooperation. For this reason the People's Revolutionary Government has pursued an active policy of principled relations and cooperation with all countries of the world.

It is also for this reason that at the 9th General Assembly of the Organisation of American States in La Paz, Bolivia, in October 1979, Grenada took the initiative to secure the passage of a resolution that the Caribbean Sea be declared a Zone of Peace. Subsequently at the 35th session of the U.N. General Assembly in October 1980, Grenada proposed specifically that the Member States adopt measures to:

1) Prohibit the introduction of nuclear weapons in the region;
2) Stop all military manoeuvres in the region;
3) Dismantle all foreign military bases that exist in our area;
4) End the colonization of all territories once and for all;
5) Establish machinery to end all forms of aggression, including assassinations, mercenary invasion, propaganda intervention and diplomatic and economic pressure.

IN NOBODY'S BACKYARD

"No, we are not in anybody's backyard."

This fact, stressed by Prime Minister and Minister of Foreign Affairs, Maurice Bishop, aptly sums up the PRG's foreign policy. It is realistic, active, consistently principled, uncompromisable, and an outgrowth of the national, grassroots democracy formed by the Revolution.

Shortly after the Revolution, Grenada was accepted as a member of the anti-imperialist Movement of Non-Aligned Nations, which represents the interests of two-thirds of humanity.

Speaking at the Movement's sixth summit conference in Havana on September 6, 1979, PM Bishop stressed that Grenada shared the Movement's core principles: "A firm commitment to the establishment of an international community, based on the principles of opposition to colonialism, neo-colonialism, apartheid, racism (including Zionism) fascism and imperialism."

Despite increasing hostility and pressure from imperialism, and faced with three forms of destabilisation—propaganda, economic and violence—the PRG has not bent.

This has brought Grenada international prestige and esteem, new friends worldwide and given Grenadians greater national identity, dignity and pride.

"Forward Ever" expresses a concrete direction against imperialism and towards greater self-sufficiency and genuine national independence. It expresses the desire for friendships based on mutual cooperation, respect for national goals and on non-exploitation.

Denying the right to exploit is tied directly to the principled anti-imperialist stance and the deepest desire for friendship with all peoples, including those ruled or misled by unfriendly regimes.

The PRG repeatedly stresses its fervent desire for and incessantly works towards, fraternal relations with all governments, including the United States, based on respect for sovereignty. Detente is also seriously urged.

Grenada's foreign policy asserts that the right of self-determination must be respected, fought for and protected. It recognises and advocates that the region's peoples are moving to build one united Caribbean and one united Latin America.

The PM's call for the Caribbean to be declared a zone of peace would not only reduce militarism, but would help local peoples accelerate their badly-needed economic take-off and subsequent social development.

Grenada, for instance, must now divest scarce funds, resources and personnel for defensive purposes, because of the ever-lurking menace of invasion and violent counter-revolution. This slows down the rate of overall development projects, and also puts extra financial burden on an economy already strained by previous corruption, mismanagement and the bitter tailwinds of capitalism's aggravating global crisis.

Solidarity with the struggles of oppressed everywhere is an important plank in the PRG's foreign policy. Yet Grenada does not "export" revolution; non-interference in the internal affairs of other nations is a sacred, defended principle of PRG policy.

The PRG's anti-imperialist stance is based on the sensible need to reduce what the PM calls "truly frightening" world tensions. Recognising that peace is the life-saving business of all, and that developed countries and rich war-mongers, for whom war is good business, cannot be left to decide humanity's fate, the PRG struggles for peace.

It understands that peace and justice are indivisible, and that world peace depends on reversing uneven, unequal, parasitic development. Thus Grenada joins the world's peoples in calling for a new international economic order and a new international information order, that would end imperialist manipulation of finances, resources, information, news, values and resulting attitudes and lifestyles.

Imperialism vainly tries to create the myth that Grenada is a "Cuban pawn" and the latest "casualty" of "Soviet adventurism." This is designed to obscure the genuine progress and advances that Grenada is making, with the generous and unselfish assistance of countries, organisations and individuals throughout the world.

"Don't listen to foreign propaganda. Come and see for yourself," the PM advises.

In response to its positive foreign policy role, Grenada now finds itself the site of numerous conferences and visits by special interest groups and organised tours.

It also actively participates in prestigious international fora. With a population of only about 110,000 its representatives sit on important bureaux and committees of regional and international organisations.

Since the Revolution, a number of friendship and support groups have been formed abroad to give moral and financial support and material and human assistance.

Grenada has signified its willingness to accept aid from any sources, provided it is principled, and does not come with strings or unacceptable conditions.

It has also stressed that ideological pluralism must be respected in practice, as must self-determination, and the sovereignty, legal equality and territorial integrity of the region's nations.

Exploited and developing countries must be free to organise and unite to facilitate their economic and social development, it insists.

Grenada's foreign policy is an extension of its domestic policy. The people cannot be free from exploitation and foreign domination, unless the government adopts a principled, progressive and non-aligned world policy.

Similarly, no one nation can be truly free, unless all are free. And so, Grenada's Revolution belongs not only to Grenadians, not only to the Caribbean, but to all struggling peoples.

FWI, March 13, 1981

WHY THEY WANT TO CRUSH US

Prime Minister Maurice Bishop last Sunday night gave to over 5,000 Grenadians, a number of reasons why imperialism is bent on crushing the popular Grenada Revolution.

He was addressing a rally at the Market Square, St. George's, to commemorate the 94th birthday of Jamaican national hero Marcus Garvey, and to demonstrate Grenada's defiance to the threat of U.S. military invasion.

The rally was co-sponsored by the Media Workers' Association of Free Grenada (MWAFG).

Addressing the gathering was Phillip Agee, former CIA officer and representatives of progressive regional organisations.

The first reason PM Bishop gave, was that "we in tiny brave Grenada have led the first successful revolution in the English-speaking Caribbean."

"Here is a small Caribbean people, brave enough to challenge and take up arms against imperialism," he explained.

Grenada has "embarked on a new foreign policy" and "the U.S. imperialists are aware that oppressed blacks in the U.S. will identify with the Grenada Revolution," said PM Bishop.

They have also claimed that "our strategic location" along their oil and bauxite routes is bothering them, and therefore they are out to crush the Revolution.

Imperialism has tried hard to turn back this process from the beginning in many different ways, including use of the notorious "pyramid plan" drawn up by the CIA.

"We have seen propaganda destabilisation and economic warfare against our country," PM Bishop went on, giving numerous examples.

"They used terrorist violence against innocent Grenadians, causing the loss of many young lives, but failed to turn back the Revolution. After local terrorists, with CIA backing, failed, imperialism decided on the ultimate course—direct military invasion.

"Reagan and his warlords are losing more credibility every day.

"World public opinion, as a result of the change in the balance of forces, is a very important factor," he added.

If imperialism "have forgotten the lessons they got in Cuba, Vietnam and Angola, among many others, we will teach them all over again," PM Bishop stated to thunderous applause.

PM Bishop also explained that "Garvey fought a struggle to bring justice to the common man. For this he was imprisoned and persecuted."

Parallels can be drawn here today, he said. Imperialism is attempting "to persecute and confuse our people, because we too struggle for a better and brighter day."

Referring to U.S. Rear-Admiral Robert P. McKenzie's criticism that Grenada, Cuba and Nicaragua, are one country, PM Bishop said he was correct. "We are basically one people, united in the anti-imperialist spirit."

FWI, **August 29, 1981**

HISTORY IS ON OUR SIDE

Within the past few days, peace-loving Grenadians have viewed with increased concern, but not surprise, U.S. imperialism's escalating campaign of lies and slander against the Cuban, Nicaraguan and Grenadian Revolutions, and its announced plans for military action against the three freest countries of the Western Hemisphere.

Because of our close fraternal bonds with the Nicaraguan and Cuban peoples, we are gravely concerned about the imperialist threats to their freedom, as we are concerned about the threats to our own national security.

We are not surprised by imperialism's criminality, because we understand that when the peoples of Cuba, Nicaragua and Grenada cast aside the yokes of dictatorship and begin to chart their destiny along freedom's road, they created a shining moral example for the oppressed masses of Latin America and the Caribbean, an example deemed dangerous by imperialism.

History has taught us that whenever a freedom-loving people choose their own path to development, resist all attempts at exploitation, break out the chains of economic and cultural dependency and ideological hegemony and begin to create the conditions for social equality, justice and progress, the forces of reaction will rant and rave with predictable hysteria.

These three revolutions in the Western Hemisphere have created popular people's democracies (as distinct from parliamentary hypocrisies) in a part of the world which has been under U.S. imperialism's dominance for generations.

They have begun to pose serious alternatives to the capitalist system of economic and social organisation. Indeed, they have called into question the most fundamental precepts of Western civilization.

Imperialism will not leave us alone because it cannot. It will oppose us because it must. It acts according to a law of history: the law of opposing and contending forces. Furthermore, its deepening economic crisis forces it to invent scapegoats, to fabricate enemies. For the military-industrial complex which dictates imperialism's foreign policy, the only solution to the economic crisis in capitalism is the production and sale of more and more arms which inevitably means military aggression and war.

And what more convenient targets for a war policy than three small revolutionary countries which are bold and brave enough to defy imperialism and everything it symbolises.

So first, we see and hear on the empire's mass media the vile propaganda weaved on the looms of the psychological war machine: lies, slander, deceptions, distortions, disinformation–all designed to "soften up" public opinion to accept the pretexts and justifications for the guns, the tanks, the bombs and the planes that will wreak murderous destruction on innocent people, whose only crime is their love of freedom and justice.

And just as the system of imperialism must oppose the courageous efforts of these three revolutions, so too must they obey an historical law to resist with sweat and blood its wicked attempts at re-enslavement.

The peoples of Cuba, Nicaragua and Grenada must obey the historical law which demands that they deepen their unity, strengthen their discipline, increase production, step up their vigilance and fortify their military defences.

History can rightfully make these demands because history is on our side.

FWI, November 14, 1981

THE CARIBBEAN IS NOT AN AMERICAN LAKE

Ronald Reagan is in Barbados, on the second leg of his two-island jaunt through the Caribbean, which began with a brief stopover in Jamaica on Wednesday.

Two things stand out in the U.S. President's brief passage through our region. The first in Jamaica, where Reagan, while holding extensive talks with his close ally, Jamaican Prime Minister Edward Seaga, refused to meet with constitutional Leader of the Opposition Michael Manley.

This decision goes against all the traditions of that country where the post of leader of the opposition is deeply respected and where the polls indicate that the holder of that post is still the most popular political figure.

But Reagan has never been a respecter of our traditions. In the same way as he has chosen to ignore and undermine the Caribbean Development Bank and Caricom by his "Bi-lateral" aid agreements under the Caribbean Basin Initiative (CBI), he now chooses to slap the Jamaican people in the face by ignoring their institution of Leader of the Opposition.

The other thing is the report that from Barbadian soil Reagan will issue the second in a series of radio broadcasts on major issues to the American people.

If nothing else underlines the contempt with which Reagan and his entourage view the Caribbean people, then this decision to use our soil to speak to the United States on issues like El Salvador, where he backs the bloody junta, like the Caribbean Basin Initiative, which has nothing in it of substance for the islands, is sufficient confirmation.

But before fully establishing himself on Barbadian soil, Reagan has launched another full scale attack against Grenada, saying we are threatened by Marxism and that Grenada will now attempt to "spread the virus among its neighbours."

While Ronald Reagan was spreading this slander, over two hundred managers of state enterprises were meeting here to democratically discuss how they will put together the first Three Year Plan of economic construction beginning in 1983.

While Ronald Reagan was spreading this slander, members of the Seamen and Waterfront Workers Trade Union together with representatives of the People's Revolutionary Government and the public were opening Otway House, another symbol of workers' unity and workers' strength in Free Grenada.

Reagan in his slander may really have a message for the Caribbean people. Yes, the Grenadian Revolution may well be spreading a virus. But it is the virus of democracy, the virus of unity, the virus of freedom for the people of the region.

Reagan, remember, we are the sons of slaves and indentured servants who made the journey across in shackles and poverty. We may have our differences, but these are our rocks in the Caribbean Sea. We will solve our problems without you dictating to us what we are or what we must be. The Caribbean is not an American lake.

We will decide our own destiny.

FWI, April 10, 1982

FORGING A PRINCIPLED FOREIGN POLICY

The recent state visit to France by Prime Minister, Maurice Bishop has been an extremely significant, historic and beneficial one in a number of important ways. However, there is one area which stands out, above all else, as the most singularly important one to have benefitted from the visit, and that is Grenada's foreign policy.

From the earliest days of the Revolution, its leaders have explained in very clear and precise terms, the principled foreign policy which would guide and shape the nature of the relationships Grenada would have with countries throughout the world. From the earliest days too, Grenada reserved the fundamental right to develop an independent, non-aligned foreign policy, without pressure from any quarter. In much the same way that no country would influence our internal political affairs, so too, no country would influence our foreign policy.

One major, single important feature of Grenada's foreign policy, even from the earliest days of the Revolution, has been its commitment to the process of regional integration in general, and the genuine concern for the development process as it relates to small poor states, such as comprise the Organization of Eastern Caribbean States (OECS).

Grenada has consistently struggled on behalf of the small poor states of the Eastern Caribbean at every major regional and international forum at which it was represented. This has been Grenada's position at the United Nations General Assembly, at the OAS General Assembly, at the Commonwealth Heads of Government Conference, and at the Non-Aligned Summit.

Grenada's commitment to the small poor states of the Eastern Caribbean has been so in the forefront of its foreign policy, that it led to Grenada's appeal on behalf of Dominica, before the Havana Non-Aligned Summit in the wake of Hurricane David.

Recently, however, it has led to the extension by France, of the Fund for Aid and Co-operation (FAC) to the small poor states of the Eastern Caribbean.

Grenada's principled foreign policy in the post-revolutionary period, is in glaring contrast to the non-policy programme of the former regime. This foreign policy reveals, in very concrete terms, that the way forward can no longer be based on insular positions taken by individual small territories, since the survival of the region as a whole, and of the Eastern Caribbean in particular, depends on firm, principled unity.

The upcoming Caricom Heads of Government conference must, therefore, be used as yet another base for concretizing action plans for cementing Caribbean unity in a very serious way. The time has certainly come when all the glib talk of unity must give way to concrete action. Already, by its actions on several occasions, Grenada has shown itself ready and committed to action in the cause of forging genuine unity.

FWI, September 29, 1982

17
New Issues for an Activist Policy

Introduction

The new militant foreign policy caused revolutionary Grenada to adopt positions on many issues that most Caribbean nations have traditionally ignored. Support was forthcoming for the Polisario Front and for struggles in East Timor and Kampuchea. Unlike the rest of the English-speaking Caribbean, Grenada supported Argentina in the Malvinas (Falklands) War against Britain. The PRG supported the Palestine Liberation Organization and denounced Zionism. It called for the Indian Ocean to be made a zone of peace and protested U.S. development of the neutron bomb. And the Reagan administration in the United States took especial umbrage at Grenada's vote against a United Nations draft resolution alleging a Soviet invasion of Afghanistan.

GRENADA'S POSITION ON AFGHANISTAN

The following is the text of a message by Prime Minister Maurice Bishop following Grenada's vote against the United Nations draft resolution condemning the Soviet presence in Afghanistan:

Our position was based on the fact that all the evidence that we had, very firmly indicated that this was not an invasion. This is really, I think, what we need to stress. But it really amounted to a call, which is a fairly usual and common call, for assistance from one independent country to another in circumstances where a military invasion by other forces—what we will call the rebels from Third World countries (at least one Third World country)—was definitely on the horizon. And in this situation, it seems that we have a duty to support what is a well recognized position that is enshrined in the United Nations Charter: that one country can always respond to another sovereign country's appeal for assistance in the face of a military threat. This is how we see the Afghanistan situation primarily.

I will point out additionally, that the Union of Soviet Socialist Republics and Afghanistan have a defense treaty as of the middle of 1978, and that again, of course, is their sovereign right. They do have a right to engage in mutual defense pacts and to bring those treaties into force once external invasion or other forms of aggression contemplated by the treaties are in fact imminent. We certainly support fully, the right of Afghanistan to call on any country, including the Soviet Union, which she decides to do, in any circumstances or rather in circumstances as these, where external aggression is being faced.

One of the things that has come out of this whole situation is the open hypocrisy of several countries around the world, some in the region—countries that have, for example, [never] condemned the white South African troops that are today in Rhodesia; countries that have never supported economic sanctions against South Africa; countries that have remained completely silent when France last year went into the Central African Empire to topple Bokassa. Now some of these same countries that were silent are coming out and making all kinds of noises. We cannot support that "two-stand" position.

As a revolutionary country, we see the world revolutionary processes as being of paramount importance; and therefore, it's our firm view that we have a right, a duty and a responsibility to support any principled position that would assist the movement forward of the world revolutionary process.

I will end by saying that in our view, the situation in Afghanistan is not really a threat to international peace and security. We are not aware of any third country being threatened by events now taking place in Afghanistan and we believe that is also an important factor.

Grenada News, January–February 1980

PRG CONDEMNS ISRAEL

The People's Revolutionary Government (PRG) has said that it and the entire people of Grenada "join in the worldwide condemnation" of last weekend's savage massacre of over 3,000 Palestinian refugees in West Beirut, Lebanon.

"This wanton butchery of innocent and defenceless men, women, children and babies in their homes and in the streets of West Beirut," the PRG said, must be recorded as one of "this century's most bestial crimes against humanity."

It added: "Apparently not satisfied with the destruction, pillage, pain and suffering they inflicted through their systematic bombardment of Palestinian refugee camps since they invaded sovereign Lebanon on June 6, the Israeli Zionists have now callously allowed their right-wing Falangist clients to gun down hundreds of unarmed Palestinians in a monstrous display of 20th century barbarism.

"The United States Government cannot escape moral responsibility for this horrific act of genocide since they have armed the Zionists and their Falangist puppets to the teeth and have consistently refused to pressure the fanatical elite that rules Israel into abandoning its policy of terrorism against the Palestinian and Arab peoples."

The PRG said that Wednesday's rejection by Israel's fascist rulers of their own people's call for a full-scale investigation into the massacre, "clearly indicates that the terrorist Begin regime is guilty of the Beirut atrocity and is as contemptuous and intransigent towards Israeli public opinion as it is towards the outcries by the world's peoples for justice towards the Palestinian people."

The PRG called for Israel's "immediate and unconditional withdrawal from Beirut, from Lebanon and from the occupied territories on the West Bank."

It also reaffirmed "staunch support for the Palestinian Liberation Organisation (PLO) and for the immediate establishment of a peaceful, independent and sovereign Palestinian state on the West Bank and Gaza."

The Grenada Peace Council (GPC) has also condemned the massacre, as "the worst human disaster in recent times, so reminiscent of the Nazi tyranny and butchery of World War II" and as "direct threats to peace in the Middle East and a wilful and blatant attempt at frustrating peace initiatives throughout the world.

FWI, September 25, 1982

PRG PROTESTS DREADED BOMB

"With shock and concern," the People's Revolutionary Government (PRG) has joined other peace-loving governments and organisations throughout the world, in condemning U.S. President Ronald Reagan's decision to go ahead with production of the dreaded neutron bomb.

The neutron bomb is designed to kill people and all living creatures by intense radiation within 70 kilometres of wherever it is dropped, without damaging buildings or property.

The PRG says its concern "is based on the knowledge of the danger that such a weapon can cause to humankind."

"That this bomb kills people and does not affect property, clearly shows its inhuman and anti-human nature," it adds.

The PRG said it does not accept the U.S. argument that when produced, the bomb will only be stockpiled within the U.S., and not in any other country.

Clearly production is the first step before pressures are mounted on North Atlantic Treaty Organisation (NATO) allies in Western Europe to station such a bomb there, it predicted. "This will mean an increase in deadly weapons in Europe, with all that this implies."

In any event, the PRG stated it is "clearly opposed to production of this bomb, regardless of where it is to be stored."

That Reagan cynically chose the 36th anniversary of the day in 1945, when the U.S. dropped the world's first atom bomb on Hiroshima, Japan, to announce his decision, "borders on sadism."

It "clearly shows the contempt which the present U.S. administration holds for the people of the world, who have been repeatedly expressing their opposition to the production of the neutron bomb," the PRG said.

Put in the context of the Reagan administration's refusal to ratify the Strategic Arms Limitation Treaty (SALT II) with the Soviet Union, or to sit down and discuss practical methods of reducing the arms race, the PRG said, "it becomes clear that no one in the world would be safe, once the U.S. has manufactured this weapon."

Grenada stands fully committed to peace, "so fully necessary for the development of the underdeveloped countries of the world," the PRG stressed.

"The massive sums of money being spent on the development of such weapons and the arms race, would serve a better purpose if channelled into assisting the world's poor countries in developing their economies and raising the quality of life of their peoples," the PRG concluded.

Britain's Opposition leader Michael Foot said his Labour Party is "deeply hostile" to the neutron bomb's development, which would not help disarmament.

"One of the most dangerous and nauseating features of the neutron bomb is that it lowers the nuclear threshold, and could lead us further towards the maniacal idea of a form of so-called limited nuclear warfare," Foot said.

The Soviet news agency Tass described the nuclear warhead as "the most inhuman type of weapon of mass annihilation," adding that the U.S.

had deliberately ignored a Soviet proposal for mutual reunification [sic] of neutron weapons.

"The step designed to bring the world closer to a nuclear catastrophe is depicted in Washington as the prerogative of the U.S. administration," Tass said.

The Soviet Union "cannot remain an indifferent bystander and will have to respond to the challenge in a manner demanded by the interests of the security of the Soviet people and their allies," Tass observed.

FWI, August 15, 1981

18
The Caribbean

Introduction

The Caribbean area in general, and the English-speaking territories in particular, provided Grenada's most intimate traditional links. The immediate official reaction to the events of March 13, 1979 in most of the English-speaking countries was one of shock mixed with fear and disapproval. The governments of Forbes Burnham in Guyana and Michael Manley in Jamaica were the major exceptions. They both immediately welcomed the new regime and delivered emergency supplies of food, arms and technical expertise.

NJM emissaries were intercepted in Trinidad waters, detained and expelled without acceptance of their requests to meet with government officials. Prime Minister Eric Williams of Trinidad refused to open letters addressed to him by Prime Minister Bishop. Trinidad defended its refusal to extend formal recognition to Grenada by saying that Trinidad had no policy of recognition or non-recognition. Resumption of normal intercourse would be tantamount to recognition.

The West Indies Associated States (WISA—precursor to the seven member Organization of Eastern Caribbean States) initially refused to recognize the new government. Its Eastern Caribbean Currency Authority withheld delivery of currency notes due to member state Grenada. The money was eventually delivered after a threat by Grenada to develop its own independent Central Bank. An April 1979 meeting of the Caricom (Caribbean Community) council of ministers had to be postponed due to refusal of most of the WISA states to meet with Grenada.

Shortlived liberal administrations in St. Lucia and Dominica gâve Grenada an opportunity to break out of this attempt at isolation by WISA. And so on July 14, 1979 the Declaration of St. Georges was signed by the new administrations of George Odlum (St. Lucia), Oliver Seraphine (Dominica) and the People's Revolutionary Government. Both St. Lucia and Dominica were before long to change to regimes less favorable to Grenada but the declaration helped Grenada break out of the attempted isolation. Its Eastern Caribbean neighbours were strengthened in their acceptance, however grudging, of the fait accompli *in Grenada.*

Prime Minister Tom Adams of Barbados early loomed as the NJM's major adversary in the region, a position he maintained up to October 1983. Grenadian government officials were often harassed and refused normal diplomatic privileges when passing through the Barbados airport. PRG minister, Unison Whiteman, was manhandled at the airport in November 1980. This incident fuelled an intense war of words between the two countries. Adams attacked Grenada during a November 1980 broadcast on the night of President Ronald Reagan's election victory in the United States. The Grenada press was by now referring to Adams as "Uncle Tom" and a "yard fowl." Prime Minister Bishop suggested that Adams had advance knowledge of a June 19, 1980 bomb blast aimed against the PRG leadership.

The relation of forces against Grenada was strengthened considerably by late 1980 with the accession to power of Eugenia Charles in Dominica, Edward Seaga in Jamaica and Ronald Reagan in the United States. Charles replaced the pro-Grenada interim Seraphine administration. Seaga replaced Michael Manley, Grenada's staunchest friend in the Anglophone Caribbean, and Ronald Reagan replaced the less hostile (though not friendly) Jimmy Carter. This sudden change in the political climate of the region augured ill for revolutionary Grenada. The three newly elected leaders, together with Adams, kept up a sustained onslaught against the PRG which was to culminate in the United States invasion of October 1983. Significantly, Adams, Charles and Seaga were Reagan's main accomplices in the October invasion.

Still, the new conservative axis could boast of no early dramatic victories against the PRG. Without the gratuitous assistance of the ultraleft coup of October 1983 they may have grown into nothing worse than a constant thorn in Grenada's side. For the Grenadian revolution had by 1980 consolidated to the point where it was able to score some impressive victories against the conservative regional onslaught. Early coolness in the two major regional associations had been all but overcome. In fact, Grenada had quickly emerged as a dynamic and influential member of both Caricom and WISA.

By 1980 Grenada was able to host a Caricom health ministers conference and the community's foreign ministers met there in 1981. The Caricom summit of 1982, the first in over a decade, was a diplomatic victory for Grenada. It first beat back attempts by the conservative axis to expel

Grenada, raise "human rights" as a Caricom issue and insist on Westminster type political systems as a condition of Caricom membership. The Grenada delegation then went on to win acceptance for its own priorities. The Declaration of Ocho Rios which came out of this meeting included the following concerns of revolutionary Grenada—an acceptance of ideological pluralism; non-interference in the internal affairs of member states; disapproval of foreign military activity in the region; and an insistence on external aid with no strings attached. Grenada also performed well at the summit conference of 1983 in Trinidad.

The Organization of Eastern Caribbean States (OECS) treaty was signed in St. Kitts but launched in Grenada on July 4, 1981 during the Caricom foreign ministers' meeting. This was not much more than two years after the predecessor organization, WISA (West Indies Associated States), had sought to ostracize Grenada. There were seven signatories to the treaty, namely Grenada, St. Vincent and the Grenadines, Antigua, Dominica, Montserrat, St. Lucia and St. Kitts-Nevis. The OECS treaty provided for mutual defense and security but would, as the executive secretary of WISA explained in June 1981, "constitute no threat to national sovereignty...." Other major areas of concern for the treaty were foreign affairs and regional unity and cooperation.

Grenada's support for Caricom and the OECS was reflective of its deep commitment to regional integration. The PRG strongly supported the preservation of the University of the West Indies as a regional institution, proposed common textbooks for West Indian school students, advocated cheaper regional transport and urged the elimination of visas for travel within the region. It emphasized the need to break down the barriers separating the Anglophone Caribbean from the rest of the region.

The PRG's West Indian initiatives won some support even from the hostile conservative axis. This was dramatically illustrated in 1981 when the United States attempted to exclude Grenada from U.S. funds loaned to the Caribbean Development Bank (CDB). Both Tom Adams and Eugenia Charles supported the regional refusal to countenance such an undisguised interference in the region's internal business. Charles nevertheless complained that Grenada's politics constituted a barrier to the flow of foreign funds to the CDB.

Grenada's successes in Caricom, the OECS and the CDB did not, of course, signal an end to the problems in the region. Grenada's nationals and residents were sometimes subject to harassment and expulsion at the region's sea and airports. Trinidad and St. Vincent were among the nations joining Barbados in occasionally making life difficult for visiting Grena-

dians. Trinidad's harassment of Grenadian residents and visitors predated (and continued after) the revolution, despite the Grenadian origin of a sizeable proportion of its own population. The PRG's minister of education, Jacqueline Creft, had had her work permit revoked while employed in Trinidad in 1977.

Much official West Indian hostility to the PRG was doubtless due to the fact that revolutionary Grenada became a rallying point for a wide assortment of Caribbean old and new left groups. These included the Workers' Party of Jamaica, the Working People's Alliance (Guyana), the National Joint Action Committee (Trinidad), the Movement for National Liberation (Barbados), the People's Progressive Movement (Trinidad), the Dominica Liberation Movement, the Puerto Rican Socialist Party, the Communist Party of Guadeloupe, the Antiguan Caribbean Liberation Movement and the People's Progressive Party (Guyana).

Only in the case of Guyana, where Forbes Burnham's ruling People's National Congress had been one of Grenada's earliest supporters in the region, did the NJM's support for opposition groupings not lead to strained relations. Cheddi Jagan and Walter Rodney, leaders of Guyana's major opposition parties, were both very popular in Grenada. Maurice Bishop pointedly insisted on calling Rodney's death in 1980 an "assassination," as against one of his own ministers, who had sought to use more neutral language in the interest of good relations with Burnham. Burnham apparently remained unruffled and was among the minority of Caricom states opposing the United States invasion of 1983.

OF YARD FOWLS, UNCLE TOMS AND POLITICAL CRAPAUDS, OF HYPOCRISY, SPITE AND INTIMIDATION

Despite the accelerated movement toward progressive political change in the Caribbean, imperialism still has a substantial influence on governmental decision making and the formation of public opinion in many territories in the region.

The influence on governmental decision making is facilitated by the economic dependence on imperialism and is exercised through imperialism's relationship with, and sometimes, control of, certain Caribbean political leaders.

The influence on public opinion is facilitated by and exercised through imperialism's relationship with, and sometimes, control of, certain newspapers and radio stations in the region.

This is what Finance Minister, Brother Bernard Coard, was talking about on November 4 at the mass rally at Queens Park when he described certain Caribbean political leaders as "yard fowls and uncle toms" and on November 18 at the "Bloody Sunday" commemoration rally at Seamoon when he again lashed out at them, this time describing them as "political crapauds."

It is in this context that we must see the attacks on the Grenada revolution by Antiguan Deputy Prime Minister, Lester Bird and Barbados Foreign Minister Henry Forde. (A Barbados newspaper recently commented on the apparent influence which Washington exercises over Bridgetown's foreign policy direction).

It is in this context that we must see the continuing attacks on the revolution by the regional (and lately the international) media, led by Ken Gordon's "Trinidad Express."

It is in this context that we must see the continuing refusal of the Trinidad government to recognise the PRG as the legitimate government of Grenada, to the point where the head of government in that country does not even bother to open, much less read, letters sent to him by Prime Minister Maurice Bishop.

These are well planned and orchestrated actions which result directly from the substantial influence, and in some cases, control, which U.S. imperialism and its allies in the industrial developed world still exercise over events in the Caribbean and in particular over some of the region's political leaders.

But imperialism's control of "yard fowls, uncle toms and political crapauds" cannot by itself turn back the democratic struggles of the Caribbean people. So we get threats of naval blockades, U.S. military manoeuvres in Caribbean waters, increased U.S. military presence in Florida and Guantanamo Bay, the involvement of "American ships" in a murderous and destructive plot to overthrow the PRG and most recently the refusal of the British government to allow Grenada to buy two armoured cars in the U.K. to strengthen our security forces.

Consider this hypocrisy: Britain has been known to sell offensive weapons to racist and fascist South Africa. She allows British based Barclays Bank to give its South African employees paid leave to go and kill black freedom fighters.

She said not a word when two of her European allies collaborated in boosting South Africa's nuclear potential. And then she turns around and refuses to sell two paltry armoured cars to Grenada, a country under constant threat of outside aggression. This position is hypocritical and spiteful, and smacks of an attempt to intimidate the PRG. And then again maybe it is not in Britain's interest to assist Grenada in preparing to resist outside aggression.

But not to worry. We will get our armoured cars elsewhere.

In the meanwhile let the imperialists understand that the attempts to intimidate our government and demoralise our people will fail just as the destabilization attempts of their "yard fowls, uncle toms and political crapauds" also failed.

FORWARD EVER BACKWARD NEVER.

FWI, December 8, 1979

PRG OPPOSES SEPARATE FINANCING OF UWI

The People's Revolutionary Government (PRG) is opposed to the proposal that the University of the West Indies (UWI) should be restructured with each of the three campuses in Trinidad, Barbados and Jamaica, funded by their respective governments.

A release from the Ministry of Education states that while the Government recognizes the need for restructuring and supports the idea of campus councils with more decision-making power at the campus level, the financing of UWI should remain centrally controlled, and countries should continue to pay their contributions to a central University Grants Committee.

This position was taken in the interest of regional integration and broader educational opportunity for Caribbean people, it said.

It added that Grenada opposed the proposal for separate financing of the three campuses for five main reasons:

Firstly, it said, the PRG is "convinced" that separate financing will inevitably lead to the break up of UWI as a regional university, because real financial control and decision-making will be in the hands not of a central body—but of the government of the individual campus territory.

It should be noted, the statement said, that the inter-government committee set up since 1975, under the chairmanship of eminent Caribbean scholar William Demas, reported that central financing was essential to prevent the total disintegration of UWI.

"Such a fate for UWI would be a severe blow to the regional integration movement, since UWI is one of the few regional institutions that brings together Caribbean people around common objectives and aspirations and which embodies the concept of a one, united Caribbean identity."

Secondly, it said, the PRG has noted that the people closest to UWI, such as the Guilds of Undergraduates and the West Indies Group of University Teachers, have all publicly opposed the idea of separate funding.

The PRG said it also supports the argument originally raised by the Mona Academic Board that separate funding will lead to a drop in standards. "A strong regional university is better able to maintain academic standards and attract the most competent lecturers than a loose association of three universities."

Standards will also decline from a lack of finance for staff and facilities because any time one island has financial problems, the university will suffer, the statement said.

"UWI's strength and the widespread international recognition for its degrees have come about largely because it has been regionally integrated and centrally funded."

Fourthly, the PRG believes the islands which would lose most by this arrangement will be the smaller, lesser developed, non-campus territories of the region. Given their smaller economies and population, it will be difficult to have universities of their own.

The idea of subordinating the Extra-mural departments into the respective national education systems of the smaller islands is further evidence of the disintegration of UWI's regional character, with the lion's share going to the campus territories.

With separate financing, students from the smaller non-campus territories are likely to face increased costs and disproportionate competition for university placement.

Finally, the PRG said, it opposes the proposal because it firmly recognises that UWI "is one of the few regional institutions that has concrete practical relevance to the people."

This is so because it provides an internationally recognised university qualification to those who enter it and a mechanism for further cementing a sense of regional oneness and identity through the lasting friendships which are made by students from the region who attend it.

The statement concluded: "UWI was established since 1948. It has grown up with the region. The resources of Caribbean countries have been collectively invested in it. The hopes of Caribbean youth for more and better university education are set on it. Its degrees are internationally recognised, Let us keep it regional, united and strong."

FWI, October 2, 1982

PRESERVE UWI IN RODNEY'S MEMORY

The New Jewel Movement says that the most fitting honour to the memory of Guyanese politician-scholar Dr. Walter Rodney, would be preservation of the University of the West Indies (UWI) as a regional institution.

Dr. Rodney, a graduate and lecturer of UWI in Jamaica and leader of Guyana's Working People's Alliance (WPA), was assassinated by a bomb blast in a car in Georgetown on June 13, 1980.

In a statement marking the third anniversary of his assassination, the NJM called Dr. Rodney "one of the most outstanding intellectuals of the Caribbean and a champion of the struggles of working people in the region and, in particular, in his native Guyana."

His contribution was however not limited to the Caribbean, NJM said, noting that Dr. Rodney has been publicly commended by Tanzanian President Julius Nyerere and Zimbabwe Prime Minister Robert Mugabe, "for his support of and contribution to the national liberation struggles in Africa."

Dr. Rodney also lectured at the University of Tanzania, and among his works were "How Europe Underdeveloped Africa" and "A History of the Upper Guinea Coast, 1545–1800."

His murder, NJM said, took place only a short time after the assassination of Archbishop Oscar Romero of El Salvador and was followed, almost immediately, by the attempt to wipe out the entire NJM leadership, with the bomb blast at Queen's Park on June 19, 1980.

This, said NJM, "was a true reflection of the desperation of imperialism in that period, a desperation which has since increased."

It said that Dr. Rodney's life and work will always be remembered and honoured by all democratic and progressive forces in the Caribbean and throughout the world, and the anniversary of his death is "a time for us to reflect" on UWI's future.

Dr. Rodney, NJM noted, was a product of UWI, a staunch regionalist, a supporter of genuine academic freedom, and an academic who saw his education as coming through the sweat of the working people and used it to further their interest.

"It is for this reason that he was expelled from the UWI campus in Jamaica in 1968," it said.

NJM therefore called for the preservation of UWI "as an institution of the highest academic standards, free from interference by those opposed to the unity of the Caribbean people, and opposed to the struggle for bread and justice for the people of this region."

Dr. Rodney's brother, Donald, who was driving the car in which the bomb blast occured, is now working in Grenada with the Ministry of Construction.

FWI, June 18, 1983

PM MAURICE BISHOP'S SPEECH TO ARUBA SOCIALIST CONFERENCE

On behalf of our party, the New Jewel Movement, our Government and the people of Grenada, I want to thank M.E.P., (the Electoral Movement of the People of Aruba), for extending such a generous invitation for me and my delegation to be here.

I extend the fullest fraternal, cordial and sincerest best wishes and congratulations to the leaders, founders, officers and members of M.E.P. on the outstanding occasion of ten years of your founding as a popular people's party.

We congratulate you also on the occasion of five years of the launching of a flag and an anthem of the proud people of Aruba. The formation of a popular people's party, and the launching of both a flag and an anthem signify most clearly to all the world that the people of Aruba are indeed serious and committed to the forward march for self-determination and independence.

In Grenada you must know, that the people of Aruba have a very deep assurance that in us they will always have a true friend, a true ally, and a true supporter.

I am particularly happy and enthusiastic to be here, because we in the party and Government of Grenada have a deep commitment to the process of Caribbean independence and liberation, and as importantly, to Caribbean integration, solidarity and cooperation.

It is our very firm view, that though we were colonialized by different masters, and therefore have had different colonial experiences which have served to divide and separate us in order to rule us better, we are essentially and fundamentally one Caribbean people: hard working, patriotic, democratic, progressive, anxious to have a better life, anxious to develop our own processes free from all forms of outside direction.

Under colonization, we were taught different languages, different European cultural traditions and we were encouraged to ape our respective masters.

In addition, the long and bitter rivalries between colonial powers themselves, ensured that we did not have much opportunity for contact with each other. Thus, they carved up our region, and gave rise to artificial differences of language and alleged cultural differences, strengthened no doubt by our geographic separation.

But many island states (such as the Seychelles and the Bahamas – with some 600 islands) have shown that geographic barriers are in fact surmountable.

Indeed, you the six members of the Federation of the Netherland Antilles have given the world the next proof that despite geographical separation, you are committed to and can, in fact, work together in the interest of all the people of the six islands. And it is for this and other reasons, that we believe that part of the process of regaining our sovereignty in the Caribbean must include the struggle to remove all artificial barriers.

Thus, one of our main concerns as an English-speaking Caribbean country is to actively develop the closest possible ties and cooperation with the Dutch-speaking, the French-speaking, the Spanish-speaking, and indeed American-speaking sister islands. To this we are committed as a party, as a Government and as a people.

I am particularly happy also today to be here, because this, in effect, has become a mini-gathering of the Socialist International. It has provided an opportunity therefore to meet with some friends from the old days, in particular to meet once again with Comrade Gallardo of Guatemala, a comrade who has been in the forefront of his own struggle, a man who has given his entire life to the struggle for his people, a man therefore this entire conference, I am sure, will want to go on record as recognising the tremendous contribution that he has made over the years.

This conference also provides for me an opportunity to meet with the distinguished and illustrious Secretary General, Brother Carlson of the Socialist International.

In approaching the question of development, we see it as an ongoing scientific activity, having as its primary goals the attainment of the fullest social, cultural, spiritual, political and economic potential of any people.

Particularly for poor, exploited and oppressed countries of the world, we see the task of development as one having both a political and economic dimension, and we say clearly then, that there is an unbreakable link between economic transformation and political independence.

For us, there is a clear link between the price we pay for essential goods and services and the political outlook of the ruling party of any country. Hence, we are convinced that there can be no strict separation between politics and economics. The two, inextricably linked, give rise to the political economy of development.

Indeed, this approach to the question of development is indispensable to our very survival, being as we are, countries with long histories of colonial exploitation, backwardness and underdevelopment.

And, therefore, in any genuine effort to go forward, raising the standard of living for our people, moving from ignorance, superstition, illiteracy, backwardness and widespread poverty, to jobs, decent housing and all the basic human needs of our people, we must register the greatest possible political commitment, the firmest political will and the highest political unity as poor nations in the struggle for economic and social justice.

Small island states, such as Grenada, and no doubt Aruba, are characterised by a variety of features, considered "normal" for poor underdeveloped countries. These include:

1. very low and generally grossly uneven per capita incomes;
2. a low level of scientific and technological development, as well as;
3. a lack of institutions and organizations designed for modern production.

In addition, small island states obviously have small land sizes and small resource bases; countries falling into this category generally have a land size no larger than 500 sq. miles (approximately 1200 sq. km.).

The limitations of such small land base are many, including the need for a much stricter economic and social use of the limited land.

Land use policies are therefore often indispensable to orderly housing, agricultural, recreational, and other developmental needs.

As we meet here to consider the political and economic development of our micro-states, we must know that the world economy is riddled with an economic crisis of massive proportions.

In its most recent report on the world economic situation, the International Monetary Fund begins with the statement that, "The world economic picture is rather grim."

The international monetary and economic crisis in the industrial western world is manifested in many ways:

1. Unemployment of phenomenal proportions.
2. Runaway inflation.
3. Prolonged decline in industrial output:
4. There is also the worsening of the balance of trade, especially for developing countries. It is accelerating at a rate faster than recovery is possible.

5. Further worldwide environmental decay and industrial pollution of land, of air, of sea, of rivers.
6. There is too the deterioration of the condition of the rural poor in particular in developing countries; illiteracy rates are actually increasing in some of these countries, especially among women. Malnutrition, famine, and hunger are also on the rise.

We in Grenada recognise the tremendous obstacles that we face, particularly as in addition to the economic crisis we also have to contend with increasing military threats and destabilisation of all forms against our country.

Yet, our experience over 2 years has been concrete proof that it is possible to move forward and to make progress even in the face of adversity.

How is this possible? Our experience has taught us that if the following guidelines are observed, then progress is possible even in the face of the most tremendous odds.

1. Always be honest with the people. Always tell the people the facts. Never attempt to fool the people. Never make the people believe that manna will fall from heaven. Always attempt to raise their consciousness as to the reality of the world, the reality of our region, the reality of their own economy and in particular the difficulties that lie ahead.

We in Grenada are quite convinced that peace, peace in the world and peace in the region, is essential for our development. There can be no peace if there is rampant poverty, backwardness and plunder of the poor of the world. Equally, there can be no development without peace.

Because the resources of the world, the vast resources of the world, must be used for the poor, the hungry, the sick, the handicapped, the dispossessed of the world, we must have peace if we are to attain and maintain peaceful development and progress.

Grenada seeks no quarrels, Grenada seeks no interferences, for we have a firm belief in peaceful co-existence, in good neighbourliness, in mutual respect for all; we believe firmly and passionately in the legal equality of all states regardless of size, in territorial integrity and in sovereignty.

We believe that we have a right to live in peace. We have a right to develop our own resources for the benefit of our own people, and not for the benefit of a tiny handful of transnational corporations around the world.

We believe we have a right to build our own economy, free from the strings of foreign aid dependency.

We have a right to live a life free from the threat of military power, nuclear threat, and destruction of our land and sea resources.

We have a right to develop relations with whomever we want as long as the people of our countries want these relations. We have a right to be free of tensions, free of fears, free of instability, free of the threat of mercenary or other invasions, free of terrorism.

This is why Grenada in November 1979, initiated in the Organization of American States, a resolution calling on all in the region to strictly respect the Caribbean as a Zone of Peace.

We want to repeat today:

Our call for disarmament.

Our call for detente.

Our call for resumption of Salt II talks.

Our call for peaceful co-existence and mutual respect for all countries.

And, Mr. Chairman, today in Aruba on your soil, on this historic occasion in the presence of so many illustrious fighters for the rights of their peoples, Grenada firmly renews this call and pledges to do all in our power to obtain these lofty objectives.

As we say in Grenada: A people that is united, conscious, organised, and vigilant can never be defeated.

FWI, March 28, 1981

PM INVITED TO VISIT MARTINIQUE

Prime Minister Maurice Bishop has accepted an invitation from the prefect of Martinique to pay an official visit to that Caribbean island in the near future.

Prior to the PM's visit, a technical delegation will visit the French department to hold discussions with officials in tourism and agro-industries and to explore other areas of co-operation.

On his way to and from France recently, the PM and his delegation made technical stops in Martinique where they were met by the prefect and by Aimé Césaire, the mayor of Fort-de-France, Martinique's capital.

At a dinner in his honour, PM Bishop held "useful discussions" with leaders of different political parties in Martinique. He described his stopover as "educational, informative and interesting."

FWI, September 25, 1982

PRG PROTESTS BLATANT ATTACK BY BARBADOS

The People's Revolutionary Government has sent a diplomatic note to the Barbados government protesting "the blatant, unprovoked and unwarranted attack on the person and privacy" of Agriculture Minister Unison Whiteman and his personal assistant, Rudolph Hagley, last Saturday.

Brothers Whiteman and Hagley were in Barbados, intransit to London that same day, on official business. Both carried valid diplomatic passports, which entitle them to privileges and immunities, the right to inviolability and the right of innocent passage.

However, Brothers Whiteman and Hagley "were subjected to the grossest form of humiliation and intimidation and physically manhandled" in Barbados airport, the PRG note said.

Barbados immigration, customs and security authorities, in flagrant violation of international law, denied them the right to VIP facilities.

They made Bro. Whiteman wait in a queue and insisted on searching him. When he protested, a customs official took out a knife, and threatened to slash his suitcase open. Bro. Whiteman opened his suitcase.

About 20 security men then dragged Bro. Hagley by his shirt into a private room and searched him.

The Barbados government's attempts to pressure the Grenada revolution and all associated with it increased last week Tuesday, the night of the U.S. presidential election.

Adams, U.S. Ambassador Sally Shelton and about 100 associates were gathered at the St. Michael's home of the first secretary of the U.S. embassy, Ashley Wills, for an "election watch" party.

As soon as it became clear that ultra-right Republican Ronald Reagan was in the lead, and while the votes were still being counted, Adams rushed to air his pleasure on radio, no doubt prompted by his American hosts.

Said Adams: "It is time that the government of Grenada understood that the spirit of Caricom is in the direction of elections.

"No doubt I am going to be quoted," he added. "And I don't care."

Adams said a government needed to be established in office in Grenada that has demonstrated its popularity "other than its use of the M-1 rifle and the Molotov cocktail.

"If Bishop cannot understand that he will put himself in the old cellar of vagabondcy that Eric Gairy occupied, if he continues to promote a government about which there is any possibility of saying that it is repressive, then Bishop does not deserve support."

"Let him hold elections. Let him legitimise himself," he added.

A PRG spokesman later said: "Adams and other members of his government cannot expect to attack Grenada and expect the Grenada government to remain silent. This foolishness has to stop sometime."

"We would really like to know how many times he rang the U.S. Embassy and State Department before this latest step."

The PRG official made it clear that Grenada would not withdraw normal diplomatic courtesies and privileges to Barbados government ministers and officials.

"We have no intention of descending to Tom Adams's level of pettiness and childishness," he said.

FWI, November 15, 1980

WHAT DID MY HUSBAND DO TO TOM ADAMS?

The Editor:

As wife of Minister of Agriculture Unison Whiteman, it took me three days before I really accepted the treatment meted out to my husband, when he landed on Tom Adams's precious soil on Saturday November 8.

My mind was working like a clock, questioning myself, but when I arrived at the final question—What has my husband done to Tom Adams?—I decided to express my feeling to Tom, telling him he is really a heartless creature, to touch a quiet, peaceful and kind-hearted person like my husband.

However, since March 13, 1979, passing through and from Barbados has been rough. I experienced it myself when I accompanied my sick husband to Cuba. When we landed no one met him, and when he asked if they had not been informed of his arrival—pretence it was.

So he went through customs etc. like everybody. The many hours we waited for the Cuban flight were very uncomfortable for him, but what could he have done?

On my return, I travelled with some other Grenadians and the so-called smart Bajans tried to trick us, but it was too vivid. When we got to LIAT's counter, I told the attendant that we had confirmed flights straight to Grenada, and if because of their dishonesty, I had to pay $35 (U.S.) to overnight, police would have to manhandle me.

Again, it was the nice loving, helpful Cubans who paid the cake after LIAT stooges tricked us.

That night in the nice hotel in Barbados, I was just scared. One of the comrades who travelled with me came and knocked on my door so I could get some supper. It took me about 10 minutes before I responded, in a real frightened mood.

I was full, although I had not eaten for a few hours. I just wanted to get home, and I do know that many other people passing through Barbados feel this way too.

That's why our international airport is a must.

I spent two weeks with my husband in Cuba, and the place and people were really touching. I travelled to and from hospital with a driver, with whom I could not communicate because of the difference in language, and I was very relaxed and comfortable.

I spent one night in Barbados, and although I was travelling in a car with other people, I was scared. Why? The atmosphere was very different. So when people try to spoil the good name of the Cubans, those of us who know must put up a fight to defend them.

I first explained the treatment people receive on Tom Adams's precious soil, and as a result of our constructing an international airport, Tom's hostility is getting worse daily. But nothing like that dog could stop it.

I will also like Tom Adams to know that he doesn't have a nook of the qualities of my husband and other peaceloving Grenadians, and because he is an empty shell, he made and will always make a fool of himself.

Tom, may I inform you, that my husband is a man with potential, integrity, peace-loving and kind, and his personality and the qualities he possesses are really above question. To cover this praise:

On Bloody Sunday, 1973, one of the secret police said: "Whiteman, run, you are a good boy." But he was never a coward and decided to remain with his comrades, despite the consequences.

Tom, we know why you are behaving so, but you can't stop us. Grenada is the peoples' and Barbados is yours. When Gairy's downfall was near, that's exactly how he behaved. He started on the foreigners and ended on his own people. So Barbadians take warning.

Nothing like Greedy Tom could stop our revolution, because the quality of our people is what made the revolution a success and will always be.

Claudia Whiteman

FWI, November 15, 1980

DON'T EVEN DREAM OF OVERTHROW, ADAMS

Prime Minister Maurice Bishop has warned Barbados Prime Minister Tom Adams against harbouring any thoughts of supporting the overthrow of the People's Revolutionary Government (PRG).

Addressing the massive Bloody Sunday rally at Seamoon, last Sunday, Cde Bishop accused Adams and his Foreign Minister Henry Forde of attacking the Grenada Revolution ever since it occurred 20 months ago.

"If Uncle Tom is seriously thinking of maintaining any dreams of overthrowing this revolution, maintaining any dreams of helping people to attack our country, if most amusingly of all, Uncle Tom is thinking of himself coming down to our country in a hostile way, he will discover that the people of revolutionary Grenada are ready, willing and prepared to fight and die to defend our revolution," Cde Bishop declared.

He read a letter sent to Adams last December 5, sharply protesting the searching of Agriculture Minister Unison Whiteman that September while he was passing through Grantley Adams International Airport, and the hostile treatment given to other PRG ministers and officials at the same airport.

The letter pointed out that the last thing the PRG wanted was a war of words with the Adams administration. Certainly, it said, such a conflict would not be in the best interest of Caribbean unity and ideological pluralism.

Cde Bishop also accused Adams of suppressing "key and vital" information threatening to the survival of the Grenada government.

Adams, PM Bishop feels, is indirectly responsible for the June 19 bombblast at Queen's Park.

Adams told a BLP public meeting in Barbados, that he had knowledge of "something about a bomb . . . a bomb being put into a refrigerator."

But according to Cde Bishop, he never informed Grenada about that until after the bomb had exploded.

[Name withheld] a notorious CIA functionary wanted in Grenada in connection with that same bombing, is given armed protection by the Barbados government whenever he is there, Cde Bishop disclosed.

Adams, Cde Bishop continued, had also attempted to prevent LIAT, the regional airline, from flying to Grenada, had tried to thwart the island's aid talks with the European Community by "using all kinds of lies," and had tried to destroy the friendship between Grenada and Cuba.

But, the PM added, "They will never be able to destroy the unshakeable friendship between our people and the Cubans."

PM Bishop rejected a comment by Adams that Grenada's failure to hold general elections could adversely affect the flow of funds into the Caribbean Development Bank.

In fact, he said, because of this revolution, the U.S. government has now been "trying to pump money into some of these islands, as a means of trying to hold back progressive change."

"The truth of the matter," he added, is that many more Caribbean territories today have been able to receive much more assistance from the United States."

Although Adams is now trying to pretend that it is through his efforts the PRG received international recognition, Cde Bishop revealed that Adams had tried to block recognition of the PRG by the U.S., Canada and Britain in the early days of the revolution.

However, Cde Bishop feels that what pro-imperialist Adams and his friends are really afraid of is the grassroots democracy blossoming in our country, "where the people themselves, on a daily basis, are involved."

"They have preferred to pretend that the Westminster kind of democracy is a real democracy, when, in fact, it is Westminster hypocrisy.

"Once in every five years, for five seconds, you put an 'X' after you eat some corned beef and drink some rum, and after that, for the remainder of the next five years, you are no longer a human being. We do not regard that as democracy," Cde Bishop declared.

The U.S. and its puppets in the region, have long recognized the potential of the Grenadian Revolution, because "they see that a whole new civilization is being born here."

This, he stated, is part of the overall process of creating a "new kind of civilization" not only for Grenada, but for the entire Caribbean.

In his hour-long speech, the PM also explained why he had referred to Adams as Uncle Tom.

"In the days of slavery," he explained, "there were two types of slaves: the field slave and the house slave. The field slave cut sugar-cane under the master's whip and only thought about freedom and how to plan revolution. They were the genuine fighters and Grenadians are their descendants."

The house slave, on the other hand, did no work in the fields and every time the master passed by, they were smiling, "bending, bowing and scraping." And every time they saw the master, they would say: Yes, master; no, master; thank you, master; please kick me, master."

It was the house slave who was called an "Uncle Tom," Cde Bishop added.

He also observed that the U.S. still believes the Caribbean is in her backyard and "whenever they spit, we must open our mouths and catch it."

"But Grenadians," he added firmly, "have said that they are not in anyone's backyard."

Cde Bishop cautioned, however, that the people of Barbados must not be drawn into the present conflict, and Grenadians were not prepared to start a war with the people of Barbados, since traditionally, very good relations have existed between the two peoples.

"A sharp, sharp distinction must be made between Uncle Tom and the people of Barbados. Tom Adams, as an individual, must be treated with the contempt he deserves," PM Bishop concluded.

FWI, November 22, 1980

LETTER TO TOM ADAMS

The Editor:

We, the members of the Grenada Revolutionary League, strongly protest the blatant interference in the internal affairs of Grenada by Barbados Prime Minister Tom Adams.

Isn't it peculiar that within days of Seaga coming to power in Jamaica and Reagan winning the American election that Uncle Tommy chose to come out and openly blast and condemn the policies of the progressive and popular government of Grenada? A Government that was elected on March 13, 1979, when the people openly took up arms against the fascist dictatorship of Uncle Gairy.

Who is Adams to tell Callaghan whether or not to acknowledge the Grenada Government?

Who is Adams to call for an election in Grenada?

What is it about the Grenada Government that he and people like himself are afraid of?

Is it because of our drive to wipe out illiteracy; the tremendous decrease in the school fees; the free medical and dental care that our people are now receiving; the record-breaking economic progress made by the People's Revolutionary Government in such a short period despite natural disasters and disasters created by reactionary forces?

Is he also afraid of the unification of the people of the Caribbean and Latin America?

Is Uncle Tommy thinking of sending troops to Grenada as he did to Union Island in 1979?

Take a look at all the Caribbean Islands where elections are held. The people's conditions are still deplorable; while their elected ministers are riding around in big expensive cars, country-hopping all over Western Europe and leaving tips that can clothe and feed three families of their country for a whole year.

Elections were held in America 13 years after the American revolution; the country which Uncle Tom holds in such high esteem. We say uncle Tom must check his history.

Why isn't Uncle Tom and his friends calling for an election in Haiti? A country where black people are starving to death; where everyday they are being brutalized by the dreaded Ton-Ton Macoutes who are trained by the American CIA?

We see this attack on Greanda as being highly hypocritical and feel contemptuous of the Barbadian Government.

We also call on Tom Adams to stop his barking immediately and stop the harassment of Grenadian nationals.

Grenada Revolutionary League, New York

FWI, November 29, 1980

ADAMS BANS NEWS FROM GRENADA

In its continuing hostility towards Grenada, the Barbados government has decided to ban all information about Grenada on State-owned CBC radio and television.

The decision was handed down in a directive from the board of directors of CBC to the newsroom of the two Barbados media last weekend.

First news of the ban reached Grenada in a report over Radio Free Grenada by Lou Smith, who has been CBC's correspondent in Grenada for the past few months.

Smith said that when he called the Barbados station last weekend to file his report on the terrorist attack, which left five Grenadians dead, he was told that CBC staffers had been ordered not to carry any news at all on Grenada.

The ban also extends to forbidding the appearance of spokesmen of the Barbados Movement for National Liberation (Monali), and Bobby Clarke of the People's Progressive Movement. Monali and Clarke are among Grenada's firmest supporters in Barbados.

The CBC directive did not go down well with CBC journalists, who have protested that it "inhibited a professional approach" to their work, and called for its withdrawal.

Clarke, a Barbadian attorney, says he intends to challenge the CBC decision in court. He told FREE WEST INDIAN that he will sue CBC for infringing on his constitutional right to freedom of speech and expression.

Monali also intends to take action against CBC. Rickey Parris, a Monali leader, said his organisation intends to demonstrate outside CBC offices this weekend, and has sent a letter to CBC's chairman David Simmonds, seeking clarification of the company's position on releases from Monali, which have been stifled on several occasions since relations worsened between Barbados and Grenada.

Monali believes, said Parris, that Barbados media workers and journalists need to have greater say in policy-making in the media.

The workers' rights have always been trampled upon, he said. Monali will be calling for the formation of a genuine journalists' organisation to protect media workers' rights in Barbados, he added.

A Broadcasting Authority has been formed in Barbados, he explained, but is under the influence of right-wing, anti-Grenada elements, who have succeeded in pushing for such actions as the recent ban.

Smith too, shares the view that the board's action is a violation of the right of journalists and of the concept of a free flow of information.

He says that he has written to the Caribbean Press Council drawing the matter to its attention.

At a time when the Barbados government has been coming under increasing pressure from Barbadians for its mishandling of the dispute with Grenada, leading political observers in Barbados feel that the latest move arises from the exposure of Prime Minister Tom Adams and his External Affairs Minister Henry Forde's efforts to turn back the Grenada Revolution.

The revelation of their efforts, made by Grenada's Prime Minister at the "Bloody Sunday" rally a few weeks ago, pointed out that Adams himself had admitted that enemies of Grenada had approached him on several occasions for assistance to overthrow the Grenadian government.

Adams also disclosed that he had had prior knowledge that "something would have happened in Grenada on June 19 last," when a bomb to assassinate the leaders of the Grenada revolution exploded, killing three persons and injuring 94 others.

These and other revelations of Adams's several attempts to isolate Grenada politically and diplomatically are having tremendous effect on the Barbadian public, who are now beginning to question their government's actions.

By banning circulation of such information, Adams is hoping that he can bring an end to such exposures in Barbados.

With an election due in Barbados soon, Adams fears the consequences of these exposures to the Barbadian public.

But, the growing support for Grenada in Barbados became more evident last weekend, with the appearance of pro-Grenada slogans on walls and public buildings.

FWI, November 29, 1980

BARROW—WE'LL BETTER RELATIONS WITH GRENADA

Barbados Democratic Labour Party (DLP), led by former Prime Minister Errol Barrow, has said that if it is elected, it would move to restore good relations between the governments of Barbados and Grenada.

Making the promise, the DLP said that deteriorating relations between the two countries have been caused by "ill-timed and ill-advised statements and expressions" from the Tom Adams regime, and noted that this is the first time in the island's history that relations with a Caricom partner have deteriorated to such depths.

The campaign for Thursday's election is in full gear, and the two contending parties have released their manifestoes.

Adams's Barbados Labour Party (BLP) is carrying out a millionaire-style campaign, being managed by an American who managed the last election campaign for former U.S. President Richard Nixon.

The BLP's media campaign, said to be costing some $10 million (B'dos), is being managed by a high-powered Madison Avenue public relations firm. It includes frequent whole-page advertisements in the island's leading dailies, and TV and radio slots.

Analysts say the millions being poured into the campaign to re-elect the BLP is an indication that it feels severely threatened by the DLP, which it ousted in 1976, after 15 years of DLP rule.

In its manifesto, the DLP is accusing the Adams administration of defending the interests of the rich at the expense [*sic*] the poor Barbadians.

It says that "the Barbados economy is entering into a state of deep crisis, despite BLP rhetoric to the contrary." It accuses the administration of allowing a chronically high level of unemployment, increased crime, alarming inflation, an impending balance of payments problem, a burdensome increase in indirect taxation, a rapid increase in the national debt, low levels of agricultural productivity, and economic privation facing small farmers.

"The nature of these problems is a clear reflection of the BLP government's policy trend to assist the privileged few" in the Barbadian society, "at the expense of the struggling masses and the middle classes," the manifesto said.

FWI, June 13, 1981

STRONG REACTION TO ADAMS ATTACK—KEEP YOUR NOSE OUT, UNCLE TOM

The people of Grenada and the People's Revolutionary Government (PRG), have reacted strongly to Tom Adams' latest attack on the Grenada Revolution.

In a statement on the issue, the PRG said that "Tom Adams is in no position to talk about freedom and democracy in Grenada, because the people of Grenada have been benefitting tremendously from the many popular programmes of their Revolution, which have brought a significant improvement in the life of the Grenadian people."

The statement went on to compare the situation in Grenada with the situation in Barbados: "After two years of their Revolution, the Grenadian people are already receiving free medical attention, free and increased educational opportunities, increased national unity, and a significant decrease in the crime rate. But after almost six years of rule by Tom Adams' Barbados Labour Party (BLP), the Barbadian people are finding it more difficult to survive from day to day. Cost of living is increasing, while workers wages are decreasing; crime in Barbados is rising at an astronomical rate and the poor are getting poorer while the rich are getting richer in Barbados."

Tom Adams' latest attack was made in London earlier this week while he was there to attend the wedding reception of Prince Charles and Lady Diana Spencer. He called on the Government of Grenada to hold elections and expressed his concern about alleged human rights and press freedom violations in Grenada.

The PRG's statement pointed out that Tom Adams obviously loves royalty, because he always chooses royal occasions to do his master's work. "He last poked his nose into Grenada's business when he was at the home of CIA royalty, Ashley Wills, well-known head of the CIA's operations in the Eastern Caribbean," it said.

The statement asks why he didn't use his platform in Britain to join the PRG in condemning the racist British Nationality Bill, and the increasing repression being faced by brothers and sisters of the Caribbean and other parts of the world in England.

It emphasized that the people of Grenada and the PRG have no quarrel with the Barbadian people but continue to regard them as brothers and sisters in the struggle.

"The people of Grenada, however, stand ready to deal with all the imperialist and CIA yardfowls, pawns and puppets who stand in the way of the Revolution and who choose to join the United States Government's plan to isolate and turn back the Grenada Revolution," the PRG stated.

Two Barbadian political organisations have supported the PRG in its condemnation of Tom Adams' attack on the Grenada Revolution. They are the People's Progressive Party (PPP) and the Movement for National Liberation (MONALI).

Both Bobby Clark, leader of the PPP and Rickey Parris, chairman of MONALI, agreed that Tom Adams has no right to talk about democracy because the recent elections in Barbados which kept him in power were considered undemocratic.

Thousands of Barbadians found that their names were not registered for voting while many were registered in several places. Some of the ballot boxes were misplaced and some were not even counted.

They said the election proved that free and fair does not mean democratic. It means that whoever controls the apparatus leading up to and on the night of the election, runs the Government of Barbados.

They both pointed out that Tom Adams has nothing to say about the racist regime in England which denied young blacks equal opportunities in the educational system, nor the repressive regimes in South Africa, the fascist Pinochet regime in Chile and the repressive Haitian Government.

Bro. Clark said that continued interference in the Grenada people's affairs, can only lead to a further disenfranchisement of the people's needs in the Caribbean, and the defeat of the common goal of Caribbean unity.

Bro. Parris commented that Tom Adams has no love for democracy. "It is a straight case of a dog barking for its master. He has always been at the centre of the forces of destabilisation and counter revolution seeking to turn back the Grenada Revolution," he said.

Elections, he pointed out, have in recent times become the tool through which the forces of imperialism have oppressed the Caribbean masses with some of the most conservative governments and through the tight media control coming out of their relationships with the Inter-American Press Association and other reactionary media bodies.

He reiterated his party's support for the Grenada Revolution.

"In the face of this new uprising in hostility to the Grenada Revolution, we in the progressive movements in Barbados remain convinced of the just path which the Grenada people have chosen and of the new democracy that has evolved. We are overcome by the unity of the people of Grenada and the PRG, and we say to you, stand firm. FORWARD EVER, BACKWARD NEVER."

FWI, August 8, 1981

BARBADOS PAPERS HIT REAGAN'S TREATMENT OF NEWSMEN

The Barbados "Nation" newspaper on Wednesday followed in the steps of the "Advocate News" and lambasted U.S. security officials for ill-treating local journalists during U.S. President Ronald Reagan's four-day working holiday in Barbados, last week.

The "Advocate News" in its editorial Tuesday suggested that there were racial overtones in the officials' attitude towards the West Indians, saying they were treated like intruders in their own country.

Barbadian and other Caribbean journalists were denied entry by White House security men at the Sandy Lane Estate, where Reagan was staying, while the all-white foreign press corps were ushered in without any problems, CANA reported.

The previous day, at Ilaro Court, the official residence of Prime Minister Tom Adams, Barbadian journalists were initially denied entry again by the White House officials and physically assaulted when they asserted themselves in an effort to cover the proceedings.

Calling for a clarification of the mess, "in the spirit of good relations," the "Nation" said: "We would not like to think that the Reagan visit to Barbados will be remembered for this unsavoury aspect, which could be the case in the absence of a full statement of explanation at the earliest possible opportunity.

"We found that the security staff were almost inhuman in their dealings with local journalists, which in the circumstances of race (they were white and we were black) and indeed in the circumstances of country (they were big America and we were small Bajans) could have led to entirely unnecessary confrontation and embarrassment," the daily said.

"The result was that the snubbed journalists had to play second roles to their counterparts, which was professionally undesirable and personally distasteful," it added.

"The visit of Ronald Reagan to our shores was not the biggest thing to have taken place here. In fact, we are quite accustomed to the big event and all that is required by the media. We had a proud track record."

The editorial said any post mortem of the Reagan visit must address itself to the problems encountered by the journalists and the reasons why matters got out of hand.

The editorial page carried a big splash by a local cartoonist of jacketed U.S. security men blocking the entrance of Ilaro Court and a local journalist, note-book in hand, sitting on the steps "depressed."

FWI, April 17, 1982

PEOPLE'S REVOLUTIONARY GOVERNMENT OF GRENADA CONDEMNS ACTIONS OF GOVERNMENT OF DOMINICA

The PRG last week issued the following Press Release on the Dominica situation:

The People's Revolutionary Government of Grenada feels that the reported acts of violence against unarmed people in Roseau, Dominica, last Tuesday was the culmination of a growing South African influence in official circles in Dominica.

In the circumstances, the People's Revolutionary Government, conscious of the stand already expressed by the Caribbean Conference of Churches, the Caribbean Congress of Labour and the Caribbean Human Rights and Legal Aid Company condemns in the strongest possible terms the recent activities of the Government of Prime Minister, Patrick John.

At the risk of being accused by the Dominican Government of interference, the People's Revolutionary Government wishes to make it abundantly clear that any form of relations between a Caribbean Government and the racist apartheid regime of South Africa is a matter of the gravest concern to the Grenadian people and Government and, we feel certain, to the region as a whole.

This relationship between a Caribbean Government and South Africa is a slap in the face to the aspirations of millions of people the world over and to scores of countries in the United Nations, the Organization of African Unity, the Non-Aligned Movement and other international organs that are concerned and working to bring about the defeat of the racist, fascist, repressive regimes in Southern Africa. Such developments also pose a direct threat to the security and integrity of the entire Caribbean region which has already had to contend with Chilean influence.

We therefore call upon the Government of Dominica to immediately end all relations with South Africa and to respect the will of the Dominican and Caribbean people for true independence, social progress, human rights and participatory democracy.

FWI, June 9, 1979

EUGENIA CHARLES ACCUSES GRENADA IN OVERTHROW PLOT

As the Eugenia Charles government approaches its eighth month in office, political confusion and instability continues in Dominica.

The state of emergency, declared last month, continues and the government is taking numerous emergency measures in its effort to come to grips with the general unrest following the killing of two Rastafarians by police and the abduction of farmer Ted Honeychurch by a group of Rastafarians.

Former Prime Minister Patrick John, Defense Force Commander Frederick Newton, former director of information and broadcasting Dennis

Joseph, and an executive member of Patrick John's Labour Party, Julian David, have all been arrested, accused of being part of a plot to overthrow the Charles government on March 14.

The 97-member Defense Force has been disbanded, and called upon to turn in their arms.

And while a number of persons have been detained, the government has announced new measures under the emergency regulations giving the commissioner of Police power to open mail addressed to any detainee or relative, or other person residing at his home.

Ms. Charles in a recent radio interview, tried to associate Grenada with the alleged overthrow plot, saying that it was timed for March 14, the day after the second anniversary of the Grenada Revolution.

But this contention was negated by "The New Chronicle," Dominica's only weekly newspaper, which supports Ms. Charles's government. It said last week that "the Grenada situation is poles apart from what is transpiring in Dominica."

At the same time that she pointed an accusing finger at Grenada, Ms. Charles said that her government has been able to secure assistance from three major Western countries—France, the United States and Britain—to train the local army in engineering, construction, "and other areas."

While military detachments from these countries have been assisting and instructing Dominican military personnel since the kidnapping, there are also reports that days after, a plane from the Jamaica Defense Force landed a shipment of American-made arms on the island.

Reports also indicate that members of the Defense Force refused to co-operate with the foreign military personnel in their efforts to track down Honeychurch's kidnappers.

Spokesmen for the major trade unions, the Rastafarians and the opposition Dominica Liberation Movement Alliance claim that these forces have come under a vicious propaganda onslaught to implicate them in the unrest on the island.

Meanwhile, the regional newspaper, "Caribbean Contact" has said that it is reliably informed that Honeychurch is alive and well. But his whereabouts remain a mystery.

FWI, March 21, 1981

ADVOCATE KNOCKS PM CHARLES TOO

Even the Barbados "Advocate News" has taken issue with Dominica Prime Minister Eugenia Charles, over Grenada.

In an editorial Wednesday, the oldest daily in Barbados said Ms. Charles's speech at last weekend's convention of the ruling Dominica Freedom Party (DFP) indicated that she was definitely becoming anxious about the economic future of her young nation.

Ms. Charles charged that by refusing to "legitimise itself by holding free and fair elections," the PRG was blocking the flow of much-needed aid into the region. She referred specifically to the Caribbean Development Bank's (CDB) refusal of a U.S. loan of $10.8 million with the condition that Grenada would not benefit.

The "Advocate News" suggested that by so chastising the PRG, Ms. Charles was perhaps hoping that her cry would reach Washington, causing the U.S. Government to realise that Dominica was suffering from its aid stipulations and possibly review its approach to "maybe . . . a bilateral basis."

But there is little hope that the PRG will be moved by Ms. Charles's cries, the paper said, merely for the sake of "imperialist dollars."

Besides Ms. Charles, all the region's governments had sided with the PRG against the Ronald Reagan demand, the "Advocate News" pointed out.

It added: "It is Miss Charles who has been the first to shift the criticism from the Reagan administration and put the blame squarely on Maurice Bishop. It only shows how our perspective can be coloured by where we stand."

The paper also pointed out that the elections issue was not as simple as Ms. Charles made it seem, as the PRG would hardly be minded to hold elections merely to ensure a flow of funds into Dominica and other Caribbean states.

FWI, August 29, 1981

NOEL—YES, RODNEY ASSASSINATED

Vincent Noel, Secretary for Home Affairs in the People's Revolutionary Government, has cleared up the misunderstanding which arose from a recent interview with the Guyanese press.

Bro. Noel, who gave a news conference in Guyana to discuss the Grenadian situation, was asked about the PRG's attitude to Walter Rodney's assassination.

In an interview with RFG News last Monday, Bro. Noel confirmed that he had erroneously stated in the Guyana press conference that the PRG had not used the word "assassination" to describe Dr. Rodney's death.

Grenada's position, however, had already been made quite clear by two PRG statements on the matter and by the fact that Soweto Day, June 16, had been declared a national day of mourning in Grenada, in memory of Dr. Rodney.

On that day too, at the request of the PRG, the Grenada Conference of Churches held a special memorial service in St. George's Roman Catholic Cathedral, attended by Prime Minister Maurice Bishop, Education Minister George Louison, Communications and Works Minister Selwyn Strachan, Agriculture Minister, Unison Whiteman as well as other members of the PRG, New Jewel Movement, and other organisations.

Bro. Noel, who had been fully aware of all these actions, told Radio Free Grenada he had, however, not been aware of the exact wording of the second PRG statement.

The statement, issued on June 14 by a PRG spokesman, had registered the PRG's deep shock at the major loss to Guyana, the Caribbean, and the freedom-loving people of the world, at the untimely death of the Guyanese revolutionary, and had called for an urgent investigation into the full circumstances surrounding the incident.

The second statement, however, was issued on June 15 by Cde Bishop, condemning utterly the "sickening and cowardly assassination" of Dr. Rodney.

Elsewhere in the statement, Cde Bishop said that the "assassination" was seen as "signifying a dangerous regional development." "Only imperialism and reaction can benefit from this murder," it continued.

In his RFG interview, Bro. Noel reiterated that the position of the party and government was that the assassination was the work of imperialism in conjunction with local reactionaries, who were not named specifically, but who aimed at destroying all the progressive forces in the region.

The party and government showed clear links, he said, between Dr. Rodney's murder and events in Chile, El Salvador, Jamaica and Grenada.

On the national day of mourning, flags were flown at half mast and members of the PRG, and the public wore black armbands.

Bro. Noel, a senior member of government and of the political bureau of the NJM, left Grenada on June 20 to attend a memorial service for Dr. Rodney in Guyana the following day.

This he did, and returned to Grenada on June 22 as planned, as events in Grenada made it impossible for him to stay for the funeral on Monday, which had not yet been scheduled when he left home.

The implication of a CANA story on Wednesday, which quotes a Guyana government statement as naming Bro. Noel as an official who left Guyana "without attending the funeral" is therefore false.

Grenada still mourns the loss of Dr. Rodney, and repeats its call for a full investigation into the "sickening and cowardly assassination" of this great man.

FWI, June 28, 1980

ST. VINCENT DEPORTS FWI JOURNALIST

St. Lucian journalist Earl Bousquet, who has worked with FREE WEST INDIAN for the past 14 months, was deported from St. Vincent this week, after arriving there to cover the budget debate in parliament.

Said Bro. Bousquet: "I arrived in St. Vincent's airport on Wednesday morning, on a chartered flight from St. Lucia. Accompanying me was a British-born businessman with a chain of stores in the islands, who had chartered the plane to carry goods to his St. Vincent store.

"We took the line to the immigration desk, where we were asked to stand aside while our passports were taken to another room. The immigration officer returned and asked how much money we had. My friend said he had $47, and I had $75. We were told we did not have enough money to enter.

"The immigration officer, WPC 392 Marshall, told us we would be deported back to St. Lucia on the next flight. The businessman argued that he had been travelling to St. Vincent for over 14 years, and had never been turned back, and further, that he had thousands of dollars worth of goods for his store on the plane. More, he had a friend who had come to meet him, and since he was only staying overnight, he did not need more money.

"When his friend came up, and the Police Commissioner came to the office, the businessman was allowed to enter the country.

"The Commissioner then left, without even considering my case. The immigration officer told me that I would take the next plane, expected in an hour, for St. Lucia. I was put in a room under police guard.

"I protested, asking the grounds for my deportation. She said she did not have to explain, but when I pressed, she said I was "an undesirable Grenadian element." I showed her my passport, proved I am St. Lucian, and she laughed, saying, 'Bishop can give anybody a false passport.'

"I continued to protest, pointing out that I'm a journalist, and I was coming to her country to cover the budget debate, going on that same day. I also added that I had been to St. Vincent at least three times on that same passport, the last time being immediately after Hurricane Allen, when I toured the island with other regional journalists, Prime Minister Milton Cato and other government officials.

"She took my passport again to the adjacent office, and after a telephone call, she returned saying that her immediate boss, a senior policeman named Stoddard, said I should not be allowed entry. I was to be deported to St. Lucia.

"I told her I had a confirmed flight and ticket to Grenada from St. Vincent that same day, and requested that I be sent to Grenada instead. Marshall laughed, saying this confirmed that I was really a 'Grenadian revolutionist' with a false passport.

"I reiterated that I worked in Grenada, and showed documents to prove it.

"She said, I would be put on the next plane to Grenada, as I requested.

"I, therefore, had to wait two hours under guard for the next plane to Grenada.

"While waiting, I spoke to a sympathetic Customs Officer, who had been listening all along. He said the only reason I was being deported was because of my "dreadlocks" hairstyle. Many other persons with dreadlocks had been deported earlier, he said.

"At 2.30 p.m. Wednesday I was escorted to the waiting LIAT plane, and put on board. My documents were then handed to me, along with two copies of a deportation order, one of which I was told to hand to immigration authorities in Grenada.

"On the order, under the heading 'Reasons for Deportation,' one word had been inserted: 'undesirable.'"

FWI, July 25, 1981

REVO RALLY IN TRINIDAD

On March 13, while thousands of Grenadians and scores of guests from all parts of the world celebrated in a mass rally the first anniversary of the revolution, their brothers and sisters in Trinidad and Tobago demonstrated their strong bonds of solidarity with the struggle in Grenada by also holding a mass rally in Port-of-Spain.

The rally, organised by the National Joint Action Committee (NJAC) drew crowds which packed the OWTU House of the People to capacity and overflowed the yard into the streets.

No matter how many lies are being spread by hostile elements, the masses of people turned out to show their approval of the new direction being taken by Comrade Prime Minister Maurice Bishop and the People's Revolutionary Government and the people of Grenada.

Despite the threatening attitude of the Trinidad state to those who identify with the Grenada revolution, several prominent artistes turned out to make their contributions.

Among the calypsonians appearing were Chalkdust, King Austin, Commentor and Short Pants. Other artistes included Andre Tanker and the Village Drummers.

Several organisations presented solidarity messages at the rally.

The feature address was given by Makandal Daaga, formerly Geddes Granger, chairman of NJAC. He condemned forces in Trinidad and Tobago who were making a determined effort to subvert the Grenada Revolution, and he warned the newspapers to stop printing their lies and distortions.

He asked the people not only to express a sense of solidarity, but to commit themselves to sacrifice for the defense of the revolution in Grenada, which is the most advanced stage of the revolution in the English-speaking Caribbean.

The people expressed their total support for the progress taking place here by thunderous shouts of power to the people of Grenada.

FWI, April 19, 1980

ANOTHER GRENADIAN HARASSED IN TRINIDAD

Ever since the people's revolution of March 13, and more so during recent weeks, there have been reports of Grenadians as well as visitors to the country, being subjected to harassment and intimidation at certain airports in the region.

Now comes the news of a Grenadian, David Lynch, being deported from neighbouring Trinidad, where he had lived for the past 50 years.

In January 1979 Mr. Lynch left for a visit to Grenada. After being in Grenada for 15 months, he decided to return to Trinidad.

When he arrived at Piarco Airport he was told by immigration authorities that his papers were no longer valid, and he would have to return to Grenada to have them renewed.

He objected, saying he had been living in Trinidad for over 50 years, and Trinidad would be the appropriate place for renewing them.

The authorities refused to accept his reasoning and recalled an aircraft, already 10 minutes in flight, to have him flown back to Grenada.

On boarding the plane, Mr. Lynch told the captain it was not his wish to be on board and that it would be dangerous to have him on the flight.

The captain reported this to his seniors, and Mr. Lynch was taken off the aircraft, had his documents taken away from him, and was detained at the Arouca Police Station, until April 21.

He was then brought to the airport in handcuffs accompanied by two immigration officers, and put aboard an aircraft for Grenada.

Mr. Lynch stated that he had been quite active in the social and political fields in Trinidad.

At the time, he was employed as a travel assistant, which entailed helping people overcome their travelling difficulties. This occupation, he noted, meant that he had close contacts with, and was known to, the Trinidad immigration authorities.

No valid reason has been given Mr. Lynch for his treatment but disparaging remarks passed by certain immigration officials suggested to him that the fact of his being Grenadian was enough reason for his harassment.

Similar incidents have been noted by the PRG and each case is being fully investigated.

FWI, May 17, 1980

TRINIDAD BARS BLACK SOUTH AFRICAN LEADER

General secretary of South Africa's Black Allied Workers Union (BAWU), Drake Koka, who was an invited guest at Grenada's recent African Liberation Day celebration, was barred from entering Trinidad and Tobago, because he is South African.

Koka left for Trinidad last week, to address the African Liberation Day rally organised by the National Joint Action Committee (NJAC). With him was Babatunde Ron Smith, chairman of the Pan African Congress Movement of Britain and France, another speaker for the rally.

But on arrival at Piarco airport, Guyana-born Smith was allowed entry, while Koka was told he could not enter, because Trinidad and Tobago was against South Africa, and therefore, "no South Africans" would be allowed entry.

Koka told immigration officials that the law banning entry to South Africans was probably aimed at expressing disgust for the apartheid practices of the racist government, and it was necessary to distinguish between the perpetrators and the victims of apartheid.

He also pointed out that he was not carrying a South African passport, but a United Nations travel document.

He was then told that he did not have a visa, and although he pointed out that there were no visa facilities in Grenada, from where he had travelled, within 35 minutes, he was put on the next plane to Grenada.

But that did not prevent the rally from coming off and being "a great success," according to NJAC officials.

Kasala Kamara, editor of NJAC's "Liberation" newspaper, said his organization contacted Trinidad's Ministry of National Security, and it had promised to put the situation straight. But by the time they got back to the airport, Koka had already been deported.

Kamara said he found the immigration officials' action contradictory to the government's position at the United Nations, that it is against apartheid.

Koka himself found these actions contradictory. "We are very concerned that a state which has a large black population should continue to victimize Africans who are fighting apartheid."

"Such actions," he added, "are in direct contravention of the United Nations Convention on Refugees, to which the Trinidad government is signatory. They ought to respect that convention, and they must see us South African freedom fighters in exile as refugees in the spirit of the Convention."

"By banning us from entering their countries, whether it is through misinterpretation of the law or not, governments which take such actions are acting only in direct support of the racist South African regime, because the regime's wish is that we continue to be harassed and victimised in other countries," Koka said.

Koka is well known in South Africa for his role in the political struggle against the colonialist regime. He was a co-founder and the first secretary-general of the Black People's Convention, a political party under the Black Consciousness Movement, and a close friend of the murdered black leader, Steve Biko.

Koka was forced into exile by the white minority regime for his leading role in the struggle. In 1973 he was served a five-year order, keeping him under house arrest on weekends and holidays, and in November 1974, he was arrested, detained for eight months, and placed in solitary confinement in a maximum security prison. A few months after the June 1976 Soweto rebellion, he was forced to flee to Botswana to avoid arrest.

FWI, June 6, 1981

WISA BEING TRANSFORMED

Seven Caribbean islands, Grenada, St. Vincent and the Grenadines, Antigua, Dominica, Montserrat, St. Kitts-Nevis, and Saint Lucia, will sign a treaty establishing the Organization of Eastern Caribbean States (OECS) on July 4, the eighth anniversary of the birth of Caricom, to which they belong.

It will culminate two years of preparation to transform the 14-year-old West Indies Associated States (WISA) into a legally-established body to help the smaller Caricom territories deal with the rest of the region and the world.

And as part of the communications and education programme designed to disseminate information on the OECS, WISA and the People's Revolutionary Government will jointly sponsor a one-day seminar at York House, St. George's next Tuesday.

The seminar will be open to the public, and panelists will include Augustus Compton, WISA's executive secretary and Charlesworth Edwards, executive secretary of the Eastern Caribbean Common Market (ECCM).

The OECS is being launched to promote co-operation, unity and solidarity, to help member-states to discharge their obligations to the international community, to seek the fullest possible harmonization of foreign policy, and to promote economic integration.

It provides for mutual defense and security, and for twice yearly meetings of heads of government, with annual rotation of the chairmanship among member states in alphabetical order, starting with Antigua.

One early plan of the OECS is to set up a pool of experts to share available expertise and increase levels of expertise in the area. This scheme will focus on agriculture, industry, transport, tourism, fiscal policy and planning services, trade, information and integration services, finance, personnel and general administration, health services and port management.

Sharing of diplomatic missions abroad is one of the main items on the agenda, to reduce the cost of overseas representation.

Minister of Legal Affairs Kenrick Radix, said recently that Grenada has gone down on record as having offered to share its many missions in other parts of the world with fellow members of the OECS.

FWI, June 6, 1981

OECS—STEP IN LONG SEARCH FOR UNITY

"The establishment of the Organization of Eastern Caribbean States (OECS) is a forward step in the movement towards regional integration, and towards the coming together of the smaller states of the region."

This was the view of Minister of Education George Louison, as he delivered an opening statement on behalf of the People's Revolutionary Government (PRG) at a one-day seminar, held at York House, St. George's, on Tuesday.

The seminar, held to promote public discussion on the OECS, was also attended by Gus Compton, executive secretary of the West Indies Associated States (WISA), and Charlesworth Edwards, executive secretary of the Eastern Caribbean Common Market (ECCM), who answered questions from members of the public.

Noting that regional integration had been discussed "for decades" in the region, and the role of such Grenadian stalwarts as William Donovan and T.A. Marryshow, Bro. Louison said that "we must see the signing of the OECS treaty as part of our people's long tradition of trying to forge unity among ourselves."

He traced the several attempts among small Caribbean states to forge such unity, and said "this new initiative should give us new perspectives on approaching the problem," adding that since March 13, 1979, Grenada's position has always been that it wants unity, not only among the English-speaking islands, but also among the French, Dutch and Spanish-speaking countries of the region.

Bro. Louison, who also has responsibility for relations with Caricom countries, urged, however, that "popular democracy, respect for workers and social and economic justice for all," should be a component of any regional movement, such as the OECS.

He cited the signing of the "Declaration of St. George's" between Dominica, St. Lucia and Grenada on July 14, 1979, when the three committed themselves to such policies, and urged that "it would be a fundamental duty for the OECS to look at some of the issues and clauses enshrined in that declaration."

Other issues worth looking at, he felt, were energy, travel among member states, and fiscal and monetary policies. The PRG held that the OECS should consider the developing countries' struggle to restructure international trade to get "a better deal," and thus, a position should be taken on the new international economic order, he said.

Peace is another major issue the PRG would like the OECS to look at seriously, Bro. Louison said. "Peace for mankind, and for the region, requires a common approach on our part," he said.

He recalled that in October 1979, the Organisation of American States (OAS) general assembly in Bolivia adopted a resolution submitted by Grenada, calling for the region to be declared a "zone of peace," and added that "it is our view that there must be stability and peace for development."

By calling for peace, he said, it would mean prohibition of all military bases in the region, an end to all military manoeuvres, an end to colonialism so that all countries in the region would have the right to choose their own paths of development, an end to assassinations, mercenary attacks, propaganda and economic destabilisation, and an end to the exploitation of the land and the seas of the region, against the will of its peoples.

"Peace represents the aspirations of all our people to end all forms of domination," Bro. Louison concluded.

Compton, of St. Lucia, gave a general outline of all issues concerning the transformation of WISA into the OECS.

"The OECS will constitute no threat to national sovereignty, as governments will retain their political independence, and will adopt collective approaches on common issues," he said.

He pointed out that the OECS will be "totally silent" on ideology, since "ideological pluralism is an irreversible factor in international relations, and should constitute no barrier" in relations among member states.

"There is no incompatibility between OECS and Caricom, as the OECS will definitely enhance the work towards the achievement of Caricom's objectives," he concluded.

FWI, June 13, 1981

PM'S BISHOP, CATO TALK

Prime Minister Maurice Bishop and Foreign Minister Unison Whiteman yesterday held informal talks with St. Vincent and the Grenadines Prime Minister Milton Cato.

Cato was intransit at Pearl's Airport on his way to the United States Virgin Islands for a vacation. PM Bishop and Min. Whiteman went to Pearl's in the morning specifically to meet him.

The two Caricom leaders discussed several matters of mutual and regional interest.

The discussions took place against the background of the upcoming Caricom heads of governments meeting scheduled to be held on Jamaica's north coast tourist resort area next month, and the People's Revolutionary Government's (PRG) recent initiatives, which have secured additional aid for the Eastern Caribbean Islands from the French government, through its Fund for Aid and Development (FAC).

The meeting also came against the background of last week's re-affirmation by the PRG of its unwavering commitment to regional unity and, in particular to joint efforts to solve the pressing economic problems of small island states.

FWI, October 6, 1982

PM AT OECS MEETING IN DOMINICA

Prime Minister Maurice Bishop is now in Dominica, attending the Heads of Government meeting of the Organisation of Eastern Caribbean States (OECS) which began Thursday.

Before he left, PM Bishop said that at the meeting, which will discuss energy, trade and sharing of certain facilities among OECS member states, Grenada will present proposals on a number of issues, including the restructuring of the University of the West Indies (UWI).

Grenada will present a paper, aimed at ensuring that any restructuring does not break up the university, compromise its integrity or sever unity in the region, he said.

Grenada's position, he said, is that the education cost for each student should be dependent on the campus being attended, since there are big differences in cost among each of the three UWI campuses, in Jamaica, Barbados and Trinidad and Tobago.

This would mean a reduction in university fees for many islands, he stated.

Grenada will also follow up a number of proposals it put forward at last November's OECS meeting in St. Lucia, including the bulk-buying of goods among member states, organising cheaper means of regional transportation, and the purchasing of common textbooks for Caribbean students.

All these have beneficial economic implications, not only for Grenada, but for all OECS members, he stated.

PM Bishop said he hoped the meeting would take a final decision on converting the Eastern Caribbean Currency Authority into a central bank.

He called the moves towards forming such a bank a historic and fundamental achievement, and evidence of the advances which the OECS had made.

OECS now has an institutional structure, he said, with the establishment of different offices, including its headquarters in St. Lucia, and its economic secretariat in Antigua.

On several fronts, the OECS has begun to achieve its objectives of helping to bring about greater co-operation among member states, he declared.

Speaking on the recent trade impasse among some Caribbean Community (Caricom) countries, PM Bishop emphasised that Grenada is not willing to become involved in retaliatory or discriminatory actions against its Caricom partners.

"Our concern now is to try and develop structures that will ensure that this kind of thing does not happen again; that before people move to any direct action, they engage in different forms of dialogue and communication," he stated.

FWI, May 28, 1983

OECS AGREES ON CENTRAL BANK

Last weekend's Organisation of Eastern Caribbean States' (OECS) heads of government meeting in Dominica has helped to advance further the OECS's possibilities and potential, said Prime Minister Maurice Bishop.

Assessing the meeting's outcome to the press, he said it was able to agree on a number of issues.

Among them is the decision to convert the Eastern Caribbean Currency Authority (ECCA) into a central bank within the next few months.

PM Bishop revealed that the meeting also made progress on the future of the University of the West Indies (UWI) but added that another meeting will have to be held before July's Caribbean Community (Caricom) Summit meeting in Trinidad to settle remaining problems.

Grenada, he said, gave full support to the proposal to offer contracts to West Indian cricketers to coach in different Caribbean islands in the off-season, so as to keep off the lure of tempting financial offers to play cricket in racist South Africa.

The two day meeting also discussed, among other things, energy, trade, OECS preparations for July's Caricom summit, and the sharing of certain facilities among OECS member states.

FOLLOW GRENADA'S EXAMPLE CARICOM MINISTERS URGE

Grenada's Prime Minister Maurice Bishop came in for special praise from the participants at the sixth conference of Caricom Health Ministers which ended at the Dome Thursday.

According to the head of the Health Desk at the Caricom Secretariat, Dr. Philip Boyd, "The conference has never had so comprehensive an account of problems in health and other health issues. It was an extremely healthy account of problems facing primary health service."

Dr. Boyd was referring to the feature address which was delivered by the Prime Minister at the opening session of the conference on Tuesday.

Grenada was also praised as the first Caricom member state to have set up a Food and Nutrition Council, and the conference urged all members to follow Grenada's example.

At Grenada's initiative, the conference discussed low-cost housing. A paper was presented by Grenada, and the conference urged the Caricom Secretariat to seek funds from the World Bank and the United Nations for low-cost housing for the region's people.

In it's paper, Grenada's delegate insisted that every home should have running water safe for drinking, proper sanitary arrangements, proper refuse disposals, and possibilities for repair.

Focus on the conference was on the special problems of smaller member states of Caricom, and a number of decisions were taken to deal with some of these.

The smaller states insisted that staff for projects oriented primarily for them should be located in their territories. They also called for a pool of specialists to serve them.

They also made a special call to attract regional specialists now working in North America and Europe.

They called on the Secretariat to seek external finance for development of rural health services, especially rural health centres.

At the same time, the conference urged that women be more involved in the decision-making and implementation of proposals for community health problems, and that member states begin to involve the masses in solving their health problems.

The conference called on the community to import drugs collectively and in bulk, to escape the high costs imposed by the monopolies overseas.

It called for the development of a drugs-testing laboratory, and for the maintenance of existing hospital equipment.

FWI, July 19, 1980

BISHOP ADDRESSES CARICOM FOREIGN MINISTERS

Prime Minister and External Affairs Minister Maurice Bishop opened the sixth meeting of Caricom Foreign Ministers at the Dome on Tuesday, with a strong call for an end to imperialist intrigues in the region, for a new international economic order, for stronger regional unity, and for the long overdue meeting of Heads of Government of Caricom member-states.

Delivering the feature address at the opening ceremony, PM Bishop said the meeting was taking place in the context of a tense international situation, and outlined many developments on the international scene, to which Grenada felt the ministers should address themselves.

In Central America, he said, there were signs of a possibility of external intervention in El Salvador, which could plunge the region into a dangerous conflict.

Reiterating Grenada's commitment to peace, he said: "We cannot shirk our responsibilities towards peace, and therefore, all our diplomatic efforts and support must be on the side of those struggling for peace and freedom."

On Southern Africa, PM Bishop called on the ministers to note increased United States support for the racist minority regime in South Africa and the condemnation of "the unholy alliance" between the United States and South Africa by all 50 member states of the Organisation of African Unity (OAU) last weekend.

"Nor can we ignore the latest developments in the Middle East," he said, referring to Israel's bombing of Iraqi nuclear installations. This act, the PM said, "constitutes a breach of international law, and a violation of Iraq's territorial sovereignty, and was aimed at cheap electoral gains."

He said that Grenada demanded compensation for the loss of life and damage caused by the Israeli attack, and called on the ministers to note that situation in their deliberations.

On the international economic situation, PM Bishop pointed out that the world faces a grim crisis, the brunt of which was on the developing countries. This crisis, he said, stems from the industrialised capitalist countries, and he pointed to the decline of tourism in the region, the rapid decline in the price of exports from the region and the escalation of the cost of imports "in dangerous and disastrous proportions" as some of its effects on the region.

To help resolve this, he said, Caricom had to join the militant struggle for a new international economic order, which would replace the present exploitative world economic order.

He reiterated Grenada's call for an end to the vast spending on armaments by the industrialised countries, and for the use of these resources in the interest of international peace, security and development. "This tremendous waste can be of benefit to developing countries, especially those as small as ours," he said.

"We cannot isolate ourselves from the concerns of peace, security, justice and progress in the world," he said, urging that these too be considered during the meeting.

The recent loss of Trinidad and Tobago's Prime Minister Dr. Eric Williams places the burden of struggling harder for regional unity on the shoulders of the Caricom member-states, he said, and called for one minute's silence in his memory.

PM Bishop said that in the context of the international situation he had outlined, "a meeting of Caricom Heads of Government seems the next logical step," and urged strong recommendations on this.

In 150 years after the end of slavery, the region had made some progress, but it was still vulnerable to external threats and pressures.

Grenada was not opposed to Caricom member-states receiving assistance "from whatever sources available," he said, "but what we take exception to is the manipulative and divisive use of funds to compromise our regional institutions and our people's integrity," he said, obviously referring to the recent U.S. efforts to force the Caribbean Development Bank to accept aid with political strings.

He welcomed the region's rejection of the U.S. attempt, and affirmed that Grenada would continue to condemn imperialist and neo-colonial tactics at all times, whether such tactics are "disguised, dressed-up or naked."

He reiterated Grenada's support for continued efforts at regional unity, and urged the region: "Let us face the world conscious of our collective strength."

On the Organisation of Eastern Caribbean States (OECS), which is being formally launched today, PM Bishop said it is an encouraging and significant development for the region. "It will help further consolidate the process towards regional integration started since 1967, and will certainly help bolster Caricom itself," he said.

He reiterated Grenada's and other regional states' call for the region to be declared a zone of peace, which would mean prohibition of nuclear weapons in the region, an end to military manoeuvres, withdrawal of all military bases, decolonization, and an end to foreign intervention, and mercenary invasions.

"When all these conditions are fulfilled, our region will definitely be closer to peace," he said.

PM Bishop also stressed Grenada's support for Belize in its struggle for independence and territorial integrity, and urged the meeting to put its support for Belize on record.

At the end of the opening ceremony, the ministers voted PM Bishop as chairman of the meeting, and the formal chairmanship of the committee was passed onto Grenada, which will hold the post until next year.

Also addressing the opening ceremony were Caricom secretary general Dr. Kurleigh King, St. Lucia's Foreign Minister Peter Josie, Guyana's Foreign Minister Rashleigh Jackson, and Belize's Education Minister Assad Shoreman.

FWI, July 6, 1981

CARICOM SUMMIT—A SUCCESS FOR GRENADA

The Third Caribbean Community (Caricom) heads of government meeting ended in Jamaica on Thursday with dramatic success for Grenada and a resounding diplomatic and political defeat for the governments of the United States, Jamaica, Barbados and Dominica.

The main issue receiving attention in the lead up to the conference, that of elections in Grenada, was not mentioned anywhere in the twelve page communique issued at the end of the meeting.

Instead, economic issues which Grenada and other progressive governments and parties in the region said must be the meeting's main focus was what dominated the final document. Secondary issues on human rights, which was raised by the rightwing governments, was only briefly referred to in the second of two appendices in the communique.

However, this reference to human rights reflected the broad spread of human rights components which was acceptable to the only people's democracy in the meeting—Grenada.

In contrast to the satisfaction expressed by members of the Grenada delegation at the outcome, Jamaica Prime Minister Edward Seaga, told a press conference at the end of the meeting that "there were things which I had hoped to have discussed which were not decided on at the conference."

He said that in the meeting no tempers were lost and, "the danger I perceived at the early stages was that it was going too smoothly."

Prime Minister Tom Adams of Barbados, who suffered the greatest personal defeat by the outcome of the meeting, left Ocho Rios early Thursday for Europe without a comment on the summit.

His proposed amendment to the preamble of the treaty of Chaguaramas about free elections proved technically impossible and politically unfeasible, given the hard work and prestige of the Grenadian leader, Prime Minister Maurice Bishop and his delegation at the meeting.

Also among the most disappointed elements is the U.S. government which both officially and unofficially sought to influence the meeting against Grenada, and against progressive movements and the peoples of the region.

An eight man U.S. congressional delegation took up residence next to the conference centre and a large American press booth plied Caricom leaders with questions designed to get negative responses against Grenada.

The U.S. chargé d' affaires in Jamaica, Robert Warne, remained in close personal touch with certain Caricom leaders and the press throughout the meeting.

For the Grenadian people, the decisive factor at the meeting was the consistent firmness and preparations of PM Bishop in defending the people's democracy and sovereignty of the Revolution.

The other leaders, many expecting apologies and promises, found Cde Bishop's clarity and conviction disarming.

For all those who participated, the meeting will be a memorable lesson in how firm preparation and principled positions can neutralize unprincipled opposition and strengthen the revolution.

The next Caricom meeting takes place in Trinidad on July 4 next year, marking the tenth anniversary of the treaty establishing Caricom, which was signed at that same venue in 1973.

FWI, November 20, 1982

SUMMIT—A RESOUNDING VICTORY FOR GRENADIAN AND CARIBBEAN PEOPLE

Prime Minister Maurice Bishop on Sunday told a cheering crowd of thousands of Grenadians that the recently concluded Caribbean Community (Caricom) heads of government meeting in Jamaica "was a massive and resounding victory for the government and people of Grenada."

He said every single one of Grenada's objectives were fully met at the three-day meeting.

PM Bishop, speaking at a mass rally in Seamoon, St. Andrew's, to mark the ninth anniversary of Bloody Sunday, said his delegation's firmness and principled position had defeated attempts by rightwing governments to oust Grenada from Caricom for its refusal to hold British style parliamentary elections, and so-called human rights violations.

"Those who had wanted to persecute us, became the persecuted . . . those who had set themselves up as hunters, became the hunted," PM Bishop declared.

Grenada, he said, stuck to its plan to focus on the real, burning issues facing the poor and working people of the Caribbean, such as high unemployment, the high cost of living and the falling prices for the region's raw materials, among others.

The Grenada delegation raised these questions at the conference, presented concrete proposals for solving them, and focused on additional, relevant and practical areas of co-operation, he disclosed.

The attempts by the rightwing governments of the region to isolate Grenada by amending the treaty of Chaguaramas—to make British style parliamentary elections mandatory for all members, failed miserably, PM Bishop declared.

On the contrary, he added, Grenada's plan to ensure Caricom's survival received considerable support.

He said the conference was not only a success for Grenada, but was also a victory for the concerns and human rights of the Caribbean poor and working people.

The leader of the Grenada Revolution pointed out that his delegation fought to uphold the principle of ideological pluralism, which, he said, is a fact of life recognised throughout the world.

Declaring that a major political and ideological struggle was being waged at the meeting, he said the refusal by some of the region's leaders to accept that principle showed their disrespect for a people's right to national determination and an independent path of development.

PM Bishop said the Caribbean leaders who were spearheading the attempts to oust Grenada from the 12-nation community, were shocked when they discovered that the Caribbean people are not hostile to the Grenada revolution and fully supported the process.

PM Bishop informed the meeting about the new grassroots people's democracy now being developed here, and the social and economic human rights that the revolution has brought to the island's poor and working people.

PM Bishop said he outlined to the meeting, Grenada's concept of human rights, which maintains that the majority of people are entitled to food, water, electricity, and the right to live a decent and dignified life.

"Our task is to continue the struggle for regional integration, unity, practical co-operation and greater people to people contact," PM Bishop concluded.

FWI, November 24, 1982

THE CARICOM DECLARATION OF OCHO RIOS, JAMAICA, NOVEMBER 18, 1982

We the Heads of Government of Member States of the Caribbean Community and the Bahamas here assembled—

Deeply aware of our situation as small States, for the most part newly independent, island-developing, prone to natural disasters and with small open economies particularly vulnerable to turbulence and pressures from within the international economic system;

Concerned about the global trend towards the use of force as a means of settling disputes and the assertion of spheres of interest and the hazards to which in consequence small States are increasingly exposed;

Mindful of the fact that external strategic perceptions of the Region can present both special opportunities and difficult problems for the development of our States;

Deeply aware of our common identity and of the need to consolidate and strengthen the bonds which have historically existed among our people;

Recognising nevertheless the reality of the growing heterogeneity in the social, economic and political systems of our States;

(1) Reaffirm our strong conviction that the maintenance and deepening of the Caribbean Community established by the Treaty of Chaguaramas provides the only certain way for the survival of our States as independent, free and developing societies.

(2) Declare our belief that the regional integration movement is the only viable option available for the optimal development of all the human and natural resources of the Region in the contemporary economic and political circumstances in the Region as well as in the world as a whole.

(3) Affirm our commitment to the political, civil, economic, social and cultural rights of the peoples of the Region in accordance with the Universal Declaration of Human Rights, the International Covenant on Civil and Political Rights, and the International Covenant on Economic, Social and Cultural Rights.

(4) Assert that while recognising that the emergence of ideological pluralism in the Community responds to internal processes and is in irreversible trend within the international system, we are committed to ensuring that it will not inhibit the processes of integration.

(5) Accordingly affirm our commitment to the interests of the Community as one of the main determinants in the formulation of foreign policy goals in response to regional and global issues.

(6) Reaffirm further that Member States will aim at the fullest possible coordination of their foreign policies and should seek to adopt as far as possible common positions on major international issues.

(7) Express our profound concern at the heightening of tension in the Region resulting from the recent increase in military activities in the Caribbean area.

(8) Reaffirm and call on all States to respect the principles of non-interference and non-intervention in the internal affairs of other countries.

(9) Reiterate the right of self-determination of all peoples including the right to choose their own path of social, political and economic development and insist that there can be no justification for any external interference with the exercise of that right.

(10) Assert our commitment to the maintenance of absolute respect for defined borders, and demarcated and traditional lines of jurisdiction of States of the Region.

(11) Insist that while the Member States have an urgent and pressing need for external economic assistance to achieve the goals of rapid social and economic development, the principles of international social justice require that such assistance be given in consultation with and with the fullest respect for the sovereign wishes of the recipient countries.

(12) Consider that aid programmes for the Region should therefore be truly reflective of national goals and priority areas for development.

(13) Affirm that programmes of aid channelled through regional institutions should be supportive of the integrity of such institutions and their autonomous character and should utilise indigenous resources and expertise.

Attaching the highest importance to the principles and objectives asserted herein, declare our common resolve to work together towards their maintenance and fulfillment.

Press package, Embassy of Grenada,
visit of Prime Minister of Grenada,
His Excellency Maurice Bishop to the
United States, May 30–June 7, 1983

GRENADA STANDS FIRM AT CARICOM

Amidst desperate efforts to revive the dead and decayed issues of alleged human rights violations, Grenada's delegation attending the Caribbean Community (Caricom) summit in Trinidad has once more succeeded in bringing real issues to the attention of its Caricom partners.

Grenada's stand on the proposed restructuring of the University of the West Indies (UWI) is well known and continues to lead the struggle for ensuring that this regional institution remains intact, serves the interest of the small non-campus territories and remains true to the principle of Caribbean unity upon which it was founded.

Of no less significance is the dangerously high import food bill of Caricom countries. Some $1,890 million worth of food imported into countries whose main economic base is agriculture is indeed sufficient to generate joint efforts and other forms of co-operation in a bid to increase its food production, be better able to feed its people and lessen its importation of food.

Then there is the case of multi-national lending institutions, whose conditional lending policies are highly unfavourable to the small developing countries. Caricom certainly has had the experience of Jamaica, whose economy continues to fall and stagger under the heavy blows of Prime Minister Edward Seaga and the International Monetary Fund (IMF). Unless there is some reform of those policies, as proposed by Grenada, many more will fall into this death trap.

The issues of sporting links with racist South Africa and peace and security in the region, remain high on Grenada's agenda in regional and international fora.

These are some of the many issues raised by Grenada at the summit that continues to characterise the genuine, honest and principled positions of the People's Revolutionary Government (PRG).

Having failed miserably on his home ground to achieve the isolation of Grenada at the last Caricom summit, Seaga opened the day's play, last Monday, with the usual senseless and empty attacks on Grenada. But he must realise that it is impossible to degenerate such a serious gathering of Caricom leaders to a circus show that will gladly facilitate his tightrope acts.

After all, it was Mr. Seaga's "secret police" that murdered over 700 Jamaicans during the last election campaign and hundreds more since he came to power. It is Mr. Seaga who is responsible for the thousands of unemployed, who have been thrown out of work since he took political office, and for the many ghettos in which poverty and inhumane suffering are the order of the day.

But Mr. Seaga attempts to use Grenada as a red-herring to hide his dirty tricks and his failing, bankrupt economic policies.

On the contrary, he will do well to take a leaf out of the PRG's book and endeavour to hold Caricom together through concrete proposals for solving the many political, social and economic problems that threaten the existence of Caricom and the regional integration movement.

CARICOM LEADERS AGREE ON PEACE

Caribbean Community (Caricom) heads of government began returning home yesterday, after concluding a four-day historic fourth summit meeting in Trinidad, that reached agreement on a number of key issues.

The need for regional air transport, peace and security, the Common Market Council and the Caribbean Festival of Arts (Carifesta), the region's major cultural event, were among issues agreed upon.

Proposals for the development of steelbands, put forward by Grenada, were accepted by the heads, as was a design for a new Caricom flag that will be flown in the not too distant future.

However, up to press time yesterday, it was not clear what were the final decisions on the three most controversial issues: the proposed restructuring on the University of the West Indies (UWI), the multilateral clearing facility and an official regional air carrier.

The meeting, which coincided with Caricom's 10th anniversary, was attended by all Caricom leaders except Antigua and Barbuda's Prime Minister, Vere Bird, who was represented by his son and Deputy PM, Lester Bird.

Prime Minister Maurice Bishop and his delegation were given an enthusiastic welcome by more than 150 supporters of the Grenada Revolution when they arrived at Piarco international airport on Sunday.

Responding to attacks made against the Grenada Revolution by Jamaica's Prime Minister Edward Seaga, PM Bishop said that Seaga clearly violated the accepted Caricom principle of ideological pluralism.

Seaga accused Grenada of human rights violations, through detentions without trial, suppression of an "independent" press, and failure to hold elections.

He said Seaga also abused his right to address the opening session of the summit and introduced a political red herring into a meeting expected to focus on economic matters.

"We really think that people should begin to recognise the importance of non-interference, to recognise, in fact, the importance of ideological pluralism, to abandon the dream and illusion that it is possible to shape the world after their own image and likeness, to recognise that people are always going to build their own processes in their own way, free from all forms of interference and outside pressure," PM Bishop said.

PM Bishop said that instead of being so concerned about human rights and elections in Grenada, the people of Jamaica and the Caribbean would want to see Seaga more respectful of their right to live, which is the most basic human right.

During the elections campaign in Jamaica in 1980, he argued, over 700 innocent Jamaicans were murdered, alledgedly by thugs and terrorists associated with Seaga's Jamaica Labour Party (JLP).

On the issue of widening Caricom, PM Bishop said Grenada would like to see this done on a planned basis and not in an ad hoc fashion.

"We think, in principle, that it is extremely important for us to bring in as many countries as possible into Caricom. First and foremost, give them observer status. Last, coming out of that, sign economic agreements with them. Later on we can consider associated membership and later on still, full membership."

On Thursday night, PM Bishop addressed some 1,500 Grenadian emigrants and Trinidadians at a rally held at the St. Augustine campus of the UWI.

FWI, July 9, 1983

PM FOR SURINAME

Prime Minister Maurice Bishop will leave here later this week for a five-day official visit to Suriname.

PM Bishop was invited by the Surinamese government, led by Lt. Col. Desi Bouterse. He will be the first Caribbean Community (Caricom) head of government to visit Suriname since the popularly-backed February 25, 1980 Revolution which overthrew the Henk Aaron administration.

In Suriname, PM Bishop is expected to visit various socio-economic projects, meet individuals and groups involved in building the revolutionary process, and address a mass meeting.

In his letter of invitation, Lt. Col. Bouterse, Commander of the Armed Forces and chairman of the decision-making Policy Centre, said the visit will afford PM Bishop the opportunity of "broadening his knowledge of Suriname."

It will also help to bring the peoples of Suriname and Grenada closer "for the benefit of a long-standing friendship" and will assist in strengthening Suriname's relations with the Caribbean, he said.

Lt. Col. Bouterse paid two visits to Grenada over the past 15 months. The first was to attend a Socialist International (SI) meeting here in July, during which he addressed a mass rally at the St. George's Market Square.

The second was last May for a 10-day holiday. During that time, Lt. Col. Bouterse visited numerous economic projects of the Revolution and attended various public meetings.

Fraternal and diplomatic relations between Grenada and Suriname have deepened over the past two years and both countries have accredited non-resident ambassadors to the other.

FWI, October 27, 1982

19
Cuba

Introduction

Cuba and Grenada established diplomatic relations on April 14, 1979. Cuba quickly became Grenada's closest friend in the international community and remained so until the demise of the revolution. Cuban-Grenadian friendship was cemented by the close personal relationship which developed between Maurice Bishop and Cuban leader, Fidel Castro.

Cuban friendship was manifested first in a level of material and other assistance unprecedented in Grenada's history. Some twenty-seven treaties covered Cuban contributions to such areas as the fishing industry, health, sports and culture. Cuba was an early supplier of arms to the fledgeling revolution. Grenadian students and policemen were sent to Cuba for training. Grenadians injured in the June 19, 1980 assassination attempt against the PRG received medical attention in Cuba. Weekly flights were inaugurated between the two countries and Cuban ships called regularly with supplies and passengers.

Many important Cuban political figures visited Grenada and Grenadian officials, including Maurice Bishop, visited Cuba. The Cuban publishing house, Casa de las Américas, published a volume of Bishop's speeches and a volume on the revolution part-authored by W. Richard Jacobs, sometime Grenadian ambassador to Cuba. Grenada and Cuba also worked closely together in international forums such as the United Nations and UNESCO.

Cuba's most important single contribution was its provision of the lion's share of assistance to construction of the Point Salines International Airport. Maurice Bishop called this "the greatest single piece of assistance our country has ever received from any other country, at any time in our history." This assistance included heavy equipment, technical expertise and a contingent of Cuban construction workers, many of whom eventually lost their lives during the U.S. invasion of October 1983.

The new Cuban presence revived memories of the almost forgotten earlier era of Grenadian-Cuban contact. This was in the years after World War I, when thousands of Grenadians and other West Indians emigrated to Cuba to work on sugarcane plantations. Interesting reminiscences of this period appeared in the Free West Indian.

Cuba became a major political and ideological role model for Grenada and Grenada, in turn, helped orientate Cuba towards its Caribbean reality.

WE OWE A LOT TO OUR CUBAN FRIENDS–BISHOP

On the first anniversary of friendly relations between Cuba and Grenada, Comrade Prime Minister Maurice Bishop says:

"I think the biggest value for our country and people has been the opportunity our relations with Cuba have given us of having Cubans live among us.

"As a result of this experience, our people now know first-hand the revolutionary commitment, dedication, discipline, warmth, unselfish attitude, sincerity, hard-work and internationalist spirit of our Cuban sisters and brothers.

"And remember that without the benefits of this experience, several of our people would have continued to believe the vicious lies and propaganda that imperialism is spreading every day against the Cubans, their great leader Cde Fidel Castro and their revolution.

"Our people have therefore learnt, in a concrete way over these past 12 months, about the vicious, dishonest and destabilising character of imperialism.

"They have learnt the truth about Cuba and the Cubans. They are now better able to appreciate the tremendous importance of developing the closest links with our Spanish, French and Dutch-speaking brothers in the Caribbean and Latin America, and in this way, smashing the colonialist-imperialist plot aimed at dividing us, so as to better exploit us.

"I need hardly say that we have also received a tremendous amount of material assistance from our Cuban comrades. In fact, without Cuba's assistance, we would not have achieved as much in our first year as we did.

"Can you imagine how many more people were able to receive expert medical and dental attention because of Cuba's loan to us of 12 of their hard-working and dedicated doctors and dentists?

"Again, the fact that we now have a fisheries training school is directly due to the fact that the Cubans have given us a number of their advanced fishing boats and loaned us some of their best technicians in this area.

"We have also benefitted from Cuban assistance in our army, the development of our water resources and several other key areas.

"But most important of all, on this aspect of our relations, is the massive and generous assistance revolutionary Cuba is giving us with our international airport project. Translating 25 years of talk about an airport into actually beginning construction has been due, in large part, to Cuban assistance with the required equipments, steel, cements, explosives, and, just as importantly, massive technical assistance by way of engineers, designers and skilled workers.

"On the material level, Cuban help with our airport is undoubtedly the greatest single piece of assistance our country has ever received from any other country, at any time in our history.

"I must also point to the great debt we owe the Cubans for the successful consolidation of their revolution. We have said before, on many occasions—and I repeat now—if there was no Cuban revolution in 1959, there could not have been a Grenada Revolution 20 years later in 1979. And that is a fact that we can never over-emphasise.

"Today, our relations with revolutionary Cuba are firm and deep. Despite the frantic opposition of imperialism and reaction, our relations are closer, firmer, tighter and more meaningful than they were, let us say, six months ago.

"And I have every confidence that the principled relations between our two countries and peoples—based on militant solidarity, strong bonds of friendship and firm opposition to imperialism, colonialism, neo-colonialism, racism and fascism—will continue to grow, deepen and flower in the years ahead."

FWI, April 19, 1980

NO VISA WAS NEEDED TO VISIT CUBA

Dear Editor,
In a previous article I promised to give some details of the procedures toward people of Grenada migrating to Cuba during the years 1918–1927, and conditions as existed in Cuba at that time. Well here we are.

Those steamships came to Grenada during the months of December, January and February and anchored in the outer harbour. People got to know about the time of their coming by a crier who went about ringing a bell and making the announcement: "Cuba boat coming."

There seemed to be a form of exploitation there, arranged between a man in Grenada and someone on board those ships, in that, the man in Grenada would receive information weeks in advance about the coming of a boat. He took bookings at a fee of 10 shillings in the first instance.

As time drew near, that fee would be reduced by half, then to two shillings and sixpence a few days before a boat arrived, where in fact, all that was necessary, was to pay a boatman one shilling to row one to the foot of the gangway of the boat.

No passport or permit was required to leave Grenada on those occasions, and no visa was required to land in Cuba.

The government of Grenada could not say how many people left this island for Cuba, and the masters of those ships concerned could not tell how many souls they had on board.

To prove those points, on December 29, 1925, between 3-4 p.m. five of us (friends) paid a boatman one shilling each.

He rowed us to the foot of the gangway of the "S.S. Labell Ganoy." We walked up that gangway, at the head of which a man inquired if we had tickets. Our reply was no. He made no further inquiry and we went on board.

The ticket in question was issued by the man in Grenada as a receipt for money that was paid to him. He caught many people from the country with that, but not those from the town of St. George's and the suburbs.

After my arrival on board, I saw people walking up that gangway at regular intervals until the dark of night. Even after the gangway was raised, men climbed on board by means of a length of rope let down to them by friends.

While it is true, that there was a Cuban president while I was there, the country's economy was controlled by the United States of America. I am not quite sure, but if there was any trading link between Cuba and any other country besides the U.S.A., that was very small.

The bulk of exportable products went to the U.S.A. and all consumer goods that were not produced in Cuba had the stamp or trade mark of a U.S.A. firm. There were Cuban stamped coins, but all paper currency was U.S.A. green-backs.

Employment—while the harvesting of sugar-cane was in predominance, there was a great demand for tradesmen, especially carpenters and painters.

Condition of Living—the standard of living was good if not high for migrants, with emphasis on those who could read and write. Very few Cubans enjoyed a high standard of living, because anything between 70 and 80 per cent of the population was illiterate. And according to reports received, it does not appear that any great effort was made toward the remedying of that deficit until after the Castro revolution.

Hence, to me, the great surprise of the almost incredible strides to enable Cuba to send us professional assistance on such great scale in our time of need. May I inquire of currently neo-colonialist disgruntled Grenadians: what is it that you want to see in your country? Certainly not progress.

I will supply the answer: your continued opportunity for exploitation. Well, I hope that that will never be made available again in Grenada.

I simply cannot agree with those who, from greed, would deign to hoard and amass wealth at the strength and the expense of the less fortunate. Down with exploitation in any form.

In a previous article, I promised to say something about Caio. This island is linked to the mainland by a mound of boulders that were dumped in a channel of cold water any thing between 500 and 1,000 yards wide, on which a train line is laid.

On Caio, there is a large pier, huge warehouses for sugar storage, large petrol storage tanks and soldiers' barracks.

Cuba—I remember the names of towns and villages, some where I lived and visited, others in the eastern provinces—Chaporra, Delicia, San Manuel, Manzanilla, Barques, Tualdero la Hel, Potopadre, Santiago, etc.

If I had the means, I would surely pay a visit to those places.

Cyril J. Cambridge,
St. Paul's.

FWI, April 19, 1980

INTERVIEW WITH CUBAN AMBASSADOR

Although April 14, 1980 marks one year of diplomatic relations between the governments of Cuba and Grenada relations between the peoples of both countries can be traced as far back as the 1920's.

In those times, pre-revolutionary Cuba was enjoying a boom in its sugar industry and there was a demand for surplus labour. Large numbers of Caribbean people, many from Grenada, migrated to Cuba to work in the cane fields and sugar factories. But typical of most capitalist economic fluctuations the "boom" lasted for only three years, the West Indian workers were laid off and the Cuban dictatorship at the time forced many to leave Cuba. But some stayed and were subsequently integrated into Cuban society.

Over the ensuing 50-odd years, contacts between the peoples of Cuba and Grenada remained negligible until in the late 1970's leaders of the New Jewel Movement, Grenadian youth, students and artists began visiting Cuba carrying with them countless horror stories of the Gairy dictatorship.

Cuba's dynamic, young ambassador to Grenada, Comrade Julian Rizo, says these visits contributed immensely to the Cuban people's awareness of Gairy-type repression and "made it easier for Cuba to react so quickly to Grenada's call for help in the first weeks of the Revolution."

In an interview with the "Free West Indian," the revolutionary diplomat recalled how the esteemed Cuban leader Comrade Fidel Castro gave him simple, clear cut instructions before leaving for Grenada: to do whatever was in the best interest of the Grenada Revolution, indeed a remarkable directive, revolutionary and internationalist in nature and in stark contrast to the conventional practice which dictates that diplomats act only in the interests of their own country.

"Over the last 12 months the relationship between Cuba and Grenada has developed in a material and concrete way in a very positive direction," says Comrade Rizo, a trained economist who hails from the Oriente province of Cuba. "Our 11 doctors in less than one year have attended to 41,611 Grenadians. Just as important as the medical care they provide is the open, friendly relationship which has developed between the doctors and their patients."

The ambassador points to the six Cuban fishermen now teaching their Grenadian counterparts new fishing techniques and the fishing trawler donated by the Cuban people as examples of the kind of concrete economic assistance Grenadians now receive from their Cuban sisters and brothers.

"Our assistance fits into the Grenadian plans for development," emphasised the Cuban ambassador. "Grenadians establish their own priorities and our Cuban technicians merely fit into Grenadian plans and schemes."

This is how the eight Cuban engineers who recently completed a survey of the Grenadian water system operated and in the same way the Cuban airport workers function under the direction of the Grenadian project manager.

Cuba believes not only in sending their doctors, technicians and workers to serve the Grenada Revolution but also in training young Grenadians (39 so far) themselves to become doctors, engineers, economists, dentists, etc. Some time in the future, after completing their training and returning to serve our Revolution, they too can move on to serve their less fortunate brothers and sisters in other parts of the Caribbean.

In our interview with Comrade Rizo, he remarked on how swiftly the massive international airport project got going. "On Nov. 17, 1979 the agreement for $25 million worth of Cuban assistance for the airport was concluded. The next day at the Seamoon rally Prime Minister Bishop announced it to the Grenadian people. On December 6 the Palm Island arrived with 95 pieces of heavy equipment and now only four months later work has already begun on the strip."

In the upcoming months more and more Grenadian workers will be involved in the airport construction and will receive training in middle-level technical positions.

"I see the airport project as a big school for Grenadian workers where they can receive training that will enable them on their own to construct huge projects like a new highway system for Grenada," observed Ambassador Rizo.

One area of Cuban assistance eagerly anticipated is in our Revolution's nation-wide campaign against illiteracy spearheaded by the Center for Popular Education. Comrade Rizo feels that Cuban successes in stamping out illiteracy can inspire us and their experiences in this area guide us as we move to organise and mobilise the whole nation around this cardinal task.

The Cuban ambassador also spoke of the advances made to increase bi-lateral trade between our two countries. Earlier this year a Grenadian delegation of businessmen visited Cuba and successfuly concluded a number of trade agreements.

Speaking on behalf of his countrymen now here contributing to the Grenada Revolution, Comrade Rizo said they had been impressed by the openness and friendliness of the Grenadian masses who smile and greet them as they drive through the countryside.

"For the Cuban comrades who have left their families, their homes and their Revolution their best reward here is to have the Grenadian people recognise them and be friendly to them," said the Ambassador.

Asked to comment on his most outstanding impressions of Grenada, Comrade Rizo listed among many the importance Grenadians place on education, the determination of our farmers to overcome difficult natural conditions, the humility of the PRG leadership, their sensitivity to the poor and their militant opposition to imperialism.

Finally, addressing himself to the relationship between Cuba and Grenada, he characterised it as one "based on principle, mutual respect, full understanding of the features of both revolutionary processes and commitment to establishing mutual benefits for our two peoples."

FWI, April 19, 1980

THE TRUTH ABOUT CUBA

A great many people congratulated us on our Feature Interview with Mr. Aaron Young, printed in last week's issue. As a result of the interest aroused by the article, the following letter was received from Mr. B. Edwards which asks certain specific questions about Cuba.

In order to obtain accurate answers to the letterwriter's questions, the FREE WEST INDIAN interviewed Mr. Julian Rizo, Cuban Chargé d'Affaires to Grenada. Below we publish Mr. Edward's letter and Mr. Rizo's answers.

The Editor,
The Free West Indian,
Hillsborough Street,
St. George's.

Dear Sir,

I was very interested to read the interview with Mr. Aaron Young about Cuba. Nobody is telling us about what Cuba is really like, so Mr. Editor I am asking you please to give us more information about Cuba, and hope you can tell me the answers to my questions.

1. I notice Mr. Young was allowed to leave Cuba and come back to Grenada. Is this because he was not a citizen of Cuba, or are all Cuban citizens allowed to come and go from Cuba as they please? If so, why do we not see Cubans visiting Trinidad, Grenada and so on as tourists, apart from Government officials?

2. Mr. Young said that no one owns big businesses where they can hire and exploit other workers. What about small businesses, like a small farm? Can you employ anyone to help you on your farm if you cannot manage all the work by yourself?

3. Can workers go on strike in Cuba?

4. Are Cubans allowed to criticize their government?

5. Do many black people hold big positions in the Communist Party in Cuba?

6. What percentage of Cubans are black?
7. What is the system of justice used in Cuba?

Yours truly,
B. Edwards.

Cuban Chargé d'Affaires Answers

REPORTER: Are ordinary Cubans allowed to travel as tourists?

MR. RIZO: Yes, Cubans can travel. There is no legal restriction. However, because of the trade embargo by the United States against Cuba we have a shortage of hard currency (dollars). This hard currency is needed for development–to purchase machinery from Western countries, for example.

As a result we cannot afford to give our tourists money to visit countries which use hard currency, that's why so few Cubans are able to visit Trinidad or Grenada.

Because we have trade links with the socialist countries our tourists can get their currency easily, to visit these countries.

Also, we now have developed trade and tourism links with Mexico and so increasing numbers of Cuban tourists now visit Mexico. Cubans can also visit their families living in the United States, provided the ticket is paid for in the States.

REPORTER: Can Cubans own small farms? Can they employ labour on those farms?

MR. RIZO: Yes, Cubans may own up to 34 hectares (75 acres) of land, and may employ as many persons as are necessary to work those farms.

Of course fewer workers need to be employed on those farms nowadays, because machines like tractors and harvesters are available to all the farmers.

REPORTER: Can workers strike in Cuba?

MR. RIZO: Yes, they can, but they don't! Firstly, because wages rise gradually but the cost of living doesn't increase, so that workers are getting better off all the time. Secondly, if there are problems regarding working conditions their own workers' committees inside the workplaces have power to remedy the situation. They have no 'boss.'

They receive all the benefits of what they produce, so if they strike, and produce less, they would be striking against themselves!

REPORTER: Are Cubans allowed to criticize their government?

MR. RIZO: Certainly! There is a 'Popular Assembly' (District Council) for every community of 5,000 persons in Cuba. The Assemblies meet once every 3 months and discuss all kinds of matters. For instance they may criticize the functioning of the health services or any other matter. Individuals may also criticize of course. The Cuban government welcomes criticism because that is how we can know what conditions need improvement.

REPORTER: What percentage of Cubans are black, and do many black people hold big positions in the Communist Party and Government of Cuba?

MR. RIZO: The Cuban government does not keep statistics which include people's skin colour, and besides we are very much a mixture of races, so it is hard to be absolutely accurate. But between 30%–40% of Cubans (roughly 1/3) are non-white. Black Cubans do hold big positions both in the government and the party, for instance Juan Almeida, the third in the government (after Fidel and Raul Castro) is black. But persons in Cuba do not hold positions because of skin colour, but because they are the most qualified and the most hardworking.

Before the revolution, those who had money and education were almost all white. This provided the ECONOMIC basis for racist attitudes. Now that we don't have a few privileged people, and we do have equal educational opportunities, the basis for racism has been removed. Both white and black people have the qualifications to get all sorts of jobs. Also in our schools we educate our children about why racism exists in the world and what purpose it serves, in order to prevent racist attitudes developing among our youth, through ignorance.

REPORTER: What system of justice is used in Cuba?

MR. RIZO: We have three levels of courts—National Tribunals (High Courts) Provincial Tribunals (at the level of each Province or State) and Municipal Tribunals (at the town level—like Magistrates Courts). In each type of court there is a Prosecutor and a defence attorney. Both are lawyers. An accused person may choose his defence lawyer freely. Then there are three judges. Sometimes they are lawyers, sometimes not. They don't have to know a lot of law. Their job is to decide whether the person is innocent or guilty.

With regard to laws, all laws are discussed by workers' groups, women's groups, village groups, youth organizations and farmers' organizations—all the people's organizations—before being passed by the National Assembly, our Parliament. The people's opinions MUST be considered and taken into account.

REPORTER: Maybe the demonstrations in Dominica wouldn't have had to take place if they had used that system of consulting the people before passing laws!

FWI, June 9, 1979

YOU CAN COUNT ON US, SAYS FIDEL

Among the many messages of sympathy received by the People's Revolutionary Government from regional governments on the Queen's Park bombing was one from Cuba's President Fidel Castro, received last Monday.

In his letter to Prime Minister Maurice Bishop, Dr. Castro said: "It is almost unnecessary to tell you how profound was the indignation felt by our people at the barbarous and criminal attempt on your life, on the lives of the revolutionary leadership of Grenada and its people.

"But nevertheless, this does not surprise us. We have lived through this experience.

"Imperialism does not hesitate before any methods, no matter how repugnant and uncivilised.

"We express our most profound condolences for the victims, and our sense of relief that you and the leadership of your glorious and heroic people are safe.

"Today, more than ever, I want to express our people's firm and unwavering solidarity with you, with your revolution, and with Grenada. Please know that you can always count on the unshakeable and resolute friendship of the Cuban people.

"The Grenadian revolution, like the Cuban revolution, is and always will be indestructible."

FWI, June 28, 1980

SPEECH OF MAURICE BISHOP TO THE SECOND CONGRESS OF THE COMMUNIST PARTY OF CUBA, DECEMBER 1980

On behalf of the Central Committee of the New Jewel Movement, the vanguard party of the Grenadian revolution–I bring warm, brotherly revolutionary greetings to this Second Congress of the Communist Party of Cuba.

In this room are gathered the finest sons and daughters of revolutionary Cuba–the vanguard of the Cuban people and the Cuban revolution, the undoubted inheritors of the mantle of Marti, Mella, Camilo and Che.

Cuba has been a beacon for us in Grenada. It has both taught and reminded us of many important lessons.

It has reminded us of the central role of the party in building the revolution. It has reminded us of the critical importance [?] the genuine vanguard of the people; building and maintaining close links with the peoples through the mass organizations.

Because of this, because of the exemplary success of the Cuban revolution, imperialism has unashamedly dedicated itself to Cuba's destruction. Those who have attempted, know that the revolution is indestructible.

But the newcomers seem to believe that they can turn back the clock of history; and therein lies serious dangers. We hope that we are wrong, but we see the possibility of dangerous adventurism on the horizon.

We know that there are plans to "teach a lesson," as these elements say, to Cuba, Nicaragua, El Salvador and Grenada. We know that we are not alone. The people of Cuba unhesitatingly and unselfishly came to our assistance in the first weeks of our revolution. When our revolution was at its most vulnerable stage, when imperialism and its mercenary forces threatened to blockade and invade our revolution Cuba provided us with the military means necessary to defend and secure our young revolution. That dealt a decisive blow to the designs and ambitions of imperialism.

We stand firmly on the principles of our anti-imperialist democratic revolution and we work consistently to preserve it. We have taken a wide range of measures to secure and consolidate our revolution. We have sought to strengthen and diversify our economy and sources of imports. We have practiced the principle of peaceful co-existence and stand in full support of world peace and detente. We continue to oppose colonialism, racism, zionism and apartheid and stand in solidarity with all peoples fighting for their national sovereignty and independence throughout the world.

It is clear that already plans have been drawn up aimed against the Cuban Revolution, the Nicaraguan Revolution, the Grenadian Revolution and the revolutionary process unfolding in El Salvador. We do not possess the full details of these plans. But what we do know is that we must learn from history and take the necessary measures to combat aggression, subversion and counter-revolution. What we also know is that no revolutionary process can survive—far less go forward—without the building and consolidation of the national economy. No revolution can survive without the political mobilization and organization of the masses, for this teaches them the goals, difficulties and gains of the revolution. No revolution can survive without the military capacity which provides the people with the honour of defending what they have built. These are the fundamental pillars of any revolutionary process. As we say in Grenada, the people without guns spells defeat. Guns without people means fascism. Cuba has the guns and the people—that is revolution.

Viva the Communist Party of Cuba!

Viva proletarian internationalism!

Viva the fighting people of El Salvador!
Viva the revolutionary forces of Latin American and the Caribbean!
Viva Cuba!
Viva Fidel!
Forward Ever, Backward Never!

FWI, January 10, 1981

MODEL POLICEMEN GRADUATE

Since the middle of July, 1980, 20 Grenadian policemen and prison officers had been undergoing advanced training at the International Police Training School in Havana, Cuba. And on December 23, they, along with 33 Nicaraguan policemen, graduated in an impressive ceremony witnessed by Prime Minister Maurice Bishop, Cde Selwyn Strachan, Commissioner of Police James Clarkson and his deputy Ian St. Bernard and other members of the visiting Grenada delegation.

The graduates had successfully completed training in such diverse areas as international law, immigration, scientific socialism, counter-intelligence, military preparation and self-defence.

Speaking on behalf of the Grenadian graduates, Cde Fitzroy Bideau thanked the school for "the fraternal help in preparing us to defend our revolution and fight imperialism."

He said that because of their commitment to the Revolution and because of what they had learned during the course, the students pledged to transmit to their comrades at home all they had learned, to maintain constant discipline and dedication and to continue "our cultural and technical training to better fight against our common enemy—imperialism."

In his remarks Prime Minister Bishop congratulated the graduates and pointed out that an important feature of the course was that it addressed one of the fundamental problems faced by all young revolutions—a shortage of skills.

He said that unless we have a fully trained and skilled people we cannot have maximum productivity and that this principle was also relevant to the police and the other security forces.

"You are in Cuba at an historic period and this must help your future political development. The experiences you can get here you cannot come by them in most other countries; to live, work and learn from a disciplined, honest, firm, united people. This course has given you the opportunity to internalise these qualities," the prime minister said.

He reminded the police officers that under the Gairy dictatorship the function of policemen was to repress and brutalise the people. However, the new policeman being groomed for the new society cannot be apart from the people but must be a part of the people, friends of the people who do not harbour colonialist or imperialist ideas and attitudes but possess a clear, anti-imperialist line.

Cde Bishop revealed that many of the "artificial distinctions" which separated the police from the army and the police from the people will be removed in this new year.

"In this dangerous period of imperialist war-mongering our intention is to build one united force of army, police, militia and people trained and ready to defend the Revolution," he said.

The prime minister concluded by saying he had "absolutely no doubt" that using their new knowledge and consciousness the 20 graduates would return to Grenada and be models that other police officers could emulate.

Cdes Clarkson and St. Bernard were "exceedingly impressed" by the spirit, enthusiasm and consciousness displayed by the graduates and also by the thoroughness, efficiency and humility of their Cuban professors.

FWI, January 10, 1981

LEARNING HOW NOT TO ADD TO BRAIN DRAIN

Grenadian students in Cuba can conceive and appreciate a new system of education for the Third World man. Why?

Well, firstly, what we see and understand is that we are studying under a different educational system than what we were accustomed to.

What used to happen to students from poor, underdeveloped countries like ours, is that when we went to study in countries like England, Canada, or the United States of America, we got education of a high academic level and learnt the new advances in science and technology, but we did not understand the need to come back to our underdeveloped country, where we know we will receive a small salary, and with limited scope of advancement.

Under these circumstances, without understanding what is true patriotism and loyalty to our country and people, our students chose to seek employment in the advanced capitalist country where he or she was studying. This led to the brain drain of our best students and youth, making our country remain underdeveloped.

In Cuba, students learn what is true dedication and patriotism to [their] people and country. The fundamental difference for a student in Cuba is that he first understands that the revolutionary government of Cuba has given him a scholarship so that he can be trained and develop professional skills, in order to go back to his country and help in the process of nation-building.

One also sees that the need to struggle for an education, helps in the full and allround development of our students. We can almost guarantee that when we return home we will be well prepared to continue the process of revolutionary economic and political construction of our country.

FWI, August 11, 1982

CUBAN BUILDERS HERE BEST IN NINE COUNTRIES

Cuban construction workers at the international airport project in Point Salines have been named the most outstanding Cuban internationalist contingent in nine countries for the first six months of this year.

The honour came last week during Cuba's National Union of Construction Workers' fifth Congress in Havana. The Cuban workers here, known as the "20th Anniversary of the Victory of Girón Construction Brigade," received a gift and flag as the best Cuban contingent serving abroad.

The union presents the emulation award bi-annually after evaluating the work of Cuba's nine construction teams, working in Nicaragua, Iraq, Angola, Guinea, Ethiopia, Libya, Vietnam, Laos and Grenada.

Brigade chief Eduardo de la Osa revealed that during the six months, the Cuban and Grenadian workers at the airport had fulfilled their production tasks 123 per cent, "23 percent more than what was expected from them."

Fulfilling production targets and work discipline are the criteria on which the construction brigades are judged, he pointed out.

Prime Minister Maurice Bishop, on behalf of the New Jewel Movement (NJM), the People's Revolutionary Government (PRG) and Grenadian people, has congratulated the brigade for "winning the very valuable and highly sought-after bi-annual prize."

In a letter to Cde de la Osa, PM Bishop stated that the project "commands the highest priority of our party, government and people, since we regard it as absolutely crucial to our entire future economic development.

"The fraternal and selfless assistance of your party, government and people in continuing to assist us to complete this project is really deeply appreciated by all of us in Grenada, particularly as we are very conscious of the severe economic difficulties facing the Cuban people at this time," the letter stated.

The letter pointed to the tremendous sacrifices being made by the internationalist workers, which have been a source of inspiration for all Grenadians."

PM Bishop recalled, "with great emotion," the accidental death of internationalist Ramon Quintana, killed in January, when a bulldozer overturned on him while he was working voluntarily at the Mt. Hartman stone-crushing and asphalt plant, which was subsequently named after him.

"The commitment and hard work of this comrade and of all the Cuban internationalist comrades, have been, for our people, a lesson in internationalist solidarity, in the true meaning of fraternal relations between countries, and in the level of commitment and discipline necessary to build our Revolution.

"The high levels of production, the excellent worker relations at all levels and, of course, the training that this project has made possible for our workers, are worthy of the deepest emulation in this year of Economic Construction and beyond," he added.

PM Bishop also paid tribute to "our dedicated Grenadian workers on the airport site," adding that this prize represents a real and concrete victory for both Cuban and Grenadian workers "who toil daily together in admirable co-operation and unity to make this project a reality." The brigade has pledged to maintain high production levels and discipline so that it can be honoured as the best for the year and keep the flag.

A delegate from the brigade represented it at the congress, which also discussed problems faced by construction brigades abroad.

FWI, October 2, 1982

CASTRO CONDEMNS U.S. ATTACK ON INTERNATIONAL AIRPORT

Prime Minister Maurice Bishop returned here Thursday afternoon after a three day visit to Cuba where he attended various activities marking the 30th anniversary of the attack on the Moncada Garrison, in 1953, which signalled the final phase of the struggle to free Cuba from its long history of foreign domination.

The past 30 years have seen Cuba liberated in 1959 and go on to become the first socialist country in the Western Hemisphere, surpassing all its neighbours in its efforts to bring the best social benefits to its people.

It was this that formed the basis for the massive celebration on Tuesday with representatives of governments, parties and progressive forces from throughout the world.

PM Bishop, however, was the only head of government there in a delegation that included Foreign Minister Unison Whiteman.

The PM had a busy schedule during his visit: he attended the main rally held in Cuba's second largest city, Santiago de Cuba, addressed a ceremony opening one of the largest textile complexes constructed throughout Latin America; visited and met residents and officials of the city of Holguin, toured a massive technical complex which produces equipment for the Cuban sugar industry; laid a wreath at the monument to Cuban national hero, Calixto Garcia; opened a new restaurant, and visited several important project/sites in Holguin, fulfilling a promise made to the residents there during a visit last year.

As always, PM Bishop was well-received by the Cuban people. He received a thunderous and sustained applause when introduced (next to President Fidel Castro) at the July 26 Moncada rally, attended by over 200,000 people from throughout Cuba.

The entire Cuban people were able, once again, to listen to him on a television transmission of his brief address to the opening ceremony at the new Celia Sanchez Manduley textile complex in Santiago.

He paid tribute to the international significance of the Moncada attack, and in reiterating the strong and everlasting bonds of friendship between the Grenadian and Cuban Revolutions and people, he presented President Castro with one of the .303 rifles captured during the pre-dawn attack on the True Blue barracks on March 13, 1979.

Receiving the rifle, President Castro said it was similar to some used by the Cuban revolutionaries in the Sierra Maestra mountains on the eve of the Cuban Revolution. It would be placed in a museum, he said, but added that it, too, would be put into use, if necessary, in the event of an imperialist attack on the Cuban Revolution, as being advocated by certain sectors in the current U.S. administration.

PM Bishop told the Cuban people that the textile complex, built with assistance from the Soviet Union, demonstrated the everlasting significance of "proletarian internationalism." It was this same spirit of internationalism, he said, which had seen Cuba giving invaluable assistance to the Grenadian Revolution in its four years.

Hallmark of this was the building of Grenada's new international airport at Point Salines, which is now nearing completion in time for the fifth anniversary of the Revolution next March.

"Thanks to the Reagan administration, Grenada is building the most publicised international airport in the world, and when it is completed next year, we will have to thank President Ronald Reagan for all the free publicity he has given to us," he said. The PM's address was punctuated on numerous occasions by applause.

In his lengthy address, President Castro hit out hard against Reagan's claim that the Point Salines airport posed a threat to U.S. national security, calling this "ridiculous." This very airport would be used even by Americans, who may wish to visit Grenada, to enjoy the sunshine and beautiful beaches, "because the airport's main aim was to improve the development of tourism, which is a vital pillar of the Grenadian economy," President Castro pointed out.

PM Bishop also reiterated Grenada's continuing support for and solidarity with the Nicaraguan Revolution. He said that the People's Revolutionary Government (PRG) also supported the initiatives of the Contadora Group of Latin American countries who were calling for a peaceful and negotiated settlement of the Central American crisis. And he expressed Grenada's support for the six-point plan unveiled by Nicaraguan leader Daniel Ortega, at the fourth anniversary celebrations of the Nicaraguan Revolution last July 19, saying that this plan, if agreed to by all the parties to the Central American conflict, would do well to bring much-needed peace to that part of the region.

During his visit, PM Bishop was able to discuss issues of mutual importance with President Castro.

FWI, July 30, 1983

PREPARED TO GIVE THEIR BLOOD—CUBAN SAILORS

Two of its generators were bad, but that didn't stop the "Gonzalez Lines" from setting sail to Grenada and beating the clock to bring its gifts on time for March 13.

Carrying an ice-plant from Bulgaria, the "Sandino" construction plant, materials for building the international airport terminal and thousands of tons of cement from Cuba, it was a priority for the ship's crew to get its treasures here in time for the Third Anniversary of the Revolution.

The ship left Havana on March 8 and stopped at Mariel (a port in Cuba), to have one of the two bad generators repaired. It then set sail for Grenada with three generators in working condition.

The ship's doctor and first secretary of its branch of the Communist Party of Cuba (PCC) Delbis Monteagudo, its Chief Engineer Reinaldo

Salinas, its Assistant Chief Engineer Fiodor Kandaurov from the Soviet Union, and its first Secretary of its branch of the Union of Young Communists (UJC) explained that a ship sailing under the conditions under which the "Gonzalez Lines" was sailing, would make the trip from Cuba to Grenada in five days. And a ship in good condition would make it in 3 days.

They described how the ship's crew worked day and night with their slogan being "to arrive in Grenada for March 13," and how the security workers in the port in Havana worked on Sunday, a day on which they don't normally work, to get things ready so that the ship could sail.

Their determination and hard work was not unrewarded, because they had the satisfaction of reaching here on March 12, making the trip in four days and 16 hours. The men said that they felt it their duty to get the ship here when they did, because it was the Third Anniversary of the Grenada Revolution, in the Year of Economic Construction, and their cargo was necessary to help in the overall economic development of Grenada.

The men proudly explained that this was their first internationalist duty. Other ships had already been on internationalist missions to Angola, Ethiopia, and Nicaragua.

On their impressions of Grenada and the Grenada Revolution, Dr. Monteagudo said that since the triumph of the Revolution, he saw Grenada becoming more democratic, mainly as a result of the high political direction with which the people are led. He feels that Grenada has its own convictions to make its own friends and follow its policies without intervention.

They all felt that Grenada has pretty beaches, and that the people's approach to them was friendly and warm. While here, the crew went to cultural performances, and said that although they don't speak English, they understood what was being said and felt.

The men explained that they went to Queen's Park on March 13, and saw the enthusiasm of the Grenadian people, which they said, reminded them of the early days following the triumph of their revolution. They commented on the warm response countries like El Salvador, Nicaragua, Cuba, USSR and most of the other socialist countries received, when Deputy Prime Minister Bernard Coard announced them at the rally. This they saw as an indication of the internationalist spirit of the Grenadian people.

They said that they would never forget the few days they spent here and would like to return to help Grenadians in whatever ways they can. They touchingly said that they weren't only prepared to give technical aid to Grenada, but if necessary, their blood.

FWI, April 3, 1982

20
The Communist World

Introduction

Relations with Eastern European and Asian communist countries grew steadily, though they never approached the intensity of the Grenadian-Cuban relationship. Deputy Prime Minister Bernard Coard toured the Soviet Union, Czechoslovakia, Hungary, the German Democratic Republic (GDR) and Bulgaria in 1980. He returned to the USSR for a month's holiday in 1982. Prime Minister Bishop visited the Soviet Union in 1982. Such visits resulted in commitments of aid and trade in a wide variety of areas, including agricultural equipment, scholarships to Grenadian students and the sale of nutmegs to the Soviet Union. The GDR provided equipment and technicians to upgrade the printing presses of the Free West Indian.

Grenada and the USSR exchanged resident ambassadors relatively late, in 1982.

MILLIONS IN AID FROM SOCIALIST STATES

Grenada will be receiving millions of dollars in aid from the East European socialist countries in the months and years ahead.

This is the result of trips made to the Soviet Union, Czechoslovakia, Hungary, the German Democratic Republic (GDR) and Bulgaria by Deputy Prime Minister Bernard Coard and a delegation of Grenadian officials during the past few weeks.

Speaking at a press conference here on Wednesday, Cde Coard, who also holds responsibility for Trade, Finance and Planning, outlined the areas in which agreements had been reached between the various socialist countries and Grenada.

The Soviet Union has agreed to provide $3 million worth of agricultural machinery to Grenada. This machinery comprises: 16 tractors, 12 six-ton trucks, 20 irrigation pumps, and 15 four-wheel-drive cross-country jeeps.

In addition, the USSR has agreed to provide two years' worth of spare parts, which will be shipped to Grenada, while Grenadians will be trained to use and maintain this equipment, all free of cost.

The agreement signed with the Soviet Union lays the basis for future trade between the two countries, and agreements have also been reached for Grenada to sell nutmegs directly to the Soviet Union. At present, Grenada sells 1.3 million pounds of nutmegs to Holland which in turn sells the same amount to the Soviet Union. The new agreement will eliminate Holland as the "middle-man," and bring the extra earnings directly to Grenadian farmers.

Grenada and the Soviet Union have also signed an agreement for the purchasing of machinery and equipment for the next five years. On a state basis, this can be purchased with up to 10 years credit, at 4½ per cent interest, but the agreement also covers purchasing of machinery and equipment by the private sector, at a rate of five per cent interest.

Cde Coard also indicated that Grenada has requested that the Soviet Union carry out a study of the feasibility of establishing a deepwater port in Grenville. However, he said, no commitment was made on this request.

A trade agreement was also signed with Czechoslovakia, and Grenada has requested a feasibility study to determine whether Grenada's rivers are capable of producing hydro-electric power generation.

If this is possible, Czechoslovakia, the GDR, Bulgaria, and Hungary, have all agreed to provide and install the generators.

Czechoslovakia, Hungary and the GDR have also agreed to send technical experts to investigate the possibility of developing light agro-industries in Grenada, and Bulgaria has agreed to provide the machinery and equipment for this, Cde Coard said.

Yet another trade agreement was signed with Bulgaria, which has agreed to construct two ice-making plants in Grenada. One will produce 10 tons of ice per day, and the other will produce 30 tons daily.

These plants will produce ice for storing fish caught by the 10 fishing boats provided by Cuba, as well as for other industries that need ice for storage. The plants are expected to be in production within 12 to 18 months, Cde Coard said.

He indicated that the GDR has agreed to provide some 800,000 worth of medical equipment, medicines and sporting equipment.

Hungary, he said, has agreed to train Grenadians in co-operative development.

Cde Coard disclosed that through the Hungarian medical complex, Medimpex, a credit line worth $2.7 million (EC) has been agreed upon for Grenada. The Hungarians will also provide technical assistance to Grenada to set up a formula for importing medicines by their generic names, instead of by their label names, as has been done in the past, which will mean foreign exchange savings.

Cde Coard, who was accompanied by a team of economists on his trip, said that all the East European socialist countries which the Grenada delegation visited have agreed to provide scholarships free of charge for Grenadians to attend universities and technical colleges, and to receive training in co-operative development and other fields.

However, he indicated that a large number of scholarships have also been offered by other countries, including France, Venezuela, Canada, Malta, Panama, Kenya, Tanzania, and other countries in the Caribbean.

The Soviet Union, he said, is offering 20 university scholarships every year.

"This is all part of the general strategy of the PRG of diversifying our trade, economic and aid relations with all countries," said Coard.

FWI, September 6, 1980

STRACHAN IN DPRK

The Minister of National Mobilisation is expected to return next week from the Democratic People's Republic of Korea (DPRK) where he attended the national festival celebrating President Kim Il Sung's 70th birthday, last Thursday.

Kim Il Sung set out on the road to revolution in his early years, and ushered in the national liberation struggle by organising the heroic forces opposed to Japanese occupation, which began in 1905.

He led the anti-Japanese armed struggle for 15 years, until the Japanese surrendered in August 1945, ending World War II.

Korea was then divided into two, and Kim Il Sung became leader of the government in the northern part. He led his country through the three-year-long Korean War that the United States unleashed in June 1950, and pushed ahead with building the Workers' Party of Korea, of which he is now general secretary.

Under his leadership, the DPRK has carried out agrarian reform, nationalised industry, transport and commerce, and eradicated survivals of obsolete feudalism. In 1975, the DPRK became a member of the Non-Aligned Movement.

In 1972, the party called for reunification of Korea, and this week, President Kim Il Sung urged the U.S. to withdraw its troops from South Korea. This, and U.S. interference in Korea's affairs are the main issues to be resolved before the country can re-unite, he said.

Prime Minister Maurice Bishop, in a congratulatory message to President Kim Il Sung, has expressed "the profound satisfaction of my government and people on your attainment of this outstanding milestone in your life, and in your leadership of the Korean people."

He wished him "many more years of leadership and guidance of the Korean Revolution and people."

Min. Strachan will discuss technical and economic assistance for Grenada with the DPRK government.

He will also visit India for talks with the government of Prime Minister Indira Ghandi on co-operation between the two countries.

FWI, April 17, 1982

SOVIETS OFFER FORTY MORE SCHOLS

The Soviet Union is to establish an embassy in Grenada within the next six weeks, revealed Prime Minister Maurice Bishop, at a press conference held Thursday on his trip to the Union of Soviet Socialist Republics (USSR).

Grenada has already opened an embassy there with former Ambassador to Cuba, Richard Jacobs as Ambassador, and Bernard Bourne as Minister Counsellor.

Describing his visit as having achieved all its objectives, PM Bishop said he was satisfied with its results, which have helped to broaden and further develop relations between both countries.

Grenada has received some $24 million, $4 million of which is a gift, to purchase a satellite earth station, steel supplies, a spray plane, work clothes for farmers, and to obtain technical assistance.

Other agreements involved sending experts here to carry out feasibility studies into the possibility of constructing an east coast port, a foundary and tool shop, a cement plant, a sewerage system, and to look at ways to conserve soil and water, and to improve the fishing industry.

Another agreement allows Grenada to sell nutmegs and cocoa to the USSR at stable prices for the next five years, and also bananas at a time suitable for Grenada.

Some 40 scholarships have also been offered at university, middle and technical levels.

PM Bishop said the satellite station gives Grenada an opportunity of breaking the imperialist cultural stranglehold on the country, and would enable Grenadians to receive news from the socialist countries which can "substitute for the United States garbage" which is now received.

It will also provide an opportunity, he said, to reorient Grenadians along more realistic lines. The station has relevance not only to television, but to telephone and cable and wireless services, he said.

PM Bishop compared the aid given to developing countries by socialist countries such as the USSR, and imperialist ones such as the U.S., saying that U.S. aid is always tied to strings, sometimes cultural or military, but there are no such strings with aid from the socialist world.

He pointed out that the USSR does not have transnational corporations in underdeveloped Third World countries to reap back its aid in profits.

PM Bishop said he was impressed with the high levels of proletarian internationalism, warmth, and sincerity, which the Soviet people possess.

The concern they have for preserving history and developing their culture, evident in the many museums, mausoleums and art galleries he saw, and the economic advance they have made in the face of harsh weather conditions and just 40 years after World War II when many of their cities were bombed out, also greatly impressed him.

The PM and his delegation were able to see the level of the Soviet People's commitment to peace. Everywhere they went there were banners advocating peace, and the Soviet people always recall that Lenin was a propounder of peace.

PM Bishop feels the U.S. leaders are not much concerned about peace because not many U.S. citizens died in World War II, nor were any of their cities destroyed, as in the USSR, where 20 million people died and entire cities were destroyed.

FWI, August 7, 1982

21
Social Democracy

Introduction

The New Jewel Movement obtained observer status in the Socialist International in 1978, before seizing state power. It became a full member in 1979. The Socialist International represented a mixed bag of nominally social democratic parties, covering a multitude of tendencies from the Barbados Labour Party of Tom Adams to the National Revolutionary Movement of El Salvador. The People's National Party of Jamaica, led by Bishop's friend Michael Manley, also belonged to the Socialist International.

In many countries where mainstream social democratic parties held power (e.g. Jamaica under Michael Manley), such parties had to contend with the existence of fully-fledged communist parties, either in opposition or in alliance. In the case of Grenada the element that would normally have constituted a communist party in fact represented a left wing within the NJM, whose membership ranged from forward looking businessmen to Marxists. The pronouncements of the NJM in power, including the statements of Maurice Bishop himself, suggested that the left wing of the NJM was very much in control of the revolution's direction. These pronouncements saw the revolution in a transitionary mixed economy stage on its way to socialism (in the sense in which communist parties use that word).

The logic of all this is that the NJM's membership in the Socialist International would have had to be transitionary as well. Had the revolution continued, one of four alternatives would have become inevitable. Either (a), the proclaimed socialist goals would have been achieved, resulting in expulsion or conversion of non-Marxist and centrist elements within the NJM and, in all probability, withdrawal from the Socialist International. (The ultra-left coup of October 1983 was probably a crude and premature attempt in this direction.) Or (b), the party's center would have succeeded in turning the transition stage into a permanent social democracy. Such a move may well have been accomplished by the left wing's defection into a fully-fledged communist party, as happened in the United States in 1919 and as has happened elsewhere. Or (c), the center, having gained ascendency, may have continued the movement towards socialism, but at a more measured pace than the left, and in a less ideologically inflexible fashion. Finally, and not very likely, the right wing may have seized control, expelled left elements and settled down into a nominally social democratic, but in fact conservative mode.

The Socialist International met in Grenada in 1981 and some social democratic states, such as Sweden, were among Grenada's important suppliers of assistance. The social democratic Manley government in Jamaica was one of Grenada's closest allies, while the social democratic Adams government of Barbados was one of its most inveterate foes.

SOCIALISTS BACK REGION'S PEOPLE

The Socialist International (SI) has given its full support to the region's anti-imperialist masses, struggling for democracy and new economic opportunities.

And it has called on governments throughout the world to stop propping up violent dictators and end the flow of arms to repress the masses.

This was the basic outcome of an SI meeting, held in the last week of March in the Dominican Republic, at the invitation of the ruling Partido Revolucionario Dominicano.

Agriculture Minister Unison Whiteman represented Grenada and the ruling New Jewel Movement at the two-day meeting.

SI is an organisation of socialist and social-democrat political parties from throughout the world. In the past, it was dominated mainly by parties from Western Europe and Scandinavia. But today, said Cdc Whiteman, many parties from Latin America and Africa are taking part, "so it is becoming more of a world body, representing parties from around the world, some in power, some out of power."

The NJM, said Cde Whiteman, first acquired observer status in 1978, when NJM delegates attended the conference in Vancouver. The party was formally accepted at a conference in Lisbon last year.

Michael Manley's People's National Party of Jamaica and Tom Adams's Barbados Labour Party are other ruling-party members from the English-speaking Caribbean. Forbes Burnham's People's National Congress got observer status at the Santo Domingo meeting, as did a number of other revolutionary organisations from the region, the Patriotic Front of Zimbabwe and the African National Congress of South Africa.

About 64 organisations were present at the meeting, which focussed on the economic and political struggles in the Caribbean and Latin America, with special emphasis on Guatemala and El Salvador.

Cde Whiteman said that the chairman of SI, Willy Brandt of West Germany, outlined the organisation's twin struggle for world peace and against world hunger.

He discussed the disturbing breakdown in political detente and the danger that "mankind will arm itself to death." And he pointed out that the fate of the Shah of Iran and Somoza of Nicaragua was sufficient indication that military solutions can no longer work in the world today.

"The social accounts with the broad masses of the people must be settled," he said. For a hungry people would fight for their liberation.

Bernt Carlsson, general secretary of SI, pointed out that it was not only a political organisation, but a socio-economic one. The opponents of SI, he pointed out, are the "large multi-national corporations and the political parties that are financed by them," noting the rapidly-growing phenomenon of imperialism through transnationals in the region.

But, he said, "the recent triumph of Grenada and Nicaragua provides great hope for the people."

Cde Whiteman said Grenada's contribution was a discussion of the poverty in the region and identification of its source. He told the meeting that whereas the price of Grenada's imports had gone up by five times in recent years, the price of its exports had gone up by only twice.

He drew attention to the low prices Grenada was getting for its goods—for example only five cents on the banana dollar—and, since this was the common plight of most of the other countries in the Caribbean and Latin America area, the contribution was well appreciated.

Robin Sears of the opposition New Democratic Party of Canada said some forces allowed political democracy, but not economic democracy; he noted there were no sanctions on multi-nationals. His country needed to recognise this, he said, since Canada itself is suffering from imperialist penetration.

Cde Whiteman said NJM's membership in SI opens up a number of contacts with progressive forces around the world, who could give moral or material aid, and opened up avenues for publicising Grenada's struggle abroad.

It also, he said, "is part of our internationalist duty to give solidarity to other peoples' struggles and to join in the fight against fascism."

FWI, April 19, 1980

SOCIALIST INTERNATIONAL SUPPORTS GRENADA

Member parties of Socialist International (SI) have expressed support for the Grenada Revolution, in a resolution passed at the end of the two-day meeting of SI's Latin America and the Caribbean Committee, yesterday.

In the resolution, the SI committee urged that special attention be paid to "the pressures of imperialism, propaganda and otherwise, to disrupt the efforts of the Grenadian people to build their own revolutionary process."

The committee once more declared its "firm support and solidarity with our brother-party, the New Jewel Movement (NJM), and with the government and people of Grenada in their efforts to build a just society of their own choosing," and agreed to form a solidarity committee of member parties "to assist Grenada in this period when it faces grave dangers from U.S. imperialism."

The committee proposed that "a serious campaign be launched to alert world public opinion fully to the dangerous and deadly implications of the imperialist tactics of propaganda, political and industrial destabilisation, economic aggression and mercenary threat to Grenada and Nicaragua."

The campaign's aim, the resolution said, "would be to ensure that these covert tactics of imperialism are treated with the same indignation and condemnation, and eventually amount to a breach of international law, in much the same way as the direct invasionary landing of troops are now regarded."

Signing the resolution were Movementu Antiy [?] Nobo (MAN) of Curacao, the National Revolutionary Movement of El Salvador (MNR), the Democratic Socialist Party (PSD) of Guatemala, the Movimiento Electoral del Pueblo (MEP) of Venezuela, the People's National Party (PNP) of Jamaica, and the New Jewel Movement (NJM) of Grenada.

Support also came from the British Labour Party, which was not represented at the meeting, but which sent two messages. A telegram, read at the closing session, expressed "warmest solidarity and support for the Grenada Revolution, the People's Revolutionary Government (PRG) and the Grenadian people" and said that although the party was not able to attend the meeting, "we have been actively pressing our Conservative government to take a sympathetic and generous attitude towards Grenada's requests for aid," particularly those for assistance for the new international airport.

"We believe the Grenadian revolution deserves the support of all democrats and socialists, and together with the government for national reconstruction of Nicaragua, it offers a beacon of hope and social justice in Central America and the Caribbean—a region too long dominated by exploitation and repression.

"In the difficult times faced by the Grenadian government in the future," the message said, "we will do everything in our power to mobilise international opinion in support of the democratic and socialist aspirations of the Grenadian people."

The message also pointed out that the party's policy towards the region was clearly pointed out in a resolution passed by its international committee earlier this month, which described the U.S. policies in the region as being "thoroughly detrimental to the achievement of democracy there, and must be condemned by the British government as a breach of the principles of self-determination of a people, and a dangerous threat to world peace."

The SI committee, in its resolution, also called on the United States government to "end its support for the present junta in El Salvador," and said this was not a viable solution to prevent further bloodshed.

FWI, July 25, 1981

NJM MEMBER OF COPAL

The New Jewel Movement (NJM) was formally admitted to membership of the Permanent Conference of Latin American Progressive Parties (COPAL) on Monday night according to party sources.

The admission was done in the presence of NJM's Political Bureau member and Minister of Agriculture George Louison, and Ambassador to Cuba, Richard Jacobs, who were both attending the COPAL meeting in Mexico.

COPAL expressed solidarity with the Grenada Revolution, and observed with satisfaction the advances made in the development of social, political and economic democracy.

A statement from the meeting said it hailed the considerable advances in health, education and social organisations and the development of the island's infrastructure.

It also made special reference to the building of the international airport in Point Salines, which it saw as being essential for Grenada's economic development.

And it denounced the United States' menacing threats to the Revolution, and specifically condemned its efforts to undermine the Grenada process.

At the same time, COPAL reiterated its support for the struggles of the Grenadian people, and for their right to construct their own process without external intervention.

This meeting was attended by seven ruling parties, three former ruling parties, and 10 other opposition Social Democratic Parties from several Latin American and Caribbean countries.

FWI, October 17, 1981

SUPPORT FROM ARUBA SOCIALIST CONFERENCE

International support and solidarity for the Grenada Revolution continues to grow in spite of imperialism's desperate attempts to isolate the "Spice Isle" from the rest of the world.

The latest manifestation of such support came in the form of a resolution, unanimously passed, at the recent international conference in Aruba which was attended by a high-level Grenada delegation led by Prime Minister Maurice Bishop.

Agreeing, without exception, to the resolution were a number of socialist and social democratic parties from Aruba, Curacao, Argentina, Bonaire, Chile, Guatemala, Jamaica, St. Lucia, Santo Domingo, Mexico, Trinidad & Tobago and Venezuela.

The resolution read:

"Having heard of the progressive economic, social and political developments occuring in Grenada and viewing them as helping to advance the conditions and aspirations of the Grenadian people, we note with great concern the threats of imperialism against the Grenadian Revolution and observe the coincidence of promised unprecedented military aid to other island countries noted for their hostility towards the Grenada process.

Consequently, at this important Aruba international conference, we declare our unequivocal support for and solidarity with our brother party, the New Jewel Movement, and the government and people of Grenada in their efforts to build a new society in accordance with historic aspirations of their people.

We restate our recognition of and support for suffering people to determine their own political process and reject any suggestion that our activities in this regard should be guided by the ridiculous notion of anyone residing in anyone's backyard."

Also unanimously accepted was a Grenada-sponsored resolution calling for the unconditional independence of Belize with "full territorial integrity."

Other resolutions called for the independence of Aruba and condemned the fascist Pinochet dictatorship in Chile.

FWI, March 28, 1981

22
The United States of America

Introduction

The United States viewed the new leftist government in its normal Cold War terms as a potential threat to U.S. hegemony in the hemisphere. Early PRG protestations of a desire for friendly relations had little effect. U.S. ambassador to the Eastern Caribbean, Frank Ortiz, visited Grenada in April 1979 and read the riot act. He warned the PRG against accepting arms aid from Cuba, hinted that the U.S. might stem the flow of tourists to Grenada and offered the contemptuous sum of $5,000.00 by way of U.S. economic aid.

In the U.S. itself, meanwhile, deposed Prime Minister Eric Gairy had received asylum and had issued a call for overthrow of the PRG. And NJM activists had been arrested on charges of gun running. The Trinidad Express *of March 31, 1979, quoting* The Beacon, *organ of Tom Adams' Barbados Labour Party, reported that U.S. Ambassador Ortiz had warned Gairy two months prior to March 13, 1979, of arms shipments to Grenada. PRG demands for Gairy's extradition were refused.*

None daunted by the size and interventionist record of the United States, the PRG joined battle with the Colossus of the North. "We are not in anybody's backyard," declared Prime Minister Bishop shortly after the visit of Ambassador Ortiz. Establishment of diplomatic relations with Cuba followed the Ortiz visit by a matter of a few days.

U.S. pressure followed a predictable pattern. Articles appeared in the mass media and travel trade publications advising against travel to Grenada. An unsuccessful attempt was made to exclude Grenada from U.S. funds channelled through the Caribbean Development Bank. Equally unsuccessful was the U.S. attempt in 1981 to prevent the European Economic

Community and other donor nations from financing Grenada's airport. Following the devastation of several islands' banana crops in the wake of Hurricane Allen in 1980, the U.S. Agency for International Development (USAID) pointedly assisted all the stricken countries except Grenada. The Windward Islands Banana Growers' Association (Winban) protested such divisive tactics. President Ronald Reagan's much vaunted Caribbean Basin Initiative studiously excepted Grenada from its list of beneficiaries. The U.S. government, while stopping short of breaking diplomatic relations, nevertheless refused to accept the credentials of Grenada's ambassador designate, Dessima Williams.

Most alarming for the PRG was the stepped up U.S. military presence in the Caribbean. Throughout the entire four and a half year duration of the revolution, Grenada lived in constant fear and expectation of the invasion which eventually came in October 1983. The PRG routinely accused the United States and its agencies for covert action of being behind many of the incidents of destabilization which plagued the revolution.

The PRG for its part countered with a stream of harsh rhetoric and a diplomatic campaign which was capable of some outstanding successes, as already indicated. Expressions of solidarity poured into St. George's from nations and organizations around the world. With great boldness for a nation engaged in such a seemingly unequal struggle, the Grenadian revolution even carried the struggle to the United States itself. The hand of solidarity was extended to radical groups within the United States and also to groups from such minority communities as African-Americans and American Indians. Well-known former CIA agents came to Grenada to warn against U.S. destabilization. Grenada successfully introduced a resolution to the Organization of American States (OAS) in 1979 calling for the Caribbean as a zone of peace. The Caribbean Community later accepted a similar Grenadian initiative.

The tension was not unrelieved, however. The PRG continued to make occasional statements in favour of good relations and even sent President Reagan a nice telegram on his inauguration in 1981. Prime Minister Bishop addressed two long letters to President Reagan in 1981, suggesting high level talks and expressing a desire for better relations between the two countries. The visit of Prime Minister Bishop to the United States in June 1983 resulted in more extensive dialogue than had taken place for some time. Bishop publicly expressed satisfaction with the trip. In addition to meeting with a variety of officials, he had made the most of the opportunity to dialogue directly with the American people.

ATTEMPTS TO IMPROVE GRENADA–U.S. RELATIONS

U.S. Ambassador to the Eastern Caribbean, Sally Shelton's recent visit to Grenada has resulted in what appears to be a step forward in improving relations between the two countries. Shelton, who was in Grenada at the invitation of Prime Minister Maurice Bishop in mid-December, promised to arrange for official consultations between the U.S. Department of Justice and the Attorney General's Office in St. George's to discuss the extradition of deposed dictator Eric Matthew Gairy and to communicate the PRG's concern about Gairy's use of the U.S. media for counter-revolutionary propaganda. The PRG had earlier stated its position that Gairy's extradition was "the main stumbling block" to normalizing relations with the United States. Reportedly, those consultations were to have taken place in January, but to date, no official or unofficial word has been received from U.S. authorities.

Phyllis Coard, Deputy Secretary of Information in Grenada said that Shelton's visit led to a "clearer understanding of our genuine wish for better relations and on our part, we see no reasons why relations should not improve. The ball is now in the court of the United States." Relations between Washington and St. George's sank rapidly after the March 13th revolution when the U.S. dispatched its then Eastern Caribbean Ambassador, Frank Ortiz, who attempted to dictate to the PRG who its friends should be, pointing to Grenada's friendly relations with the government and people of Cuba. Prime Minister Maurice Bishop, in a statement prior to Ms. Shelton's visit told newsmen that the PRG desired to have the best possible relations with the U.S., but that such relations "must be based on the principles of mutual respect, sovereignty and noninterference." He pointed to the on-going interchange of nationals of both countries, including Grenadians in the U.S. and U.S. tourists in Grenada. "We have absolutely no quarrel with the *people* of America, . . . and we do not want to have any quarrel with [the] American government," said the Prime Minister. He cautioned, however, that the PRG would not "be intimidated or bullied" by anybody wishing to dictate the process of revolution in Grenada.

During Shelton's visit, Grenada requested U.S.$1.8 million in assistance from the U.S. for infrastructural repairs necessitated by torrential rains in the country and U.S.$18.5 million (EC$50 million) to assist in building the new airport at Point Salines. This figure represents twice the amount which Cuba has already pledged for the airport construction project. No response to the aid request has been received by the PRG.

Grenada News, January–February 1980

MESSAGE TO REAGAN

The Grenada Ministry of External Affairs, on behalf of Prime Minister Brother Maurice Bishop, has sent a congratulatory message to U.S. President, Ronald Reagan on his inauguration to office.
The message reads:
"On behalf of the Government and on my own behalf, I congratulate you on the occasion of your inauguration to office as the 40th President of the United States of America.

"The Government and people of Grenada wish you a very fruitful term of office and hope to be able to work with you and your administration in promoting peace, greater co-operation and development in the region. The Government and people of Grenada also look forward to developing cordial relations with the government and people of the United States of America."

FWI, January 31, 1981

LETTERS FROM PM MAURICE BISHOP TO PRESIDENT RONALD REAGAN–EXCERPTS

March 26, 1981:

"We in Grenada have heard, read and seen reports on radio, newspaper and television saying in effect that your Government is engaged in an intense diplomatic and press initiative aimed at discouraging European support for international financial assistance for our new international airport. In fact, Mr. William Dyess, spokesperson for your administration, is quoted in the Miami Herald of Sunday, March 22, 1981 as confirming this.

"If in fact these reports accurately represent your Government's views, I express deep concern and dissatisfaction with the position of your administration.

"You must know of the genuine need for and character of the airport especially because it so very clearly represents a major attempt by Grenada to break with underdevelopment and to assist in bringing economic justice to the people of Grenada. References, allegations and speculations to the contrary give greatly distorted and inaccurate views of this reality.

"My Government has *always* wanted good relations with your Government and people. All your diplomats and officials who have come to Grenada can confirm this. As we have continued to repeat, the basis for such principled good neighbourliness includes the fact that U.S. tourists come to Grenada by the thousands annually; the fact that thousands of United States citizens (residents and students) live in Grenada; included also is the fact that thousands of Grenadians live in the United States. Equally important is the fact that Grenada poses no security threat whatsoever to your country, or, indeed, to any other country.

". . . Mr. President, I would like to suggest that our two Governments hold bilateral discussions at the highest possible level to discuss developments and to clear up possible misunderstandings. I sincerely look forward to a positive response to this proposal. . . ."

August 11, 1981:

"Mr. President, my Government lays down no conditions precedent to the improvement of relations between our two countries. . . .

"Again, on the occasion of your inauguration to office as the 40th President of your country, I sent a message congratulating you on behalf of the Government and People of Grenada and reassuring you that my Government looked forward to developing cordial relations with the Government and People of the United States of America. Regrettably, there has been no positive response by your Government to any of the indications of our desire for cordial relations with your Government. On the contrary, your Administration has consistently demonstrated an overtly hostile attitude towards the people and Government of Grenada.

"Although under President Carter's Administration, relations between the United States of America and Grenada were somewhat less than cordial, nevertheless the mechanism existed through which both Governments could, by an exchange of views, seek to improve those relations. The proposal made by President Carter on March 23, 1979 to accredit Miss Sally Shelton as Ambassador to Grenada was readily approved and agreement was accordingly conveyed on 6th April, 1979.

"On the other hand, the Government of Grenada is still awaiting an acknowledgement of receipt of its request for agreement of the United States Government to the proposal to appoint Mr. Jimmy Emmanuel, a career diplomatic officer, as this country's Ambassador Extraordinary and Plenipotentiary to your country. This proposal was submitted on January 15, 1980 for agreement to the appointment of Ms. Dessima Williams, which in like manner, was not even acknowledged.

"Mr. President, in response to the many initiatives taken by my Government to normalize relations between our two countries, the United States Administration has demonstrated indifference and hostility to the People's Revolutionary Government in a variety of ways. In what seems to be a systematic and concerted propaganda campaign against us, members of your Administration have persistently made false, malicious and misleading statements, (which they must surely know totally lack any factual foundation) concerning our development process and particularly in regard to our international airport project.

"We were quite frankly very alarmed by the massive diplomatic campaign which your Administration mounted in order to dissuade certain countries and international organizations from attending the Co-financing Conference which we convened in Brussels on 14th and 15th April, 1981 with the help of the European Economic Community Commission, for the purpose of mobilizing financial support for our new international airport. Unfounded and unreasonable fears have been expressed that, because of the proposed length of the runway strip of the new airport and the small size of the existing tourist plant in Grenada, the new airport is being constructed for other than economic reasons. We wish to reassure you, as we have already assured several of your officials that we have no intention, and have never had any intention, of using this modest international airport for any purpose other than as the means of developing our relatively untapped tourist potential and for the development and expansion of regional and international trade in fresh fruits and vegetables and agro-industrial products.

"We believe, in all humility, that this international airport is the most important project that we need to undertake to achieve further economic development. In fact, we see it as having the same socio-economic significance as the construction and expansion of the railway system had in your own country in the 19th century. The length of the runway when completed will be 9,000 feet, which will be the same length as the runways in Antigua and Trinidad and will be shorter than almost all the runways in other countries in the region where similar facilities exist. . . .

"My Government is also painfully conscious of the increased efforts by your Administration to cut off our traditional aid possibilities both regionally and internationally with a view to strangulating our fledgling economy and to subverting the political, economic and social process which we have instituted. By way of examples, I wish to refer to a few of these incidents.

"Following the devastating damage inflicted to the banana industries in all four Windward Islands (Grenada, St. Vincent and the Grenadines, St. Lucia and Dominica) by Hurricane Allen in 1980, the Windward Islands Banana Association, which is an umbrella organization comprising the four islands' banana societies, applied to the Government of the United States of America through the appropriate agency for assistance to rehabilitate the banana industries in all four islands. Aid was granted for the purpose for which it was sought but on the express condition that no part of the funds allocated should be made available to rehabilitate the banana industry in Grenada.

"During the months of January and February 1981, following the visit to Grenada by staff members of the International Monetary Fund (I.M.F.), my Government successfully negotiated a three-year Extended Fund Facility for Special Drawing Rights of $6.3 million U.S. currency (equivalent to $21 million East Caribbean Currency). This facility was, and still is, required to assist the Government of Grenada in implementing a programme designed to fundamentally restructure the local economy. On March 25, 1981 the United States Director on the Board of Directors of the I.M.F., on somewhat specious grounds, asked for an indefinite postponement of my Government's request. Our application to the Fund was prepared and recommended by the technical staff of the Board and approved by the Management of the Fund and was listed for consideration at a meeting of the Executive Directors of the Fund which was scheduled to take place on March 26, 1981.

"More recently, Mr. President, in a further demonstration of its economic aggression against Grenada, your Administration attempted to deny Grenada's having access to the funds which your Government proposed to make available to the Caribbean Development Bank to finance "basic human needs" projects. Your Government's proposal to the Bank was clearly intended to bar our tiny, underdeveloped island from benefitting from financial aid disbursed through a regional institution which has been established for the express purpose of providing financial assistance to regional governments and undertakings. We are also aware of other initiatives currently being taken against our interests in other regional bodies.

"Mr. President, I wish to refer to one other matter of the deepest concern to the Government of Grenada which seems to demonstrate your Government's hostility and indifference to the vital interests of Grenada. There are abundant credible reports currently circulating about the activities of mercenaries who are at this moment being trained on United States territory for deployment against certain regional countries including Grenada. It is impossible to believe that the law enforcement agencies in your country are not privy to those reports. Convincing evidence in support of the veracity of these reports recently came to light when a number of mercenaries were intercepted near the Mississippi state line just as they were about to embark on an invasion of the Commonwealth of Dominica, one of the four Windward Islands. Statements made by some of the persons who were apprehended reveal that the primary objective of their operation was the invasion of Grenada and that Dominica was going to be used by them as a base from which to conduct operations.

"Mr. President, you are no doubt aware of Resolution No. 35/48, which was adopted by the United Nations General Assembly on December 4, 1980 and which established an *Ad Hoc* Committee on the drafting of an International Convention against the Recruitment, Use, Financing and Training of Mercenaries. This Committee comprises thirty-five Member States, including the United States of America.

"You are also doubtless aware of United Nations General Assembly Resolution No. 35/35 adopted on November 14, 1980, operative paragraph 7 of which "reaffirms that the practice of using mercenaries against national liberation movements and sovereign states constitutes a criminal act and that mercenaries themselves are criminals. . . .

"Mr. President, it seems to me that the foregoing amounts to a virtual declaration of war by your Government against the Government and People of Grenada. When a Government of your power and influence chooses to embark on a conscious campaign of propaganda destabilization and economic warfare against a small, poor non-aligned country like ours it must raise serious concerns and questions for our people and, must also have a devastating effect on the economy of our country and thus affect its Government's modest, but totally resolute, efforts to end poverty and raise the quality of life of its people. When, on top of this, mercenaries training on your territory even boast of their plans to invade our country, without being subjected to any form of legal action, then I am sure you will agree with me that the conclusion I have been obliged to draw is, in the absence of any contrary statement from you, eminently reasonable and justified.

"If you should choose to allow this letter also to go unanswered as happened to my earlier letter to you of March 26, 1981 referring to similar unhappy developments and requesting high level discussions, then we shall have to conclude that your Government does not desire even normal and minimum relations with my Government, in which event we would be obliged to consider further measures necessary to advance, consolidate and defend the social, political and economic transformation process which we have undertaken in Grenada.

"In the hope that you will respond to this letter before the end of September, I repeat my earlier call for urgent high level talks with a view to exploring all possibilities for normalizing relations between our two Governments."

Grenada Solidarity Committee of Boston,
Facts About Revolutionary Grenada

FREE OUR BROTHERS

The Prime Minister of Grenada, Bro. Maurice Bishop, has written to United States Secretary of State Cyrus Vance, requesting the immediate dropping of charges against Chester Humphrey and James Wardally, our two Grenadian brothers arrested in February of this year on charges of exporting firearms to Grenada.

At the same time our Acting Attorney General, Bro. Lloyd Noel, has written to the U.S. Attorney General, Griffen Bell, making the same request.

In reply to Bro. Bishop's letter, Secretary Vance has agreed to recommend that charges against the brothers should be dropped. His recommendations apparently went to the American Justice (Legal) Department some weeks ago. Up to now, however, there has been no response from the Justice Department.

Grenadians in the United States have recently begun a postcard campaign asking Cyrus Vance to make sure that charges are dropped. Their postcard says "Dear Secretary Vance: In the interest of promoting good relations with the people of Grenada and protecting the civil liberties of U.S. and foreign nationals within the United States, PLEASE DROP ALL CHARGES AGAINST CHESTER HUMPHREY AND JAMES WARDALLY."

Chester and Jim are well known to all Grenadians as sincere, committed and courageous brothers long in the struggle for human rights in Grenada. At a time when we at home are for the first time in many years enjoying the smell and the taste of freedom, let us not forget that our two brothers in the United States still face the possibility of being put on trial on charges which carry a maximum penalty of LIFE IMPRISONMENT.

In the light of the delay in dropping such charges against Chester and Jim, it is time that Grenadians at home add their voices to the protests being made by Grenadians living in the States.

We are appealing to all brothers and sisters who support the Revolution, who support the cause of freedom and justice, to write to SECRETARY CYRUS VANCE, U.S. DEPT. OF STATE, 2201 C STREET, NW, WASHINGTON, D.C. 20520. Ask him to make sure that charges against Humphrey and Wardally are dropped. Our freedom must be their freedom!

FWI, June 16, 1979

SHELTON SPEAKS WITH FORKED TONGUE, SAYS PRG

The People's Revolutionary Government says it is "disgusted and disturbed" over recent remarks by outgoing United States Ambassador Sally

Shelton that Grenada had rebuffed U.S. attempts to improve relations, and that she did not pay a farewell visit to St. George's, because of the PRG's lack of interest.

Ms. Shelton's remarks came at a farewell news conference in Barbados. A political appointee of former U.S. President James Carter, she was not requested to stay on by the new Ronald Reagan administration.

Ms. Shelton's assertions, the PRG says, "fly in the face of truth and reality," since the PRG has "from the first day of the revolution, made every attempt to have good relations" with the U.S. government, "but on each occasion was rebuffed."

The PRG recalls that Frank Ortiz, Ms. Shelton's predecessor, visited Grenada in the early weeks of the Revolution, "to issue imperious threats and directives" and to offer bilateral assistance of $5,000.

The U.S. government, it also recalls, "first promised, and later, in effect, refused, to extradite Eric Gairy" to face serious criminal charges, including conspiracy to murder.

Ms. Shelton's dishonesty, said the PRG, "is staggering," noting that it had invited her on December 12, 1980, before she resigned as ambassador, to hold talks on "certain matters of mutual interest with a view to promoting and developing friendly relations between the government and people of the U.S.A. and the government and people of Grenada."

The PRG also recalled that it sent to President-elect Reagan on November 6, 1980, a congratulatory cable, stressing that "the government and people of Grenada look forward to maintaining and further developing friendly relations with the government and people of the U.S.A."

In reply, Reagan thanked Prime Minister Maurice Bishop and said he looked forward "to a mutual effort to promote friendly relations between our two nations."

Ms. Shelton's remarks obviously don't help those efforts.

On Reagan's inauguration, the PRG said it sent him another message, reiterating that "the government and people of Grenada also look forward to developing cordial relations with the government and people of the U.S.A."

In her farewell letter to PM Bishop, dated February 6, 1981, Ms. Shelton observed that "we both share deep concern about the welfare of the people of Grenada and for the future of the Eastern Caribbean.

"I shall most certainly follow with deep interest the progress of your government and I want you to feel free to call upon me if ever I can be of assistance," she ended.

"In the light of all this, how could Ms. Shelton now make these preposterous, absurd and dishonest statements, unless they were made for the purpose of advancing her own career?" the PRG asked.

Ms. Shelton told the press that "the US had demonstrated its commitment to friendly relations by continuing its economic assistance programme to Grenada, which is now benefitting from several million dollars channelled through the Caribbean Development Bank (CDB)."

On this, the PRG reminded Ms. Shelton that, notwithstanding its repeated requests, "we have never received one cent of bilateral assistance from the U.S.A." Indeed, the only offer was that of the $5,000 from Ambassador Ortiz.

While it is true that Grenada has received assistance from the CDB, the PRG said, Ms. Shelton well knows the CDB, as a regional institution, draws funds from several different governments and agencies, including the U.S.A."

Moreover, it was Ms. Shelton's government, the PRG recalled, "which tried to compromise the 20-year-old Windward Islands Banana Association and the regional integration movement, by insisting that U.S. banana rehabilitation aid to Winban, following Hurricane Allen, must exclude any benefits to Grenada."

The PRG neglected to mention that the U.S.A. has so far failed to recognise its appointed ambassador, Dessima Williams.

Finally, the PRG reiterated that "it has always been interested in developing cordial relations with the U.S. government, based upon the well-established principles of legal equality of states, mutual respect, sovereign integrity and non-intervention in each other's internal affairs."

FWI, February 28, 1981

ANTI-GRENADA PROPAGANDA BACKFIRES

Attempts by the might of United States imperialism to smash the recent co-financing conference for Grenada's international airport have failed miserably and early signs show that its vulgar propaganda has backfired in its face.

At a meeting last Wednesday at York House, Minister of Finance Bernard Coard, who led Grenada's delegation to the conference in Brussels, last week, reported that it has been a major success with some 13 countries and international organizations attending.

Attending were the host and conference organizers, the European Economic Community (EEC), Libya, Syria, Algeria, Venezuela, Nigeria, Sweden, Iraq, the Organization of Petroleum Exporting Countries (OPEC), the Iraqi Fund, the Caribbean Development Bank (CDB), and the World Bank.

After hearing the facts on the airport and its importance to Grenada, delegates issued a joint communique in support of it.

The communique called on donor countries to aid the project. In addition, representatives expressed distaste for the US attempts to bully them from attending the conference, and said that the airport's importance to Grenada was very clear to them.

The EEC representative, at the end of the conference, said their aid was not subject to favourable or unfavourable political winds and it was this character that made their aid meaningful and principled.

Bro. Coard said that prospects for aid looked very good and that bilateral talks would continue with the interested countries and organizations.

The airport is expected to cost some $71 million (U.S.) of which $41 million has already been granted by the governments of Cuba, Venezuela, Syria, Libya, Algeria and Iraq. The other $30 million the PRG is seeking to raise through grants where possible, as well as loans from international organizations and countries.

It is incredible the kinds of lies the US circulated in the mass media the world over before the conference, Bro. Coard said.

One said that the airport runway would be extraordinarily long, with several different airstrips. In fact, at 9,000 feet, the Point Salines airport will be one of the shortest in the region.

Another was that the airport is not feasible and that Grenada would not be able to repay its cost.

Bro. Coard pointed out that the net revenue from the airport, combined with hotel occupancy taxes, will easily cover both the principal and interest on these loans. This does not include, he said, revenue from hotel profit taxes and import duties on materials to build new hotels.

In fact, he said, only 10 years after its completion, the airport will earn the people of Grenada some $17 million per year, at lowest estimates.

The US acted on the assumption that countries attending the conference would not know anything about the airport project. So many studies had been done on an international airport for Grenada that the conference was able to study all, including joint Canadian, English and American studies, Bro. Coard pointed out.

FWI, April 25, 1981

U.S. FAILS TO BLOCK CDB $

The United States has failed once again, in its continuing efforts to promote economic sabotage against the Grenada Revolution.

The latest attempt came on June 18, at a meeting of the board of directors of the Caribbean Development Bank (CDB), when the U.S. representative demanded that Grenada be excluded from receiving U.S. funds channelled through the bank.

He said the U.S. took this position because Grenada did not respect human rights and did not hold elections, and that the American government had the right to decide which countries should receive its money.

But the CDB decided that U.S. money could not divide the region or dictate policy. Representatives of regional governments on the bank's board of directors voted unanimously to reject the $10.8 million (EC) grant, which was to have been part of a pledge by the U.S. government to a basic needs programme for the Leeward and Windward Islands, under assistance through the Caribbean Group for Co-operation in Economic Development.

CDB vice-president Neville Nichols said the bank had turned down the U.S. offer because to exclude Grenada would have been contrary to the Bank's charter. He quoted Article 35 of the CDB charter, which states that the bank "shall not accept loans or assistance that may in any way prejudice or otherwise alter its purpose or functions."

Nichols also quoted another section of that article, which states that the bank "shall not interfere in the political affairs of any member-country" and its staff's decisions should not be influenced by the political character of the member-state concerned.

According to this clause, only economic considerations relevant to the purpose and functions of the bank should affect its decisions, and that such considerations should be weighed impartially, to achieve and carry out the bank's purpose and functions.

First indications of reaction to U.S. pressure on the CDB came the day after the Barbados election, when Prime Minister Tom Adams said his country would not support efforts aimed at preventing Grenada from receiving funds through the CDB, and suggested that the bank should reject the U.S. grant, if the Americans insisted that Grenada should be excluded from benefitting from it.

Dominica's Prime Minister Mary Eugenia Charles, who was attending a meeting at the Secretariat of the Organisation of American States (OAS) earlier this week, said that due to the multi-lateral nature of the CDB's loans, "any insistence by the U.S. that aid should be used for only certain member countries cannot be complied with by the bank."

The Dominica Liberation Movement Alliance (DLMA) praised the CDB and PM Charles for their position, and chided the U.S. government's efforts to turn back the Grenada Revolution.

The People's Progressive Party (PPP) of Guyana, led by Dr. Cheddi Jagan, described the U.S. position as "hypocritical," and called on the people of the Caribbean to support the Grenada government in the face of the increasing U.S. pressure against the Revolution.

This latest U.S. attempt at economic destabilisation against the Grenada Revolution follows other similar attempts in the last few months. Late last year, the U.S. government pressured the Windward Islands Banana Growers Association (Winban) into excluding fellow-member Grenada from hurricane aid despite the regional grouping's protest.

And last April, the Reagan administration dispatched envoys to European countries to try to prevent them from attending a conference co-sponsored by the European Economic Community (EEC) and the Grenada government aimed at getting additional finance for construction of the international airport at Point Salines.

On that occasion too, the U.S. was rebuffed, and the conference came off successfully, with many institutions and countries pledging assistance.

FWI, June 27, 1981

U.S. AID FOR ALL BUT ONE

Prime Minister Maurice Bishop has expressed gratitude to the Windward Islands Banana Growers' Association and its member states for their principled stand in calling upon the U.S. Agency for International Development (USAID) to reconsider its refusal to assist Grenada's banana industry, ravaged by Hurricane Allen.

Cde Bishop's remarks were made in an address to the annual qualifiers convention of the Guyana-Trinidad Mutual Life Insurance Company, held at the Dome in Grand Anse, on Monday.

At its annual general meeting in St. Lucia on October 15, Winban passed a resolution deploring USAID's exclusion of Grenada from assistance to Winban member states, stating that such action was "fundamentally opposed to the concept of the unity of Winban." Winban called upon USAID to offer prompt rehabilitation assistance to Grenadian banana growers.

Winban's president, Michael Moncherry of St. Lucia, also wrote in protest to U.S. ambassador Sally Shelton and USAID's director for the region, William Wheeler, drawing their attention to the resolution, and outlining the serious damage done to Grenada's banana industry, 40 per cent of which was destroyed by the hurricane earlier this year.

Cde Bishop told the GTM convention that while Grenada wished to have normal relations with the U.S. and had made several attempts to establish cordial relations, the response of "establishment America" had been to resist.

He pointed to the U.S. refusal to accept Dessima Williams's credentials as Grenada's ambassador to the U.S.: their refusal to make security personnel available to Grenada's Finance Minister Bernard Coard while he attended meetings of the IMF and World Bank in Washington earlier this month; and their harbouring and protecting former dictator Eric Gairy while he is wanted on criminal charges, including murder, in Grenada.

Cde Bishop said Grenada has "a continental vision," which rejects the "interventionist, divisionist, hegemonic, and backyardist tendencies" of the U.S., and does not adhere to the Monroe Doctrine which, he said, is "incompatible with sovereignty and independence in the region."

Thus, he said, "the problem lies with the US, and not with us."

Cde Bishop said the Grenada revolution is a people's revolution with a Caribbean flavour" which is based on the principles of respect for sovereignty non-interference in other countries' internal affairs, and respect for the way in which any people decide to run their country."

He said that the PRG did not expect every country in the region to have the same method of governing, but that this should in no way hinder regional integration, which, for Grenada, "is of utmost importance for the region."

Grenada's wish, he said, is to establish good relations with all countries, except those like South Africa, which is well known for their racial injustice.

For this reason, he said, Grenada constantly calls for a Caricom heads of government meeting, since this would enhance the region's chances of coming together under one umbrella.

Grenada's vision goes beyond the English-speaking Caribbean, he observed. "Traditionally, because of the colonialist policies, attempts have always been made to get us to feel that people in the region coming from French, Dutch and Spanish-speaking countries are different from us," said Cde Bishop.

The PM urged representatives at the convention to work to break down the language barriers set up by colonialism as a "divide and rule" tactic.

FWI, October 25, 1980

U.S. PLAN DIVISIVE—WHITEMAN

Minister of Foreign Affairs, Bro. Unison Whiteman, has called on CARICOM countries not to allow the proposed United States version of the Caribbean Basin Initiative (CBI) to create divisions among countries of the region.

Bro. Whiteman made the appeal at the Caricom Foreign Ministers meeting which ended in Belize last Thursday.

He called on the meeting to carefully analyse the plan proposed by U.S. President Ronald Reagan, as there were dangerous, divisive and "disruptive elements" in it, aimed at breaking up the regional community.

"Caricom is to a large degree a trading community, and if the U.S. faces our region from a trading point of view, they should face our region as one bloc—not try to establish separate relations with each individual unit and try to give special privileges to individual units," Bro. Whiteman said.

In an interview before the meeting, Bro. Whiteman said that the peoples of the region had together worked out the principles on which they should conduct their relations with each other. The Articles of Caricom states that there should be harmonisation of relations between countries in the community and third countries. The Reagan approach, of dealing with countries bilaterally violated the spirit and even the letter of Caricom and the integration movement.

Philosophically, Bro. Whiteman said, the so-called Caribbean Basin plan is "nothing more than an export version of Reaganomics, which is itself under attack in Reagan's own land, for its failure to function."

"We do not know for how long Reaganomics will be in fashion," he continued. "However, what all of us would like to know is that before we are transformed into dust, ashes or clay, we will have built and left behind a solid foundation, a noble legacy of regional cooperation as a fitting monument to our ancestors who struggled for the cause of regional unity: T.A. Marryshow, Grantley Adams and Norman Manley."

Bro. Whiteman said he did not think a Third Power could tailor a plan to its liking and then dictate it to a region while ignoring the wishes and principles of the region, but if it did, then "it will be a question for the member states of the Caribbean to decide whether for a few dollars they are prepared to sacrifice their principles."

For Grenada's part, he said, "there will be no dilemma. Our position is very clear, that no outside country, no third country can use the few dollars to break us away from our Caribbean brothers."

In his wide ranging speech Bro. Whiteman also reiterated the PRG's position that the Caribbean region be declared a zone of peace and noted with concern the threats, aggressive military manoeuvres and military buildups in the area.

He recognised the sad plight of the people of El Salvador and said that Grenada is convinced that only a negotiated political settlement along the lines of the French/Mexican statement can guarantee a lasting peace.

FWI, April 3, 1982

GRENADA COMPLAINS TO USAID ABOUT EXCLUSION

A formal complaint against Grenada's exclusion from a study done by the United States Agency for International Development (USAID), has been made by the Ministry of Health's permanent secretary, Dorcas Braveboy.

The study was made in five of the six islands having family nurse practitioners, prior to USAID's consideration of funding for the family nurse practitioner training programme, after 1983.

The programme is to provide training for a new category of health worker, intended to function in primary health care, dealing with preventative as well as curative medicine.

It is sponsored by the United Nations Family Planning Association (UNFPA), the Pan American Health Organisation (PAHO) and the Caribbean Community (Caricom).

Sis. Braveboy filed the complaint at a meeting of participating governments in the programme, held in St. Vincent from May 13–14.

She said the USAID representative at the meeting gave "no excuse." However, a copy of the report on the study will be submitted to Grenada.

FWI, May 22, 1982

PM BISHOP—OPEN TALKS WITH U.S.A.

Prime Minister Maurice Bishop, now in the United States on an eight-day visit, has told black Congressmen that his People's Revolutionary Government had requested and set a totally open and unconditional agenda for talks with the Ronald Reagan administration.

He was speaking in Washington on Thursday morning to a breakfast meeting of the U.S. Black Congressional Caucus.

The Caucus, comprising the 22 blacks in the U.S. Congress, and TransAfrica, a prestigious group promoting black American interests, invited PM Bishop to the U.S.

The visit is aimed at informing the U.S. people about the objectives of the Grenada Revolution and seeking efforts to improve relations with the Reagan administration.

PM Bishop, who left here on Monday, is accompanied by Foreign Minister Unison Whiteman, Minister of Tourism and Civil Aviation Lyden Ramdhanny, Grenada Chamber of Commerce and Industry president Richard Menzes, and Grenada Hotels Association (GHA) president Royston Hopkin.

According to a report from press secretary Don Rojas, PM Bishop reiterated to the Congressmen Grenada's position that dialogue is critical for normalising diplomatic relations between the two countries.

He also told them about the state of Grenada's political, social and economic affairs.

The meeting was attended by the Black Caucus chairman Julien Dixon, House of Representatives Sub-Committee on Africa chairman Howard Wolfe, House Sub-Committee on Military Installation chairman Ron Dellums and several other congressmen.

These rounds of meetings with senior U.S. congressmen, as well as those active and influential on Caribbean and Western Hemispheric issues, Rojas reported, have been well-received.

On Tuesday, in an address to the Organisation of American States (OAS) permanent council, PM Bishop explained the need for Grenada's international airport, commented on the PRG's relations with the U.S., and called for greater unity among the Caribbean and Latin American states.

He said the airport is vital to the economy and tourism and termed its importance "unquestionable."

On U.S.-Grenada relations, he declared: "It is an unfortunate historical fact that every effort on our part to achieve these normal relations has been ignored."

Speaking to the press shortly before he left Grenada, PM Bishop said that he hoped the visit would be useful in establishing a permanent channel of communication between the two governments, that can lay the basis for normalising relations.

He disclosed that the PRG had requested a meeting for him with President Reagan and for Foreign Minister Unison Whiteman to meet Secretary of State George Schultz.

At the OAS meeting and one with Grenadian nationals in Washington, the PM expressed Grenada's support for efforts of the Contodora Group—Mexico, Panama, Colombia, and Venezuela—to mediate a peaceful solution to the political conflicts in Central America.

PM Bishop will address a mass indoor rally of Grenadian and Caribbean nationals in New York tomorrow.

Speaking to reporters in New York, after meeting United Nations secretary general Javier Perez de Cuellar, PM Bishop said his government has prepared Grenadians to withstand any invasion, and have also alerted friendly government leaders and organisations, such as the Non-Aligned Movement, the Commonwealth, the UN and the OAS.

Although he didn't think all this had changed the U.S. ultimate objectives, it would have slowed down their plans, the PM said.

FWI, June 4, 1983

USEFUL TRIP TO U.S.

PM Returns

Prime Minister Maurice Bishop returned home yesterday afternoon from an 11-day visit to the United States, expressing confidence that the trip has achieved all its important objectives.

"I would say that perhaps the number one success of the visit was the fact that we were able to bring a true picture of what the real Grenada is like, following upon all the propaganda which had been spread against the Revolution," he told the press at Pearl's Airport shortly after his arrival.

He was greeted there by Deputy Prime Minister Bernard Coard and other People's Revolutionary Government (PRG) members, and scores of Grenadians who turned out for the occasion.

PM Bishop said that Grenada's true image was conveyed to millions of people across the U.S.

"These people were not only able to receive that message, but at the same time, they were able to get a sober and responsible image of the Grenada Revolution."

His visit to the U.S. was made at the request of the Congressional Black Caucus and TransAfrica, a prestigious organisation lobbying on behalf of Caribbean and African peoples in the U.S.

Among the visit's highpoints were the PM's meetings with U.S. national security advisor William Clark and acting secretary of State Kenneth Dam, his address to the Organisation of American States (OAS) permanent council, TransAfrica's sixth dinner at a large indoor rally in New York, and a meeting with United Nations secretary general Javier Perez De Cuellar.

PM Bishop also held many meetings with congressmen and senators and was interviewed several times by the press.

The Grenada delegation met over 40 senators and congressmen, including the U.S. House of Representatives speaker, Tip O'Neill.

Said PM Bishop: "I think in several different ways, through many different media reports, briefings and press conferences, we were able to get across to the U.S. people that the Grenadian people regarded them as friends and wanted to see relations between our two peoples continue."

He described his meeting with Dam as "useful, businesslike and exploratory."

Grenada, the PM said, made a number of proposals to the U.S. on normalising relations and "in particular with resuming official dialogue and official contact through formal mechanisms and channels."

The Americans have promised to respond to these proposals within the next few weeks, he said.

According to the PM, one senator he met has agreed to come to Grenada later this year with a delegation of small businessmen to pursue possibilities for investment and co-operation in fishing.

A successful reception was also held with over 400 tour operators, travel writers and other key figures involved in the tourist industry.

PM Bishop was accompanied on his trip by Foreign Minister Unison Whiteman, Tourism Minister Lyden Ramdhanny, the Grenada Chamber of Commerce and Industry president Richard Menzes, and Grenada Hotel Association president, Royston Hopkin.

FWI, June 11, 1983

23
Latin America

Introduction

As in the case of Cuba, many of the countries of Central and South America are geographically and historically close to the English-speaking Caribbean. Yet present day contacts are often sparse, due to a variety of reasons. Grenada set about to bridge the gap separating these countries.

Relations with Nicaragua were especially close. Grenada became the second government in the world (after Panama) to recognize the Sandinista regime. Daniel Ortega, coordinator of the Sandinista leadership, visited Grenada in 1980. Cuba, Nicaragua and Grenada became a new alignment of forces in opposition to U.S. influence in the Caribbean. Prime Minister Bishop warned that Grenada was the only one of the three yet to be invaded.

In Nicaragua, as in Cuba, there was an English-speaking community descended from immigrant West Indian workers of an earlier generation. Grenadian internationalist students participated in Nicaragua's literacy campaign among this group.

The PRG also strengthened relations with Venezuela. Maurice Bishop made two state visits to that country and Venezuelan cooperation covered the fields of sports, tourism and the provision of teachers of Spanish. Venezuela also provided oil for the international airport. A Venezuelan Cooperation Center was established in St. George's. As in the case with some of its other Caribbean neighbours, Venezuela's fishing vessels caused some temporary friction by encroaching on Grenada's territorial waters.

Prime Minister Bishop also visited Mexico. The PRG supported the French-Mexican initiative of 1981 which called for peaceful negotiations among all parties to the conflict in El Salvador.

The PRG supported the freedom fighters in El Salvador and supported Argentina in the Malvinas (Falklands) War against Britain.

SPEECH OF FOREIGN MINISTER UNISON WHITEMAN TO THE UNITED NATIONS—EXCERPT

Permit me to express my delegation's deep distress at the sudden death of the then incumbent President of Ecuador, Jaime Roldos, the former Chief of State of Panama General Omar Torrijos and the sad passing of the former President of Venezuela, Romulo Betancourt. All were outstanding in their own country in their time.

Permit me to pay special tribute to Omar Torrijos, the symbol of Panamanian dignity, the leader and catalyst of the Panamanian Revolutionary process; a leader in the Central American and Caribbean region, a World Statesman. We will always remember the General who marched in the forefront of the anti-imperialist struggle. The peoples of the world who struggle for justice and freedom will not forget Torrijos' fight to restore Panama's territorial integrity and for the achievement of her complete independence and sovereignty.

For centuries, the Latin American and Caribbean peoples have been subject to some of the most barbarous tyrannies that have beset the world. The oligarchies have enriched themselves at the expense of the people. This is the age of change. The people will no longer tolerate their exploitation. Those who innocently or otherwise suggest that the popular processes of our region are orchestrated from outside are simply poor students of history, for the people who know their history cannot be fooled.

Mr. President, Grenada continues to be outraged by the atrocities against the people of El Salvador committed by the Junta. The patriots of that suffering country have long ago earned our solidarity, our brotherhood and our everlasting respect. We therefore, hail the Mexican/French initiative as an act of statesmanship. We are proud to associate ourselves with the views expressed in the recent Joint Communique. We support without reservation, the view that the alliance between the Farabundo Marti Front for National Liberation and the Democratic Revolutionary Front constitutes a representative political force, ready to undertake responsibilities and obligations with a legitimate right to participate in negotiations towards a political settlement.

Peace and justice have as their necessary pre-requisite the unconditional acceptance of ideological pluralism and respect for sovereignty and territorial integrity. No one has the right to dictate to another and we deplore the arrogant attitude adopted by some who seek to isolate those with whom they disagree. We specifically condemn all efforts to blockade Cuba or put pressure on Nicaragua via political, economic or military means.

All these points of conflict and confrontation, Mr. President, create the conditions for instability. In order to avoid the Caribbean becoming a permanent zone of confrontation and tension, we have consistently called upon the United Nations and the Organization of American States to declare the Caribbean as a Zone of Peace.

This proposal was accepted at the La Paz meeting of the OAS in 1979. At the sixth meeting of the standing committee of Foreign Ministers of the Caribbean Community, held in Grenada in June, 1981 a working committee was set up charged with the responsibility of elaborating the general proposals to give effect to the declaration.

Foreign Minister Unison Whiteman (left) and Michael Manley, former prime minister of Jamaica and vice-president of Socialist International.
Free West Indian

24
Africa

Introduction

Some elements within the New Jewel Movement had annually celebrated African Liberation Day in Grenada since 1971. The Black Power background of some NJM members predisposed them to a Pan-African outlook. Such sentiments were clearly expressed in revolutionary Grenada's first address (by Kenrick Radix) to the United Nations (reproduced here). President Kenneth Kaunda of Zambia became the first non-Caribbean head of state to visit Grenada in 1979. It may be, though, that the march of socialism in time caused some elements within the NJM to regard the Pan-African fervour of the Black Power days as a "backward cultural nationalism."

Actual contacts with African states seemed to focus largely on those which already had strong ties with the Soviet Union and Cuba. These included Libya, Algeria, Mozambique and Angola. President Samora Machel of Mozambique visited Grenada by way of Cuba for African Liberation Day in 1982.

Grenada also provided strong support for the liberation groups in Southern Africa, through rallies and fundraising campaigns at home and diplomatic efforts abroad.

At the time of the ultraleft coup of 1983, preparatory work was underway for a visit to several African countries by Prime Minister Bishop.

INDEPENDENCE FOR NAMIBIA

First Address to the United Nations by Ambassador Kenrick Radix.

Mr. President, Mr. Secretary General, Assistant Secretary General, Distinguished Ambassadors, Colleagues: On March 13th 1979, Grenada had a new Government and it is the first time we have the opportunity to address you. Allow me then, on behalf of my Prime Minister, Mr. Maurice Bishop, the members of the new revolutionary government, the people of Grenada, and on my own behalf to offer you warm and sincere greetings, and to say how proud we are as a new people to be here represented.

For too long the unpopular and oppressive government of South Africa has been defying the high organs of the United Nations and world opinion on the acute question of self determination for the people of Namibia. The question of Namibia first came to the attention of the United Nations over thirty years ago when South Africa decided to annex that territory and spread the cancer of apartheid to the Namibian land and people. Despite the brave and vigilant struggle of the Namibian people the Fascist Pretoria Regime divided up families and banned the people from owning and enjoying the land of their birth. They plundered and raped the human and material resources of the people in the false hope of fully subjecting the land of the courageous people of that territory.

The Security Council in recent years has come to regard the vicious and flagrantly illegal acts of South Africa in Namibia as threats to world peace and security. Repeated calls by the General Assembly, the Security Council, the International Court of Justice and the International Community that South Africa relinquish its illegal hold on Namibia, have fallen on deaf, racist ears. The continued illegal occupation of Namibia by South Africa is an act of war. Under the steadfast leadership of SWAPO the Namibian people have risen to fight South Africa for the liberation and complete independence of the territory.

Every day the arch enemy of mankind, South African apartheid, is driven out inch by inch from the presence of the Namibians and flung into the ocean. As the struggle of the Namibian people moves to newer and higher stages of success the fascist and racist regime becomes more and more repressive. No longer content to wage war in Namibia, acts of grave aggression with criminal intent are being waged against the fully independent and sovereign front line states by the international bandit in Pretoria. Mr. President, the massacre of men, women and defenceless children on May 4th, 1977 at Kassinga in independent Angola is one of the cowardly, brutal and nauseating acts in the total history of the modern world. Such murderous acts have been repeated, each assault being more vicious and hostile than before. It would appear that the South African fascists are bent on the complete eradication of all forms of human existence in that mineral rich land. But it is the blood of the Namibian martyrs wich is the cement upon which the nation of a free Namibia is being built.

Mr. President, the people of Grenada have only recently overthrown a brutal dictator, and in doing so released ourselves from oppression. We in Grenada have our eyes fixed on those nations who claim to support the high ideals of the Charter of the United Nations, but who in the same breath give aid, comfort, and support to the racist regime. For the sake of a few dollars, many nations sell their souls to keep that minority clique in power. But the eyes and the consciences of the world see them and know who they are. All their support cannot defeat the will of the Namibian people for their self-determination, independence, and national liberation.

The holding of sham elections by South Africa in Namibia and the pretended victory of their puppet, the Turnhalle Alliance, will not be recognized nor tolerated by the people, nor the revolutionary government of Grenada. We have suffered through the experiences of slavery, colonialism, racism and neo-colonialism, so we know first hand what racist oppression is. As I mentioned before, only two months ago, through a popular and bloodless revolution we acclaimed the right of self-determination and real independence. The majority of our people are of African descent and therefore through contemporary understanding of the plight of Black and Third World Peoples, we share each day, in an intimate and intense way, the sufferings of the Namibian people.

Grenada therefore embraces the call of the United Nations that 1979 be observed as the year of solidarity with the People of Namibia and calls for the implementation of Security Council resolutions 385/1976 and 435/1978; Grenada is also pleased to add its name to the list of co-sponsors of Resolution A/33/L37. We adopt the call by the OAU that the apartheid regime of South Africa be isolated and that maximum pressure be brought against those vested interests who act in concert with them. All forms of support will be given by the Government and people of Grenada, to the Namibian people and their vanguard SWAPO in their liberation struggles.

The time has come, Mr. President, when the United Nations with the total support of the international community must take firm and resolute action against South Africa, the only country in the world which has for so long defied not only the United Nations, but people of goodwill throughout the world.

South Africa poses a threat not only to Namibia but to the whole of Southern Africa. All peoples of the world united to defeat the fascism of Hitler. We are therefore commanded to action before the world is plunged into racial war. The time to act is now. Grenada therefore urges that the cancer of South African apartheid be removed by mandatory measures contained in Chapter VII of the Charter. The year 1979 must be recorded in history not only as the year of Solidarity with the people of Namibia, but also as the year of their total victory.

FWI, June 16, 1979

PAN-AFRICANISM SAYS WE ARE ALL ONE

Pan-Africanism is first a positive statement of identity between all those of African descent whose forebears experienced colonial subjugation and the dislocation resulting from it—whether those people live on the African continent or anywhere else in the world. It is the affirmation that "We are all an African people."

Secondly, it is a call to regain what was lost in the colonization process, namely, African sovereignty: the right to live in, develop, and govern the continent as they see fit, independent of external manipulation and control. In other words, "Africa for the Africans."

Thirdly, it is a strategic perspective which places the struggle for African liberation at the centre of the anti-imperialist struggle internationally.

FWI, May 23, 1981

WELCOME SAMORA

Mozambique President Samora Moises Machel will get a warm reception from Grenadians when he touches down at Pearl's Airport on Saturday at 2 p.m.

Scores of Grenadians are expected to be at the airport with buntings and flags in the gold, white, red and green colours of Mozambique, to welcome Pres. Machel.

Among Pres. Machel's 37-man delegation, are the Minister of Foreign Affairs, secretary of FRELIMO'S Central Committee responsible for Foreign Relations, and member of FRELIMO's Political Bureau, Major General Joaquim Alberto Chissano; and the Minister of Agriculture, and Central Committee member Colonel Sergio Viera.

Young Pioneers from Grenville will welcome Pres. Machel and his delegation with a song, and will present bouquets to them.

A 21-gun salute will announce Pres. Machel's arrival. He will then inspect the guards along with Prime Minister Maurice Bishop. Members of the People's Revolutionary Government (PRG) will be presented to him, and he will in turn present his delegation. Chief Protocol Officer Shahiba Strong will present the PRG's diplomatic corps.

PM Bishop will welcome Pres. Machel, and he will reply.

Pres. Machel will then leave the airport in a motorcade, which will travel from Grenville to St. George's. He will be welcomed by villagers lining the route.

On Sunday, Pres. Machel will visit the international airport and later will proceed to Seamoon, St. Andrew's, to deliver the feature address at an African Liberation Day (ALD) rally. Thousands of Grenadians are expected to turn out to hear him speak, and to celebrate African victories, and give solidarity to continuing struggles.

ALD is recognised as the day on which the Charter of the Organisation of African Unity was signed, on May 26, 1963 at an all-African conference in Addis Ababa, Ethiopia.

It has since been commemorated by many countries throughout the world to celebrate African victories, and to express solidarity with African countries still in bondage.

FWI, May 22, 1982

AFRICA'S STRUGGLE IS OURS

"Africa's struggle is our struggle," said Minister of Agriculture George Louison, addressing an indoor rally in St. John's to mark the 20th anniversary of African Liberation Day (ALD) on Sunday.

Speaking to over 500 persons at the St. John's Anglican School, in Gouyave, Min. Louison said ALD has been celebrated in Grenada for 12 years. "In those days, we did not function as the New Jewel Movement (NJM), the party having been formed in 1973," he explained.

"One of the things we were able to prove," he said, "was that there were hundreds of Grenadians who identified with Africa."

He said that in 1971 many African countries, including Mozambique, Angola, Cape Verde and Guinea-Bissau were still fighting for their liberation, but because of their struggles, these countries are liberated today.

"Some of these countries which went on the battlefield lost many of their soldiers, but many of them knew that their blood will be used as fertiliser for the struggle," he said.

Speaking about the apartheid system, he said it was but a child of imperialism and it was through imperialism that apartheid came to Africa.

The moving of millions of Africans in carts and trucks to special reserves called "homelands" was very dehumanising, he said.

Present at the rally were Minister of National Mobilisation Selwyn Strachan, Minister of Health Christopher De Riggs, Grenada's High Commissioner to London Fennis Augustine, Rickey Parris of the Barbados Peace Council and John Diabour, an African working with the Department of Sports in the Ministry of Education here.

Min. Strachan said that the kinds of improvement here that the People's Revolutionary Government (PRG) has been trying to bring about are similar to those taking place in the free countries of Southern Africa.

"Since 1979 the imperialists have been going all out to prevent the process from going forward, but the people of Southern Africa and Grenada will never surrender," he said.

He said that the PRG and the NJM have embarked on a major task of preparing for the fifth anniversary of the Revolution. "Since the Revolution will be five years old next March, we believe it is important to prepare for that historic occasion now.

"We have to sit down and analyse carefully where we have made progress, where we have made little progress and where we have failed, " he said.

One of the projects in preparing for the next anniversary is the Fifth Anniversary Community Project, which will repair very bad roads throughout the country, he said.

The project has already begun working on the New Hampshire, Woburn, La Borie and Shenda roads in St. George's.

Min. Strachan also urged workers to take their workers' education classes more seriously and to join the adult education programme of the Centre for Popular Education (CPE).

The minister also called upon Grenadians to step up their participation in defense of the Revolution, adding that "if we do not take defense seriously, all our gains over the last four years will be lost."

Solidarity messages were delivered by representatives of the Agricultural and General Workers' Union, National Youth Organisation, National Women's Organisation and the Productive Farmers' Union.

Poems were read by Wayne Andall of Victoria, St. Mark's, and Denis Branch of St. George's.

Parris in a short address, said that it is important to give full support to liberation struggles if the imperialist military threat was to be beaten back.

"Every blow struck for liberation touches every man and woman in our society," he said, adding: "Revolution ends that process of exploitation."

FWI, June 4, 1983

25
Afro-America and Afro-Britain

Introduction

Revolutionary Grenada was unique among English-speaking Caribbean nations in its outspokenness on racism in Britain and North America. The Afro-British population, in particular, is primarily of West Indian origin and its problems would seem of obvious concern to governments and media in the home countries. Yet this has usually not been the case.

The NJM leadership contained several persons who as university students were active in Black metropolitan communities. Prime Minister Maurice Bishop in England; Deputy Prime Minister Bernard Coard in England and the United States; Minister of Education Jacqueline Creft in Canada; Foreign Minister Unison Whiteman in the United States—all of these and others had served their political apprenticeship as activists in Black communities in the metropolis. Their knowledge of racism in these countries was intimate. And unlike other West Indian politicians of similar background, they did not forget their metropolitan experiences on the way back home to the Caribbean. Denunciations of British and North American racism were especially severe during the first two years of the revolution.

From the perspective of the United States, Grenada's stand on this subject was especially threatening, since Grenada represented something new—a revolutionary Black, English-speaking country enjoying considerable prestige in Afro-America and situated on Uncle Sam's doorstep (if not in his backyard). As a member of a visiting Afro-American delegation put it, "Grenada is an inspiration to us. We need a victory every now and then, and this is definitely one."

BLACK LAWYERS DEFEND GRENADA

The National Conference of Black Lawyers (NCBL) of North America has called on U.S. President Ronald Reagan "to cease and desist immediately from all attempts to undermine the popularly-supported government of Grenada."

In a letter to Reagan the NCBL said it was "a violation" of international law and self-determination, "to exert political and economic pressures which constitute deliberate interference in the internal affairs of a sovereign state."

The NCBL comprises 1,500 black lawyers and judges from throughout the U.S., Canada and the Virgin Islands.

It told Reagan it "is gravely concerned about efforts by representatives of your administration, which were directed at the undermining of a meeting" sponsored by the European Economic Community in Brussels in mid-April, to discuss financial assistance for the construction of the international airport.

The airport, the NCBL said, "is a major development project by the PRG to stimulate economic activity through tourism and to lay the basis for future self-sustaining economic growth and development."

Rather than impede the PRG's efforts "to develop an economy that will benefit the majority of the people," the NCBL said the U.S. "should lend its assistance to bring those efforts to fruition."

FWI, May 9, 1981

PM LASHES U.K.'S RACIST BILL

The moves by Britain's Thatcher government to pass the Nationality Bill have come in for criticism from many Caribbean governments, including Grenada.

This brand new attempt to legalise and institutionalise British racism came in for attack from Prime Minister Maurice Bishop, in his feature address at the May Day rally, in Queen's Park.

"At exactly the same time that we are ending police brutality, and discrimination against women, and removing all traces of racism from our country, there are big countries around the world that are moving to institutionalize racism and police brutality," he said.

PM Bishop pointed to the efforts by Britain's Conservative Party to pass the Bill, which he said "will ensure deep and tremendous discrimination against blacks and other ethnic and racial minorities living in the United Kingdom."

Under this bill, he explained, those people who formerly had the right to regard themselves as citizens of the U.K., who had the right to a passport and security, who were either born, had grown up or lived in the U.K., are now discovering that "the rules have been changed overnight."

"And the rules are being changed in such a way that millions of Third World people in the Commonwealth will now find themselves stateless," he said.

"Many of them will discover that they are being discriminated against because of the simple reason that they don't happen to look like the original British, regardless of what contribution they have made to that country," he added.

He urged the workers and the people of Grenada to reflect on these things, which forcefully reminds us that in our country these principles no longer apply."

"Half the time when what they call race riots take place in countries such as England, what it really represents is a serious act of resistance on the part of people who regard themselves as colonized second-class citizens who have no chance to fight back," he pointed out.

PM Bishop said that was one of the reasons behind the Brixton uprising, by thousands of blacks living in the Brixton ghetto without work, facing daily police brutality, facing arbitrary arrest or being picked up on "suspicion."

"These people, together with the poor whites in Brixton, got together and showed serious and massive resistance," he said.

He also referred to the recent situation in Lewisham, again in England, when more than 14 Caribbean children at a party were murdered by a fire-bomb thrown in the house. "Again, the Third World people living in the area came out in massive protest," he said.

These people, he continued, have not only been in the forefront of building these countries, but have also been in the forefront of fighting for their rights, always resisting oppression, victimization and racism "whenever it shows its ugly face."

PM Bishop also called on the workers and the people of Grenada to reflect on the situation in Atlanta, in the United States, where 26 young black children have been murdered in the past few months.

"Those children were murdered simply because they were allowed to go on the streets—a right that they have—and simply because they appear to have the wrong colour," he said.

"Yet, notwithstanding the mighty apparatus and mighty resources of the United States, after all these months, no justice has been done," he added.

But it is this same big and powerful country, which has been able to keep what former United Nations Ambassador Andrew Young described as "political prisoners," and which practices so much racism against ethnic and racial minorities, that can nevertheless find the time to try to squeeze the poor and working people throughout the world who are fighting for their own liberation and social progress, he said.

FWI, May 9, 1981

EXPOSED U.S. PLAN TO WEAKEN BLACKS

A leaked presidential review memorandum about the U.S. black movement and black Africa, is causing outrage in the United States.

The top secret memorandum from the National Security Council's Interdepartmental Group for Africa, is signed by the most powerful man in U.S. President James Carter's administration—national security advisor Zbigniew Brzezinski.

And it may well cost Carter the black vote—and the election. For if Carter is to retain the presidency, he must hold on to the black votes, which won him it in the first place.

The White House, of course, has disclaimed the document. They claim it is a forgery, but admit "it has all the earmarks of a very professional job." It was "prepared with some skill and care," certain phrases it uses were "in current or common usage on such papers," and it is often racist in tone.

The memorandum dated March 17, 1978, discusses U.S. interests in Africa, and the means of securing these interests, which it states are both political and economic.

Black Africa is important to the U.S., it says, as "an outlet for U.S. exports and investments. The mineral resources of the area continue to be of great value for the normal functioning of industry in the United States and allied countries.

"In 1977, U.S. direct investment in black Africa totalled about $1.8 billion and exports $2.2 billion. New prospects of substantial profit would continue," the memorandum says.

U.S. policy toward black Africa, it notes, "is to prevent social upheavals which could radically change the political situation throughout the area."

It fears the West "many face a real danger of being deprived of access to the enormous raw material resources of Southern Africa, which are vital for our defense needs, as well as losing control over the Cape sea routes, by which approximately 65 per cent of Middle Eastern oil is supplied to Western Europe."

A main threat to U.S. interests, the memorandum says, would be having Zaire, for example, go "the way of Angola and Mozambique" and having the nationalist liberative movement in black Africa stimulate organisational consolidation and sympathetic activity in the 25-million strong American black community.

Such joint actions, it predicts, "could include protest demonstrations against our policy toward South Africa, accompanied by demands for boycotting corporations and banks which maintain links with that country; attempts to establish a permanent black lobby in Congress, including active leftist radical groups and black legislators; the reemergence of pan-African ideals; and resumption of protest marches recalling the days of Martin Luther King."

The memorandum notes that . . . "this may lead to critical differences between the United States and the Third World, in general, and between the U.S. and black Africa, in particular."

To head off this threat to U.S. interests, the memorandum recommends steps to weaken the U.S. black community and to isolate it from black progressive Africa.

It suggests that "special clandestine operations should be launched by the CIA, to generate mistrust and hostility in American and world opinion against joint activity of the two forces, and to cause division among black African radical groups and their leaders."

Moreover, "the FBI should mount surveillance operations against black African representatives and collect sensitive information on those, especially at the UN, who oppose U.S. policy toward South Africa.

"The information should include facts on their links with the leaders of the black movement in the U.S., thus making possible at least partial neutralization of the adverse effects of their activity."

The memorandum analyses the present stage of the black movement in the U.S., noting its weaknesses as fragmentation, lack of organisational unity, sharp social stratification and "want of a national leader of standing comparable to that of Martin Luther King."

Then it sets out to aggravate these weaknesses. Its "range of policy options" include calls for special programmes designed:

* to perpetuate divisions in the black movement; to neutralise the most active groups, of leftist radical orientation, and to diminish their influence among blacks; to stimulate dissension and hostility between organisations

representing different social strata of the black community; to encourage divisions in black circles.

* to preserve the present climate which inhibits the emergence from within the black leadership of a personality capable of exerting nationwide appeal.

* to work out and realize preventive operations in order to impede durable ties between U.S. black organisations and radical groups in African states.

* to support actions designed to sharpen social stratification in the black community, which would lead to the widening and perpetuation of the gap between the successful educated blacks and the poor, giving rise to growing antagonism between different black groups and weakening the movement as a whole.

* to facilitate the greatest possible expansion of black business by granting government contracts and loans on favourable terms to black businessmen.

* to take every possible measure through the (American Federation of Labour-Congress of Industrial Organisations) AFL-CIO leaders to counteract the increasing influence of black labour organisations which function in all major unions, in particular the National Coalition of Black Trade Unionists and its leadership, including the creation of real preconditions for adverse and hostile reaction among white trade unionists to demands for improvement of social and economic welfare of the blacks.

* to support the nomination at federal and local levels of loyal black public figures to elective offices, to government agencies and the courts. This would promote the achievement of a two-fold purpose: first, it would be easier to control the activity of loyal black representatives within existing institutions; second, the idea of an independent black political party, now under discussion within black leadership circles, would soon lose all support.

Despite Carter's professed ignorance of the document, its policies do seem to have been effected. Since it was written two years ago, the black community has become further fragmented, no national leader has emerged and no independent black political party has come about.

FWI, October 25, 1980

ANTI-CAPITALIST BLACK PARTY FORMED IN U.S.

Once again, black people in the United States are responding to stepped up repression, isolation, and the chronic unemployment which are the major features of their lives, by a new surge of political organisation.

This time, it is the forming of a new National Black Independent Party (NBIP). At its founding congress in Chicago, Illinois, in August, delegates representing over 1600 members came from 33 cities across the country. There were industrial workers, teachers, students, professionals, and long-time community organisers: a cross-section of the black community nationwide.

Addressing the Congress, the Rev. Ben Chavis (himself a victim of Ku Klux Klan terror in North Carolina) stated: "We must build a mass-based party from the bottom up in the interests of black liberation. If we do not organise black people nobody else will."

Reflecting the state of emergency in which the black community now finds itself, the NBIP's preamble states: "We aim to attain power to transform radically the present social-economic order, that is to achieve self-determination and social and political freedom for the masses of black people. Therefore, our party will actively oppose racism, imperialism, sexual oppression, and capitalist exploitation."

While traditional civil rights organisations in the U.S., such as the National Association for the Advancement of Coloured People, the Urban League, and others still view politics within the framework of reforming the Democratic and Republican parties, NBIP's development has made a clear and unequivocal break with the capitalist system.

On international relations, the party is equally clear. NBIP stands committed to "support the heroic and just struggles of the people of Africa, Asia, Latin America and the Caribbean against colonialism and neo-colonialism and for freedom, national liberation, self-determination, sovereignty, and independence."

In the context of President Ronald Reagan's new militarism, the party's program rejects the administration's policy of preparing new Vietnams. Specifically, it states, "we believe that no black person should be forced to fight in an imperialist war of aggression for the U.S. against people who are oppressed and fighting for freedom as we are here in the U.S."

The NBIP's founding at this time is of particular importance to countries like Grenada. It increases the ranks of our allies at the centre of the world imperialist system; it demonstrates to the world that the capitalist pattern of development brings no benefits and, indeed, inflicts great hardships on the masses of its people; and it is proof positive that no matter how many individual black leaders are assassinated, jailed, or co-opted by the U.S. government, the movement of those suffering at the bottom cannot be extinguished.

***FWI*, September 26, 1981**

GRENADA IS VICTORY WE NEED, SAY U.S. BLACKS

"The decade of the 1980s is decisive for us," agreed the 25 members of the National Black United Front (NBUF) of the U.S.A., visiting Grenada on a solidarity tour.

As organisers in the black communities where they live, they pinpointed both the objective and subjective factors conditioning their attempts to forge a unified progressive movement in the U.S.A. at this time.

Although many blacks have been brainwashed by the media into identifying with and believing in the U.S. system and many others are inactive because they fear losing their jobs or their lives if they get involved in organising for radical change, they said, most realize that "time is running out."

Adeyemi Bandele, leader of the NBUF tour, said, "while the U.S. government is spending billions on bombs, they're closing down hospitals in Harlem. Our bread, our butter, and our lives are at stake.

"As pressure mounts and capitalism is unable to resolve its own internal crisis, he continued, more brothers and sisters are drawn into the struggle. Once in the struggle, they're there."

Reflecting on the lessons that black people in the U.S. have learned from the last 20 years of battles for democratic rights, electoral power, and economic justice, members of the group agreed that today, political consciousness among the masses of blacks is higher.

"It's no longer enough to be black," they said. "You must also understand that it is the whole system that needs to be attacked. We used to look just to individual leaders for direction; now leaders are rising up and coming forward from the masses in collective forms at grass-roots levels."

In this connection, they said, "Grenada is an inspiration to us. We need a victory every now and then, and this is definitely one. When more black people in the U.S. learn the truth about the process being built here and, even better, come to see for themselves, they will be strengthened in their own work and see what is possible more clearly."

Since the 1960s, there has been no national focus for the U.S. black movement. But now conditions are forcing this to change. "We either get out a programme together, or we won't survive." For this reason, Bro. Bandele stated "NBUF is especially important."

Since its formation in June 1980, its growth has been constant. A large part of the reason for this, he continued, is that "it is the only national black organisation with a consistent and progressive international posture."

"Not since the Black Panthers were infiltrated and its most impressive leaders were killed by agents of the U.S. Government has any group had a clear policy or programme to combat apartheid, Zionism, or the global effect of Yankee imperialism in the Third World."

"We, in NBUF, consider this a priority. In large part, that is why we are here. We must make those connections."

A central commitment arising out of the group's stay in Grenada is to publicise the positive revolutionary developments occurring here.

NBUF's future plans to make this commitment a reality involve organising national forums on Grenada in the U.S., educating the people about U.S. invasion plans, using their organ "Black News" and other black newspapers and radio stations, such as WLIB in New York, for consistent coverage on Grenada, and pressuring the U.S. Congressional Black Caucus to mobilise public opinion to halt U.S. intervention and economic sabotage.

"Just as Grenada has set an important example in the international community by speaking out on the situation of black people in the U.S.," they said, "so we must follow that example in our home communities and wake up North American blacks to the situation here."

FWI, September 5, 1983

U.S. CONGRESSMAN SUPPORTS AIRPORT

United States Congressman, Major Owens, ended a three-day official visit here yesterday, during which he met Deputy Prime Minister Bernard Coard and other People's Revolutionary Government (PRG) ministers and officials.

Rep. Owens told the press that his visit came out of his concern over U.S. President Ronald Reagan's claims that Grenada is a threat to U.S. national security, because of the international airport being built at Point Salines with Cuban help.

At the very beginning of his visit, he said, he became aware of the genuine need for the international airport. His party was due to arrive in Grenada Tuesday evening, but because of the lateness of their flight, and because there are no night-landing facilities at Pearl's Airport, he could not get a flight to Grenada, and had to overnight in Barbados.

Rep. Owens, in the U.S. House of Representatives for the past seven months, said he represents a district in Brooklyn, New York, where many Grenadians and other West Indian emigrants live. He wants to be able to go back and answer all their questions about Grenada, he said.

His interest in visiting Grenada, he said, was heightened by Prime Minister Maurice Bishop's successful 11-day visit to the U.S. last month. He was very impressed by his meeting with the PM and by what he learnt from him about this country.

While here, Rep. Owens toured the international airport site and visited a number of socio-economic projects undertaken by the PRG, such as the Mt. Hartman Genetic and Livestock Development Farm, the Grand Anse Housing Project, the Sandino Industrial Complex and the Agro-Industries Factory in True Blue.

Accompanying him was the Reverend Herbert Daughtry, chairman of the National Black United Front (NBUF) of the U.S.

Rep. Owens said that as a member of the U.S. House, he would like to help put a stop to the Reagan administration's errors about Grenada.

He was very impressed, he said, by the PRG's policy of involving the people in the decision-making process, its success in reducing unemployment and its fight against illiteracy.

Rep. Owens has also been serving in the New York Senate for the past eight years.

He is the fourth U.S. Congressman to have visited Grenada since the March 13, 1979 Revolution. The others were Reps. John Conyers and George Crockett of Michigan and Ron Dellums of California.

Meanwhile, U.S. Senator Clairbone Pell, senior Democratic Party member of the U.S. Senate's Foreign Relations Committee, has objected to the Reagan administration's failure to move to normalise relations with Grenada.

In a letter to U.S. Secretary of State George Shultz last month, Pell urged the U.S. to establish full diplomatic relations with Grenada.

Pell next put his call for normal relations to the Senate floor, at a committee hearing.

FWI, July 9, 1983

26
Internationalism

Introduction

In the tradition of many twentieth century revolutions, Grenada emphasized the value of "proletarian internationalism." Progressive people from around the world were attracted to the country. Progressive and left groups of all description found their way there to see what was going on and to offer solidarity. Governments, notably Cuban, sponsored internationalist workers. Many, however, came on their own. Some sacrificed jobs and careers elsewhere for a chance to work in a revolutionary environment. Grenada sponsored its own first internationalists to Nicaragua in 1981.

International solidarity conferences also played a role in Grenada's diplomatic offensive against attempts at isolation by the United States. Several of these took place, sponsored both by Grenada and by foreign organizations.

GRENADA IS NOT ALONE

The deserved praise directed at Cuban workers in Grenada often neglects an equally important internationalist display of collective revolutionary solidarity and sacrifice. Grenada's revolutionary process is being aided by peoples from all of the earth's continents.

They come from close-up, a 20 minute LIAT flight away, and from far away places requiring hours of flying time. All have similar purposes: to lend tangible support to Grenadians, and to take instruction from the masses.

They come, not as aloof "experts," but as those with specialized skills and deep enthusiasm to offer, and much knowledge to gain.

Grenada's expanding revolutionary democracy has international importance for the global anti-imperialist struggle, and for peace, regional security and working class emancipation. Its inspirational emphasis on progressive social development, creative self-reliance and international solidarity has attracted many international workers and visitors.

Prime Minister Maurice Bishop repeatedly stresses: "Come and see for yourself." And this is impressively happening. Folks are not only watching, but are experiencing social and psychological transformations by being in one of the "little giants."

Cuban President Fidel Castro has said that nothing is more beautiful than a people building their revolution. That beauty extends to all such builders. In this "big revolution in a small country," a wonderful experiment is taking place. An irreversible multi-ethnic, multi-lingual, multiracial and multi-national atmosphere exists that is unique to the English-speaking Caribbean. It is history-making.

Throughout all of this, there is a commitment to and practice of working class leadership. True, the Revolution has an essential internationalist dimension, but not at the expense of Grenadians' themselves organizing and leading the process. Hence, there is no room for propaganda to manoeuvre that "foreigners are running things."

In the Revolution's first year, mainly Caribbean progressives came to lend assistance. Since then, comrades have increasingly come also from non-Caribbean countries whose peoples are willing to sacrifice their jobs, apartments, studies and otherwise interrupt their previous activities.

Free Grenada has had workers lending revolutionary assistance from such places as Dominica, Jamaica, Guyana, Canada, the U.S.A., India, Pakistan, France, England, Ghana, South Africa, Nigeria, Australia and Suriname.

These devoted internationalists are making sacrificial and deeply appreciated contributions in countless PRG projects and ministries. They may be seen in agriculture, education, external affairs, communications, legal affairs, construction, public works, agro-industries, health, in offices, in the streets and in the fields.

A vital aspect of their work involves transmitting skills through in-service or other training programmes whose purpose is to consolidate and expand the economy. Consequently, Grenadians are building their badly-needed infrastructure which serves as the basis for economic transformation and greater productivity.

Some internationalist workers are volunteers. Others are on government contracts. Still others are on loan from their governments or jobs. Some have resigned former positions. All could be earning large salaries elsewhere or living bourgeois life-styles in metropolitan countries. Yet all testify to having had our lives changed and fulfilled by being here.

We regard it as a duty, privilege and immeasurable joy to be in Free Grenada. We have developed a deeper sense of purpose in helping to advance the Caribbean revolutionary process. We recognize that by so doing, we also aid progressive struggles elsewhere.

The Revolution has taught us that change is possible, that apathy and indiscipline are destructive. We know that as Grenada makes it, then so too will other struggling peoples. By aiding Grenada, we aid ourselves.

For us, as internationalist workers, Free Grenada is indeed our home. With humility and love, by our work and acceptance here, we are learning that the only "foreigners" are those who exploit.

All of us are being socially integrated more and more each day. The sharing of our cultures is an added personal and social benefit. Because of the Revolution's popular base, there is no sense of mythical "outside agitators taking over," or resentment against non-Grenadians.

As we enter the third year of people's democracy, our daily work routine firmly convinces us that we are not "outsiders," but "insiders," brothers and sisters in the practical revolutionary senses of these bonds. And we have learned to be better and truer patriots.

As Fidel put it, internationalism is one way of repaying our debt to humanity. For us, "forward ever, backward never" is a living reality.

FWI, March 13, 1981

WALTER RODNEY VISITS

Bro. Walter Rodney, well-known Guyanese historian and political activist has been in Grenada over the last few days.

Dr. Rodney on Tuesday gave a talk at the Anglican (Hindsey) School about the liberation process in Southern Africa.

The talk was so well attended by the public that many people could not get inside to hear Bro. Rodney.

This was the first time in years that such a meeting could be held publicly with the use of the microphone and be advertised on the National Radio Station.

FWI, June 16, 1979

REVO BELONGS TO CARIBBEAN

Minister of Legal Affairs and Fisheries Kenrick Radix asserted that Marcus Garvey was a prophet and struggler for equality and justice for the black masses. The Revolution's goals were also equality and justice for the majority of Grenadians, he said, noting that the "Revolution has rejected racism and colonialism."

On the U.S. invasion threat, Bro. Radix said the U.S. was "terrorist" in outlook and was using technology to frighten the people. He noted thousands of Grenadians had come out, thus demonstrating that we are "militant, conscious, united. The people are not afraid and are prepared."

Vice-president of the Media Workers Association of Free Grenada (MWAFG), Don Rojas, FWI's editor, said MWAFG "forcefully condemns the present U.S. military manoeuvres" noting the "concrete evidence" to show that the U.S. intends to invade Grenada. He referred to the Reagan administration's action as a most "vulgar, obscene display of international misbehaviour." Bro. Rojas quoted Garvey as saying "no ruling class will give up power willingly" and in today's context, he stressed, "imperialism through propaganda and economic sabotage was trying to turn back the Revolution."

Executive member of the UK branch of the People's Progressive Party, and of the Caribbean Labour Solidarity Movement (CLSM), Mongol Singh, affirmed that the Grenada Revolution was not only for the people of Grenada but belonged to "millions of oppressed people of the world." He emphasised that, "if they touch this island, they will have to touch all the other sister islands." His speech received thunderous applause from the crowd who sang, "Oh when they come, oh when the Yankee soldiers come, we will be in the frontline."

The general secretary of the Dominica Liberation Movement (DLM) Dr. Bill Riviere asserted that the "revolutionary forces in Dominica were in total support of Free Grenada." He commented that the "Revolution here is as much the revolution of Dominica, the Caribbean, of the Third World Revolution, and worldwide," noting that the oppressed people of the world share the common historical experience of colonialism and neo-colonialism.

He said oppressed people world-wide had identified the common enemy, U.S. imperialism. His speech was punctuated with spontaneous applause, clapping and singing of various anti-imperialist songs.

Leader of the People's Progressive Movement, Bobby Clarke, commented that the Grenada Revolution would eventually "embrace the whole of the Caribbean." He referred to the Cuban Revolution in 1959 as the first major triumph which "sticks in the throat of U.S. imperialism." Comrade Clarke underscored the fact that the PPM would "react with violence, the only language the U.S.A. understands, when the Revolution is touched."

Nicaraguan Ambassador Marco Val Martinez, noted that while imperialism is strong and a threat to the Grenada Revolution, "never can it be great and strong as our two people." He asserted that Cuba and Nicaragua were alongside the people of Grenada in their struggle against U.S. imperialism and hoped that Grenada would continue to be "an example for other people."

FWI, August 29, 1981

FIRST INTERNATIONAL SOLIDARITY CONFERENCE WITH THE PEOPLE OF GRENADA

Final declaration of First International Solidarity Conference with the People of Grenada:

"We the delegates to the First International Solidarity Conference with Grenada, representing countries from all parts of the world and meeting in St. George's from November 23 to 25, 1981, express our profound gratitude for the warmth, friendship and hospitality of the Grenadian people.

"After observing and experiencing the revolutionary process taking place in Grenada, we proudly declare our unshakeable solidarity with the revolutionary people and Government of Grenada.

"We acclaim and proclaim the enthusiastic involvement of the people of Grenada as an expression of people's democracy through the creation and growth of institutions and organisations such as Zonal and Workers' Parish Councils, the National Women's Organisation, the National Youth Organisation and the young Pioneers and other mass organisations.

"We have witnessed the participation and support of the masses of the people of Grenada for the programmes of the Revolution under the courageous, committed and inspiring leadership of Maurice Bishop and the New Jewel Movement.

"We have recognised and appreciated that despite the fact that Grenada is an under-developed country which was devastated by the corrupt Gairy dictatorship, that despite the propaganda and economic destabilisation of U.S. imperialism, the Grenada Revolution, after only two years and eight months, has been able to achieve free education for all the people at all levels, free and improved medical and health care, the creation of over 2,500 jobs, the establishment of significant agro-industries, is successfully combatting and eliminating illiteracy, has established a modern fishing industry, has firmly and clearly expanded workers' rights and the right of trade unions, has given new dignity to workers through equal pay for equal work, and fully paid maternity leave for all working women, has developed co-operatives for unemployed youth and women mainly, and has created new benefits for farmers.

"The Grenada Revolution has fought inflation through the Marketing and National Import Board by lowering the prices of essential goods and, among other things too numerous to mention, is constructing a new international airport which will advance the development of all sectors of the Grenadian society.

"We have noted the many threats of aggression, the several military manoeuvres conducted in the region and the world, the dangerous promotion of the arms race by the war-mongering Reagan Administration.

"We see all this as a deliberate and calculated attempt by U.S. imperialism to intervene in and to set back the great progress by the people of Grenada, Nicaragua and Cuba and the heroic struggles of El Salvador and other parts of the world.

"The Conference strongly denounces this policy of the Reagan Administration, which threatens world peace and stands firmly with the people in the struggle for their rights to economic and social justice and self-determination.

"The conference expresses its firm solidarity with the struggle of the people of the world against racism, colonialism, apartheid, zionism and fascism, and acknowledges and reaffirms the rights of all peoples to national independence and to choose their own economic, social and political system.

"The conference gives its fullest support to the efforts of all peace-loving countries to achieve disarmament, detente, co-operation and the preservation of world peace.

"We unanimously resolve to combat the campaign of lies and distortion against the Grenada Revolution and to provide and widely disseminate information about the great achievements and triumphs of the people of Grenada.

"We pledge ourselves to give all possible assistance to ensure the advance and development of the Grenada Revolution.

"We commit ourselves to defend Grenada against all threats and aggression and firmly resolve to establish friendship societies and solidarity committees in our respective countries to expose the reality and express our militant support for the Grenada Revolution.

"We also pledge to give the fullest possible publicity to this document."

FWI, November 28, 1981

SPREAD THE WORD, SAYS C.L.R. JAMES

What will be the future of Grenada and what will it be able to do?

Trinidad-born historian and political activist C.L.R. James offered his answers to these momentous questions and discussed the steps he feels all Caribbean nations must take if they are to survive individually and as a region.

"Things cannot continue like this until 1990," he said.

Grenada, Barbados, St. Kitts, St. Lucia, Martinique and the other nations of the region are but "small and geographically and economically insignificant islands," the 79-year-old James explained during his visit to Grenada this week.

These insignificant geographical territories must unite in some sort of Caribbean federation, James said.

"Not a federation like the one attempted in 1958. That was written in the colonial office in London," he said adding: "That wasn't a federation. It was a British crown colony get-together, a Caribbean calypso callalou."

Socialist

James explained that the federation he envisions must be socialist, and it must get rid of all these little elitest special governments, which are doing nothing but continuing what the imperialists left behind.

"What new have they introduced?" he asked. "Manley is the only one who is trying to do something, and Grenada has introduced something new."

Unlike other nations in the region, Grenada is not a former colonial territory that is dressed up as an independent one, James remarked.

"Grenada has started a new orientation. Manley is trying to get a new one—that is what he means by democratic socialism."

"The other nations are drifting along just as they were," James said. "They have flags of independence; they have prime ministers; they have national anthems; but they are still economically and socially structured as colonial territories.

"That's what they have to get out of, he said emphatically. "And the only thing I think can get them out is a Caribbean federation."

Not only must the federation be socialist, James declared, "To have some future, it must begin with Cuba." Cuba is not now considered a part of the Caribbean, but a federation must begin with it, James believes.

The next nation to join must be Haiti, then the Dominican Republic, and Jamaica, he said giving a structural analysis. "Then we'll come down to the smaller islands, particularly Martinique and Guadeloupe."

As for Guadeloupe and Martinique's saying they are provinces of France, James countered: "What kind of nonsense is that?"

"They're Caribbean and they belong to a Caribbean federation," he said flatly.

The federation should comprise Trinidad and all the other islands, James went on.

"I've spoken to the boys from the Guianas," he added, "and they want to be part of the Caribbean, too."

"They don't want to get mixed up with Brazil and Argentina and all of those. They'll get lost there."

Regarding the prospect of federation under the present governments, James said: "I don't believe the present unions can unite. That's why I am so opposed to them."

"They have no sense of the future," he added disgustedly.

James admitted his vision of the federation may sound idealistic now, but he said it was no more utopian than Garvey, Padmore and DuBois must have sounded in 1935, when they spoke of a politically-independent Africa.

James argued that the stepped-up aggression by imperialist powers will not be a big problem in the move to federation, provided the local leadership has got the mass of the population behind it.

In that case, he predicts, the Americans will have to kill half the population.

Existing conditions necessitate that the people remove leaders like Gairy. "No objective conditions are known," James said. "The Caribbean simply cannot continue as it is."

Summing up the state of the region, James quoted a 16-year-old passage from his book "Spheres of Existence," which was reprinted with two other of his books in London this month. He read: "The position does not imperatively or inescapably demand revolutionary measures . . . such as took place in France in 1791 or Cuba in 1958."

It may call for such action," James interjected, "but I don't begin with that."

He continued: "Many elements both at home and abroad recognise the explosive character of the Caribbean scene. Many elements know it can't go on this way. Many people in the islands and elsewhere know that something's going to happen."

James advised Grenadians to spread the history of their revolution around. He does not believe enough people in the region know how the New Jewel Movement was founded, what it went through, and how it seized the power by seizing the time.

"This is the message I want to bring to the people of Grenada—a revolutionary people who've broken away from the old strings and entanglements and are going into the deep," James said.

"I am looking to them to play a great role in as much as they have broken the bonds."

FWI, August 2, 1980

FEWER ARMS HERE THAN IN CHICAGO, SAYS U.S. PRESIDENTIAL CANDIDATE

In U.S. presidential elections it is often the relatively unknown third-party candidate who clarifies issues and challenges the imperial twins, the Democratic and Republican parties to take a stand.

Andrew Pulley is the Socialist Workers' Party (SWP) candidate for the presidency, in the November elections. And recently he visited Grenada to see the revolution firsthand and to help beat the imperialist slander campaign against progressive nations.

"What I've found here has been extremely inspiring and impressive, Bro. Pulley said, noting the greater availability of medical care, the creation of 2,500 jobs within the last year, and the standard of the education system.

"All of these speak very well for the future, contrary to what the U.S. press has been reporting," he said. I've seen fewer people armed here than I've seen in an area of Chicago any given day."

Bro. Pulley theorises that the purpose of the media attacks on Grenada is to make the average U.S. citizen hate this country so he'll accept whatever criminal and terrorist activity the U.S. government may perpetrate.

This is particularly true for the black communities, which would readily identify with the ongoing progressive movements in Grenada, if they knew the truth, he said.

The SWP platform is raising many key issues, Bro. Pulley said. "One is the whole question of the military drive—its intentions to build up a big army to police the capitalist world and overturn the socialist revolutions that have taken place."

His party challenges the increased military budget in the U.S. and demands that proposals to reintroduce the draft be scrapped.

The SWP is against stepped-up military interference in the Caribbean, too. Specifically it demands that Cuba, Nicaragua and Grenada be left alone; that adequate aid be sent to Nicaragua to compensate for U.S. supported damage done by the Somoza dictatorship; and that Guantanamo be returned to the Cuban people.

On the domestic front, things are rapidly deteriorating, Bro. Pulley said. Although the U.S. still boasts one of the highest standards of living, American workers have been squeezed economically and more than nine million people are out of work.

"Half of the young people in the black and Hispanic communities are permanently unemployed," he said.

Besides unemployment, Bro. Pulley explained, the inflation rate which now stands at 15 to 16 per cent means the average person is hard put to afford adequate housing, food and medicine.

SWP is committed to the nationalization of the oil industry, too. Companies like Exxon make more money than many nations," he said. "In one year they made $4.2 billion, and it was due to one of the greatest swindles ever perpetrated, a manufactured energy shortage."

"The anti-draft movement is important here, not only because it speaks out against war, but because it recognises that any war is designed to benefit the oil companies and a few millionaires and billionaires."

"Thus," Bro. Pulley said, "the anti-war and anti-draft slogan now is: "We won't go; we won't fight for Texaco—or Exxon!"

SWP also stands firmly committed to the women's movement in the United States and the passage of the Equal Rights Amendment.

Though it receives less than its share of press coverage in the U.S., SWP is one of the largest left parties there. In 1976, it got 100,000 votes throughout the country. This November, Bro. Pulley's name will be on the ballot in 31 of the 50 states, but he expects no better press coverage.

As a black, born in the south, Pulley's political education began with racism. As a youth, he began recognising a lot of injustices, but it wasn't until he went into the army and met some socialists who put those injustices into scientific perspective that he feels his most important political education began.

Eventually, he was kicked out the armed forces for handing out anti-war and socialist literature.

Bro. Pulley has returned to the U.S. to continue the struggle inside the belly of the beast. As he campaigns, he said, he will tell the truth about the Grenada revolution and share the peoples' messages of solidarity.

FWI, August 23, 1980

ANGELA ENJOYS THE JAB-JABS

Angela Davis is back in Grenada.

Coming in last Sunday from the United States, the black activist was in time for the Dimanche Gras show and the other Carnival activities. On J'Ouvert morning, she could have been seen moving through the crowd and taking photographs of the "jab-jabs" and other old mas' bands and individuals. She attended the pageant on Monday afternoon and saw the parade of the bands on Tuesday.

Grenada's carnival, she said, was one of the most fascinating experiences she has ever had. She had never experienced so much fun and festivity in an organised way, while still feeling safe, she said.

Although Sis. Davis had never seen jab-jabs before, she didn't feel threatened by them, she said. She moved around freely and some of the jab-jab dirt came off on her and her sister Fania.

She compared her experiences here with those in the U.S., where, she said, whenever so many people came together, there would be fights and pickpockets.

Here with her sister, mother and 12 other family members, Sis. Davis described this as a political holiday, which will last two weeks. She explained that she didn't see much of Grenada while she was here last March for International Women's Day celebrations, and would take the opportunity to do so now.

Accompanying her is Fannie Haughton, a close friend, who has taught for 15 years and is now training teachers. With Sis. Davis's mother, who has taught for 30 years, she will assist the Ministry of Education, while here.

Commenting on the struggle in the U.S., Sis. Davis said that although there has been a backward movement since 1971, when she was arrested, and particularly with Ronald Reagan's election, which saw racism on the increase with the rise of the Ku Klux Klan and the threat of nuclear holocaust, there has also been an increase in the level of consciousness of the U.S. people, and there is now greater potential for organised struggle.

This, she said, was because of the clearer historical direction of the entire globe, reflected in the rise of the national liberation movement within the last 10 years and the increased unity of the socialist world.

The tasks facing the Communist Party of the U.S.A., of which she is a Political Bureau member, she said, are the fights for nuclear disarmament, against racism, and decreasing unemployment, which now affects some 10 per cent of the U.S. people, and in some areas, 75 to 80 per cent of blacks.

FWI, August 21, 1982

INTERNATIONAL UNION OF STUDENTS TO MEET HERE

A high-level international youth and students' conference will be held in Grenada from June 27–30. The conference, sponsored by the International Union of Students, was originally planned for June 16–19, but was postponed.

The conference is being held in solidarity with the oppressed youth, students and people of South Africa, Latin America and the Caribbean, and will show the link between South Africa's racist apartheid regime and the fascist dictatorships in Chile and Latin America.

About 50 official representatives of youth and students' organisations all over the world are expected to attend the conference. The sessions, to be held at York House, St. George's, will be officially opened by Prime Minister Maurice Bishop. Many international figures are also expected to attend.

Grenada is not an official member of the organisation, but earlier this year was present as observers at an IUS conference in the German Democratic Republic.

Grenada's application for membership will be formally reviewed at the next IUS executive meeting in October.

Deputy Prime Minister Bernard Coard, recently visited IUS headquarters in Prague, Czechoslovakia, and talked on the progress of the Grenada revolution. Bro. Coard denounced the destabilizing meddling plans promoted from abroad with U.S. government support through the CIA.

The IUS immediately reiterated its solidarity with the Grenada Revolution with a statement and letter of solidarity to the Prime Minister Maurice Bishop.

The statement, among other things, called on progressive youth and students the world over to support the people of Grenada in their fight against imperialist destabilization and aggression.

FWI, June 14, 1980

OCLAE MEETING SUCCESSFUL

The first Consultative Meeting of the Continental Organisation of Latin American and Caribbean Students' (OCLAE) member organisations of the Caribbean, ended yesterday with an indoor rally in the St. Andrew's Junior Secondary School.

At the meeting were representatives from Barbados, Trinidad, Suriname, Guyana, OCLAE, and the International Union of Students.

OCLAE's representative, Grenadian Tarlie Francis, at the opening ceremony Thursday said the student movement in the region was included in a wave of action toward regional unity now flowing through the region, and the meeting was evidence of this.

He expressed OCLAE's commitment to democratisation of education to meet the needs and aspirations of the broad masses of students in the region, and reiterated its solidarity with students suffering under dictatorships in Latin America, and who are denied their rights to education.

The meeting reviewed OCLAE's last year's work programme, and made proposals for the coming year. It examined education and educational opportunities in the Caribbean and ways in which joint educational programmes will be implemented.

Francis said on Thursday, that OCLAE was committed to regional integration and supported bodies objecting to the proposed restructuring of the University of the West Indies.

IUS' representative Nazim Chandiraphal of Guyana, at the opening said that holding the meeting here was of great importance because Grenada's experience over the past three years can serve as an example for the student movement in the region.

Participating in the International Students' Day (ISD) celebrations here was important, he said, because the participants were able to see the extent of the enthusiasm with which students participated. ISD could only have been observed here, he said, because Grenada had a Revolution, and the state puts the interest of the youths and students in front.

He urged the students to struggle for peace and against the arms race, since it threatens their own survival.

The meeting opened at the Public Workers Centre, Tanteen, and was held at the Pope Paul's Ecumenical Centre, St. John's.

FWI, November 20, 1982

AMERICAN INDIAN MOVEMENT LEADERS IN GRENADA

Two leading members of the American Indian Movement (AIM) have described the Grenadian Revolution as "an inspiration."

Bill Means, executive director of the International Indian Treaty council, a nongovernmental organisation at the United Nations, and Bill Wahpepah, a board member of AIM, were in Grenada for the recent Caribbean Workers' Conference.

They spoke of the present conditions under which American Indians live and AIM's struggle against the U.S. Government, to better these conditions.

AIM's main objective now, said Means, "is to try to educate the international community that we still exist."

When the white colonialists arrived in North America in the 1600s, most of the continent was occupied by Indians. But, in their greed for more land, the colonialists seized Indian lands and started destroying their hunting grounds.

Most of the Indians were forced into reservations, although, for over 200 years, they have put up a continuous, determined and legendary resistance against the white invaders.

Today, related Means, the remaining 1.5 million Indians still suffer from such diseases as tuberculosis, transmitted to them by the colonialists.

The infant mortality rate is very high and the average lifespan is approximately 47 years.

"Twenty five per cent of our women of child-bearing age have been sterilized," he said.

There are about 70 Indian reservations in the United States, all owned by the federal government, although some are managed by the states in which they are located.

Means and Wapepah are descendants of the Sioux and Kickapoo peoples respectively, and veterans of the 1973 Wounded Knee uprising.

On February 23, that year, members of AIM seized control of Wounded Knee, a small town in South Dakota, in an attempt to draw the nation's attention to Indian grievances.

They occupied the town until May 7, that year. Two people were killed by the U.S. government authorities, before the town was recaptured by Army troops.

"Massive repression was unleashed against the movement by the U.S. government after the uprising," the two observed.

However, they added: "We believe we have the right to control our own lands and be respresented as Indian peoples." Land and treaty rights is an important issue in the present struggle.

Grenada, Means noted, was a small island which was successful in casting off the bonds of colonialism.

"Seeing that you don't have substantial resources, you were able to defeat some of imperialism's intrigues and manoeuvres," he said.

"The people are becoming involved in building a government from the bottom up—not from the top down.

"I am impressed by the work of the youths. And I hope many of our people can come and have a look. It's an inspiration."

FWI, January 17, 1981

GRENADA'S FIRST INTERNATIONALISTS IN NICARAGUA

Grenada and Nicaragua are united, not only as revolutionary countries, but also in their efforts to improve the standards of their people.

This is best manifested in their similar efforts to bring literacy to the unfortunate people in the two countries, who have not had the opportunity to learn to read and write.

Two young Grenadian literacy teachers are now assisting Nicaragua's literacy campaign, in the Atlantic Coast town of Bluefields, where they are teaching English to the descendants of West Indians.

Spanish is the main language in Nicaragua, but the people of Bluefields speak English, since they are mainly the sons and daughters of immigrants from the days of the construction of the Panama Canal.

The campaign in Bluefields began last October, with Ceford Robertson of St. Andrew's and John Wilson of Carriacou, among the volunteer teachers. They are due back in Grenada this month.

The Nicaraguans have asked for 25 more Grenadian volunteers to continue at Bluefields, but due to the extent of work at home, CPE has not yet been able to meet this request.

The presence of Grenadian internationalists in Nicaragua is significant, as was noted by Prime Minister Maurice Bishop in an address to the CPE Congress last October 18. He urged CPE volunteers to "use our own talent, experience and energy at the service of our brothers and sisters, in the region and the world, who are themselves struggling to free their countries from illiteracy."

Mentioning the two Grenadian volunteers in Nicaragua, he said their contribution is "extremely important" and was worth recognition of the congress.

Apart from the presence of the two Grenadians, CPE co-ordinator Val Cornwall also visited Nicaragua last year, where she attended the closing of the first phase of the Spanish literacy crusade. She also held discussions with members of Nicaragua's National Technical Commission.

FWI, February 28, 1981

Prime Minister Maurice Bishop and U.S. Ambassador Sally Shelton. *Free West Indian*

PART VI

Counter-Revolution and Threats of Invasion

Cartoon attacking Prime Minister Tom Adams of Barbados. *Free West Indian*

27
Destabilization

Introduction

Destabilization was a constant problem for the revolution. Supporters of the old regime at home and United States hostility abroad provided a formidable alignment against the new government. The near bloodless nature of the seizure of power and the relatively small number of detainees, as far as revolutions go, made for a potentially sizeable local opposition. It can be surmised that many of this group were won over to the NJM cause as time went by. But the more intransigent elements were able to benefit from a fair amount of freedom of movement.

Local opposition (and perhaps hostile infiltrators) were helped by the openness of Grenadian society. Entry into Grenada was not difficult, the country still tried to attract tourists and the traditional patterns of inter-island trafficking and emigration to North America and elsewhere did not cease.

Destabilization took many forms. First there was violence. Some NJM supporters were ambushed and shot to pieces. In the most violent act of all prior to October 1983, a bomb exploded on June 19, 1980, under a platform where almost the entire top leadership of the People's Revolutionary Government was assembled. Three young women were killed and almost one hundred persons injured. In a pattern which sadly repeated itself in October 1983, the perpetrators of this violence aimed to kill and injure a large number of innocent people along with the NJM leadership. Persons sentenced to death in 1982 for this crime were summarily released in the wake of the U.S. invasion of 1983.

Economic destabilization was also severe. The hostile media of the United States, and some Caribbean territories as well, aimed at stemming the flow of tourists to Grenada. U.S. efforts to cut Grenada off from aid sources have already been mentioned. Rumourmongering was added to the list of destabilizing tactics. The frequent threats from official U.S. sources and the constant hints of imminent invasion added to the grim picture facing the PRG.

The PRG countered these threats by every means at its disposal, including an anti-destablilization propaganda campaign of its own and its energetic diplomatic offensive. It also strengthened its army and militia. Former CIA agents were even brought in to share their knowledge of "dirty tricks." One, Philip Agee, warned that the hand of the CIA might be anywhere, "particularly when an openly hostile U.S. policy is evident to all." His comments (reproduced here) make chilling reading in retrospect.

DON'T LET THEM STOP OUR PARTY

This is only the second Christmas the people of Grenada and the People's Revolutionary Government are enjoying together, in Free Grenada.

This, it is said, is the season to be jolly, for peace and good-will, exchanging gifts and making merry with food and drink a-plenty.

But peace, food and gifts do not fall freely from Heaven. They are produced and paid for by man.

In the past year, the people and the PRG have exchanged many gifts. The PRG has given money, materials and interest. And Grenada has benefitted from better houses, roads, schools, health clinics, community centres, industrial plants and productive farm lands.

Gifts have come to Grenada from its new friends all over the world, from countries such as Cuba, Venezuela, Libya, Iraq and Hungary, from international and regional international and regional organisations such as the Organisation of American States (OAS) and from organised supporters and individual well-wishers throughout the hemisphere.

The projects and equipment they have funded or donated have provided more services, created more jobs, kept more money circulating and, therefore, provided the extra cash for the pears, wine and dolls, this Christmas.

The land-reform programme is putting on the table more meat, fruits, and vegetables; the agro-industries local hams, salted fish, tinned juices and preserves.

Various training programmes are giving us skilled workmates and offspring; the Centre for Popular Education is turning out people who can now read and write greeting cards themselves.

The country is caught up in an expansive mood of moving forward towards a definite goal, of hope in the future, of pride in achievement.

Emulation and worker of the year awards have helped underline that pride and given new encouragement to individual initiative, creativity and conscientiousness.

It is indeed a time for showing appreciation and love.

But while we sing "Peaceful night, all is bright," let us not forget there are those around us, and in our midst, who do not wish us peace and prosperity.

There are those who bear us no love or goodwill, who do not share our joys and sorrows, and who, in fact, are awaiting the chance to cause us more grief.

They come bearing time-bombs left silently for our sisters and daughters, bullets whizzing towards the loving hearts of our sons and brothers. Their gifts to us are permanent injury, the early grave, and the destruction of our dreams.

It might be wise to reflect on who these people are and why they bear us, a warm, friendly, good-natured people, such evil.

This region is dominated by a handful of large transnational corporations, whose main interest in our countries and our peoples is making money from us.

They want our natural products and our working time and energy on the cheap, to produce fancy goods to sell back at high prices. They want to lend us money at high interest rates and under stringent conditions. They want to put in little and take out a lot, as they do throughout the region.

Anytime a country attempts to break out of their parasitic stranglehold, as revolutionary Cuba did, they see it as an example to others, and therefore as a threat to their continued power, luxury and pleasures.

They must, therefore, break that country's leaders, at any cost to life and limb. They did it to Cheddi Jagan in Guyana, Michael Manley in Jamaica. They have no qualms about doing it to little Grenada.

When our country is once again dependent and securely in their grasp, it will once again be left forgotten, neglected and run down. And the brutality and torture will again be unleashed on any native who dares complain.

So this Christmas, as at any time, beware of strange smart men bearing promises.

Some will be just waiting till we get high and carefree on wine, feteing and song, to strike us down and stop the party suddenly.

FWI, December 20, 1980

THE UNSEEN HAND–THE CIA

"The CIA is employing, at this time, all the tools necessary to work against the revolutionary government of Grenada. It is not idle speculation to look for the hand of the CIA, all the time.

"As a general rule, it would be foolish not to be continually looking for the CIA hand in subversive activities against progressive movements particularly when an openly hostile U.S. policy is evident to all. It's not foolish speculation when terrorist bombs kill innocent people, or when unusual pests, blights or epidemics occur, because the CIA never sleeps and is never indifferent to political events in any country."

That advice comes from one who should know, Philip Agee, "the spy who came in from the cold" and is now visiting on a Grenadian passport.

Agee, aged 46, was secret operations officer for 12 years for what he called "a very rich, very powerful, international Mongoose Gang"—the United States Central Intelligence Agency (CIA).

A Floridian, Agee was recruited in university at age 21. Between 1957 and 1968, he served the CIA in Washington D.C.; under diplomatic cover as political attache in the U.S. embassies in Ecuador and Uruguay; and as U.S. attache for the 1968 Olympic Games in Mexico. "For 12 years I lived a lie," he comments.

His disaffection with the CIA started with his awareness of the poverty in Latin America, and, he said, "when I began seeing the type of people who were benefitting from my work. They were all wealthy, greedy, corrupt; not interested in any reform programmes."

It was gradual understanding of this, and of the CIA's role in serving these interests, that Agee said, "brought this disillusionment, which encouraged me to leave the CIA."

Since then Agee has devoted himself to exposing the CIA's dirty tricks and, as expected, his former bosses have not forgiven him. He has lived through attacks on his life, being followed, and having his room bugged and phone tapped. But Agee has learnt enough low dodges himself.

More unsettling is the harassment. Agee has been deported from several West European allied nations, and in December 1979, lost his U.S. passport. He now lives in West Germany, but only for as long as his wife, a resident, stays put.

The CIA, Agee said, was set up to handle U.S. secret foreign policy. Its goals are mainly to collect and analyse information so that the U.S. government knows what is happening around the world, and covert action, that is intervention in other countries. "The CIA has tried for over 20 years to manipulate institutions of power."

But the CIA doesn't act on its own, Agee said. Its activities flow from policy decisions made by the U.S. executive branch, particularly the National Security Council, chaired by the U.S. president.

Therefore, to put the CIA in the same category with other intelligence services is "to mix apples with bananas. Security services are as different as the governments and political movements they represent."

Agee explained: "The earnings of the corporations of industrialised countries depend on the best possible access to the raw materials and a docile labour force in much of the Third World.

"Among the imperialist powers, the CIA is the richest and most powerful of the secret police organisations designed to preserve the system on which the earnings of the corporations depend, and ultimately, of the owners and associated ruling groups in metropolitan areas."

Put in this context, and "of the priorities and escalation of U.S. efforts to prevent popular revolutions from occurring and, when they occur, from succeeding," Agee believes the threat of a U.S. invasion of Grenada is as real as the CIA.

"I myself worked in various Latin American countries, along with hundreds of other CIA officers, to subvert and destroy revolutionary movements.

"When I first went down to Latin America, our main job was to isolate Cuba.

"And when subversion by secret means is impossible, the only recourse is an attempt at violent overthrow of a revolutionary government."

The pattern of U.S. hostility against Grenada since the March 13, 1979 Revolution, including overt U.S. opposition to credit and loans for completion of the international airport, propaganda offensive to hurt tourism, and terrorism, Agee said, "are part and parcel of CIA tools and methods.

"The standard practice is to link up with opposition political forces or exiles, and supply them with money, training, arms and explosives, where appropriate, in addition to propaganda paraphernalia."

And, Agee commented, on the beaten themes used against the Revolution, "there's no area in which the CIA has been more effective than in promoting "free elections" and "free media." Anytime you hear that word "free" from the U.S. government, you have to be very suspicious, to look for the CIA. It means their freedom to intervene, to subvert.

"Human rights too," he said, "is often a diversionary ploy," as is "much of the preaching on pluralism. Pluralism always opens the door to the CIA and its operations."

The propaganda attempts to make Grenada look like a threat, Agee explained, "is to reduce support from its neighbours, to prepare them psychologically, and therefore, to reduce adverse reaction to U.S. aggression."

The "U.S. fear of tiny Grenada," Agee said, is actually fear of the awakening of confidence in revolutionary ideas and activities, and of the spread of the Revolution's influence, "ultimately back to the U.S. itself."

Grenada, Agee observed, "is a very open country. People come and go, with very little control."

And, since "the CIA routinely assigns people under non-official cover" it's logical that it would "assign people to live in Grenada, under any of a number of imaginable covers, to collect information and to provide support for subversive attempts within Grenada."

Their tasks would be infiltration and recruiting Grenadians who have access to PRG policy, military defence plans and areas of weakness in revolutionary organisations. "Just one, two or three people can do tremendous damage," he said.

Agee recommends a strong People's Militia as the best answer to the CIA, because "force is the only language the CIA understands."

"The militia's strength sends signals to the U.S. government and population that the cost is rising all the time, and is already too high, in terms of 'body bags' going back home."

And, Agee predicts that any U.S. invasion is doomed "because Grenada will win that struggle, both internally, and in the work of its many friends externally."

FWI, August 29, 1981

STAY CLEAR OF AIFLD WARNS CIWU

The Commercial and Industrial Workers Union (CIWU) has called on local trade unions to stop sending members to seminars and courses sponsored by the American Institute for Free Labour Development (AIFLD).

The call was made by CIWU general secretary John "Chalkie" Ventour, in an address to the May Day rally at Queen's Park.

Earlier in the rally, Septimus Forsythe, president of the Trade Union Council (TUC), had indicated that yet another Grenadian, Christopher Strachan of the Seamen and Waterfront Workers Union (SWWU) would be attending an AIFLD course in trade unionism.

But Bro. Ventour who is also general secretary of the TUC, said that AIFLD has obvious connections with the American Central Intelligence Agency (CIA), and has participated in the overthrow of several progressive governments in Latin America.

For this and other reasons, CIWU was calling for an end to AIFLD training for Grenadian trade unionists.

Bro. Ventour's charges against AIFLD are understated. AIFLD is an agitation arm of the CIA, and has helped overthrow many governments.

AIFLD's history is an impeccable record of counterrevolutionary achievements.

AIFLD was formed in 1962, as a junior partner to the AFL-CIO, an older U.S. trade union alliance formed to promote anti-communism after World War II. It is run by ALF-CIO leaders, and representatives of 70 major U.S. monopolies operating in Latin America and the Caribbean.

AFL-CIO's president, Layne Kirkland, is also AIFLD's president. And the present chairman of AIFLD's board of directors is J. Peter Grace, head of Grace and Company, which operates many corporations and banks in Latin America and the Caribbean.

The CIA connection goes back to 1955, when CIA operatives infiltrated all AFL-CIO affiliates in the U.S. and abroad. Their principal task was to engage in subversion and espionage in trade unions in other countries under CIA guidance. They gathered intelligence information, and brainwashed union members into organising strikes and coups.

With this foothold in the labour movement, the CIA then set up AIFLD.

The CIA men holding key posts in AFL-CIO and AIFLD affiliated unions aided the U.S. invasion of Guatemala in 1954, when the Jacobo Arbenz government was overthrown. And they gave generous assistance to Cuban counter-revolutionaries after the 1959 Cuban revolution.

In 1964, AIFLD helped bring down the progressive Guyana government led by the People's Progressive Party and Dr. Cheddi Jagan. And the year after, AIFLD set the trade unions in the Dominican Republic against the progressive government led by Juan Bosch.

AIFLD participated actively in engineering the overthrow of the progressive Salvador Allende government in Chile in 1973, and during the 1973–74 period, when Britain was in the grip of the crippling miners' strike, the CIA, through AFL-CIO, infiltrated over 40 agents into the British trade unions.

AFL-CIO bosses actively backed U.S. military interventions over a period in the Korean People's Democratic Republic (North Korea), Cuba, the Congo, Vietnam, Laos and Cambodia.

The basic foundation of AIFLD and AFL-CIO "seminars" and "courses" is anti-socialism, and with the growth of such ideas in the Caribbean, the region has been added to AIFLD's and AFL-CIO's international agenda.

Over the years, AIFLD has been able to penetrate trade unions in virtually every Caricom country, Grenada included.

Through its seminars, trade unionists are acquainted in the basic methods of attacking and combating the spread of progressive ideas in each island's trade union movement.

In Grenada AIFLD has been able to penetrate the SWWU. The heavyweight in SWWU's executive Stanley Roberts, is responsible for AIFLD's training programme in the English-speaking Caribbean. SWWU's vice-president Valentino Sawney, who attended an AIFLD seminar after the Revolution, has publicly attested to the subversive nature of such courses and seminars.

And SWWU's recent efforts to encourage work stoppages by dockworkers and public workers, as well as its boycotting of the May Day celebration, attest to the reactionary nature of its AIFLD-trained leadership.

AFL-CIO's latest documented counter-revolutionary activities are in Poland, where it stepped up its activity last year. After last September's problems, AFL-CIO's council set up a "fund" for Polish workers, saying that the money would get into "the right hands."

But the American magazine, "Counterspy," recently revealed that anti-socialist literature and printing machines were being bought with the money and smuggled into Poland, while another newspaper revealed that the AFL-CIO has illegally smuggled $165,000 (U.S.) into Poland for anti-government forces.

FWI, May 9, 1981

ARMY CAMP TAKEOVER PLAN—THREE ARRESTED

Three persons were arrested Tuesday afternoon in a combined army and police operation in St. Andrew's.

Those arrested are—Kennedy Budhlall, Dennis Charles and Brian Felix.

The police and army are still in search of several others.

Those arrested will be charged with a variety of offences, including illegal possession of firearms and ammunition and other counter-revolutionary offences.

A statement issued by the Ministry of Information noted that Kenny ('Buck') Budhlall headed a group which organised the seizure of the River Antoine Estate near La Poterie serveral weeks ago.

The People's Revolutionary Government has condemned both the seizure of the estate and the fact that the group had led the workers of the estate and the people of La Poterie to believe the PRG had authorized the seizure.

In the weeks since the seizure, there have been complaints from many persons living in the St. Andrew's area that some members of the group have threatened small farmers and shop-keepers with seizure of the property also.

Ever since the seizure, the Agricultural and General Workers Union, and Lyden Ramdhanny of the PRG, have been holding discussions with the owners and workers of the estate in an effort to bring about a peaceful solution to the problem of very bad living and working conditions on the estate while making it clear to all concerned that the estate would have to be returned to its owners.

Meanwhile, however, the police received information as to the involvement of Russell, Kenny and Kennedy Budhlall in the large-scale growing and trading of marijuana.

It is felt that the chief motive of the River Antoine estate seizure was their intention to use the estate's bay as a point for their import-export and wholesale distribution trade of marijuana, as well as to add to their stock of lands for the growing of marijuana. It recently came to light that a few months ago, Russell Budhlall was arrested in a neighbouring island, for large-scale possession of marijuana in a package marked "PRA" (People's Revolutionary Army).

Last week, the security services discovered that as a result of the PRG's campaign, to stamp out the large-scale growing and selling of marijuana, the group led by the Budhlall brothers, which included some soldiers of the PRA camp at Pearls Airport, had begun making plans to seize three army camps, moving from there to overthrow the Government, in order to protect their million-dollar marijuana investment. . . .

Last Friday, members of the Pearls army camp were suspended from duty and fresh PRA troops moved into the camp. Following this, members of the group began issuing threats to members of the St. Andrew's communities which opposed their activities.

It was also found that they had retained possession of certain weapons which they had illegally hidden and Tuesday obtained, under false pretences, large quantities of free gasoline from the Public Works Department in Grenville.

The security services, which have been monitoring the plans and activities of these individuals, learned over the weekend that the group was firming up plans to overthrow the Government, in order to defend their marijuana Mafia operations. The security services therefore moved to arrest members of the group.

The Ministry of Information's statement has re-stated the PRG's position that arbitrary seizure of people's property and large-scale growing and trading in marijuana will not be permitted, no matter who is involved.

"The full weight of the revolution will be brought against them" the statement says, "and the people are called upon to defend the revolution by revealing the whereabouts of any persons known to be wanted by the security services."

A further statement will be issued shortly concerning the group's connection with the CIA.

FWI, May 5, 1980

PM–SAVAGE BLOW

Today imperialism struck a savage, most brutal, most cowardly blow against the revolution.

Today a monstruous crime was committed by imperialism and its local agents.

Today is a sad day for our country, a day when we have gathered together to commemorate, as we have always been doing, another important anniversary, on this occasion, the anniversary of Butler and Strachan, two of our national heroes.

Before the day was ended, even while we were commemorating the lives of these two outstanding Grenadians, we find now that in the future June 19 we will be commemorating new martyrs, new heroes, new patriots for our people's revolution and our struggle.

At this point two young sisters, two young comrades of ours are dead, murdered by these cowards, murdered by these vicious beasts of imperialism. At this point two more people of our country are gone.

What we see here is a situation where our people make a bomb and do it in a very clever way, in a way that indicates very clearly, that they received training. This is not local technology, this is not the way of Grenadian people.

We must know too that this was not an attempt to kill only the leadership of our country, important as it may be and would be for any of these murderers and reactionaries to wipe out the entire leadership at one time. We must note that this plan went beyond that. By their attempts to wipe out the entire leadership of this country, these murderers were prepared to kill hundreds, dozens, maybe thousands of ordinary Grenadians. In our situations only imperialism could be responsible for this.

Can one think of any one Grenadian agreeing to plant a bomb in a rally of thousands of Grenadians? When we look at the list of those who have died, those who will die, and those who are injured, some seriously, some in a very critical way, you can get an idea of the point I am making.

We think of the scientific way in which the imperialists have evolved their concepts of destabilization, of creating political violence and economic sabotage.

We think of the local opportunists used, local counter-revolutionaries who tried to build a popular base and have failed. And as a result of having to fool the masses, they turn to the last weapon they have in desperation, the weapon of open, naked, brutal and vulgar terror.

Having given up all hope of winning the masses, these people now then turn on the masses. They now seek to punish the masses, to murder them wholesale, to plant bombs in the midst of rallies, to make us afraid to continue to assemble, to try to break the back of the popular support of the revolution.

FWI, June 21, 1980

WOMAN: I HELPED CARRY BOMB TO PARK

A 26-year-old woman of Rose Hill, St. Patrick's, has testified about helping carry a bomb to Queen's Park on June 19, 1980, and seeing her companion place it against a wall-post under the pavilion.

Giving evidence in the bomb blast trial on Thursday, at the St. George's High Court, Fitzlyn Joseph said that in a car driven by Layne Phillip, she and Grace Augustine brought the bomb to St. George's.

Both Phillip and Augustine are charged with the bombing that killed three young women. Joseph was originally charged with the other five defendants, but the charges against her were dropped.

Also charged are Russel, Kenneth and Roland Budhlall.

Joseph said that Joseph Charles, alias "Yussuf", told her and Augustine to place the bomb under the pavilion, at 2:45 p.m..

She said Yussuf instructed her to buy a "Five Roses paperbag" in which to put the bombs and vegetables that were to cover it. Augustine and the witness were given $20 each to buy the bag and vegetables, which they did.

The two women then joined a march and entered Queen's Park, with Augustine carrying the bomb.

Augustine put the bomb in position, and at about 2:40 pm., they went outside.

While they were near the Queen's Park bridge, Joseph said she heard the bomb go off and saw people running and screaming. They joined the crowd and ran to Granby Street in St. George's, where they met Phillip in his car.

Phillip told them he would return through St. David's, instead of the Grand Etang Road, for fear of being stopped by security forces.

In the car, Joseph said she expressed concern that innocent people were killed, to which Augustine replied, "Some must die for others to live."

Another witness, Eddie Richardson of Top Hill, St. Patrick's, told the court on Wednesday, that one day in 1980, using wires, batteries, "cigar-looking things," dried coconuts and flashlight bulbs Kenneth Budhlall and Joseph "Bateye" Williams constructed bombs.

Williams died in July 1980 when a bomb he was carrying exploded.

Richardson also told the court of having been in the company of Russel Budhlall, Williams, and two other men—one nicknamed "Duck" at a place called "Perrotte High Woods" in Top Hill. These men had bombs in their possession.

Richardson said Russel Budhlall told him he wanted him to go with him to "blow up some PRA." Richardson also said that he wanted bombs placed at Fir Pasture in Mt. Craven on African Liberation Day 1980, to "blow up Bishop and Coard."

Following the blast, Richardson saw "Bateye," who told him that a double bomb had exploded at the Park.

Presiding Judge Satrohan Singh had earlier overruled a motion by defence counsel Frank Phipps that Richardson was incompetent, since he was originally charged with the five accused and his name appeared on the amended indictment even though the charges against him had been dropped.

Under cross-examination, Richardson admitted to having lied to the judge earlier in the year, before hearing was adjourned, when he said that he had been tortured by security forces to give evidence. He said he was forced to lie by the Budhlall brothers, who advised him that if he stood with them, they all would be stronger.

Another witness on Wednesday was Denis Rush, a former member of the People's Revolutionary Army (PRA) who apprehended the three Budhlalls on an island off St. Andrew's, on July 3, 1980.

In all, 21 witnesses gave evidence during the week.

FWI, **October 23, 1982**

FOUR FOUND GUILTY AS BOMB TRIAL ENDS

Four of the five persons who were charged with the June 19, 1980 bomb blast at Queen's Park have been found guilty, and were sentenced to death by Judge Satrohan Singh on Monday.

The other accused was found not guilty of the charges and was discharged.

Sentenced are Grace Augustine, Layne Phillip, Russel Budhlall and Kenneth Budhlall, while Roland Budhlall was found not guilty.

In passing sentence, the presiding judge referred to evidence given to the court by Fitzlyn Joseph and Eddie Richardson both of whom were originally charged with the others, but later had charges dropped against them.

Judge Singh agreed that both Joseph and Richardson weere accomplices, adding that a conviction is not illegal just because it is based on the uncorroborated evidence of an accomplice. This, he said, is based on a law which was established in 1811. He however stated that caution was needed in approaching their testimony.

The judge said that both Joseph and Richardson had an air of confidence and were unhesitant and straight forward in replying to questions.

He said that he was satisfied beyond reasonable doubt that Grace Augustine, Layne Phillip and Fitzlyn Joseph brought the bomb to the park.

Judge Singh said the bomb placed in the park was similar to those manufactured in Top Hill, St. Patrick's, and that enough evidence was presented to prove that Russel Budhlall, Kenneth Budhlall and another person known as Bat-eye, and others formulated a plan to blow up Prime Minister Maurice Bishop and Deputy Prime Minister Bernard Coard on June 19, 1980.

Judge Singh said there was also evidence that Kenneth Budhlall and Bat-eye passed the devices to another person known as Yussuf, who then gave them to Grace Augustine and Fitzlyn Joseph to place in Queen's Park.

He drew attention to Fitzlyn Joseph's testimony that she was reminded about the time to place the bomb at the Park by Layne Phillip.

The Judge found that the only evidence produced against Roland Budhlall with bomb-making materials, adding that it proved nothing. He said that he was satisfied that Roland Budhlall lied in giving evidence, but that was however insufficient to convict him.

In his hour and a quarter submission, Judge Singh also spoke about the rule of law in Grenada. Last week defence counsels Frank Phipps and Israel Khan implored him to assure that the rule of law prevailed in the trial. The judge said that there was never any attempt to interfere with the judiciary during his two years in Grenada, and expressed confidence that the rule of law was secure.

A battery of ten lawyers participated in the two-week hearing and twenty-five witnesses were called by the prosecution.

FWI, November 3, 1982

IMPERIALISM ATTACKS WITH WORDS AND RUMOURS

"This is Major Basil 'Akee' Gahagan speaking. I would like everybody in Grenada to know that I am alive and well, in good health. I am not sick, and I am not dead."

When Grenadians heard the voice of one of the nation's most senior soldiers over Radio Free Grenada (RFG) this week, many were relieved.

And they had reason to be, because for the past few days, a strong rumour has been circulating that he was dead.

According to the rumour Major Gahagan and a large number of PRA soldiers had been killed in El Salvador, and were sent back to Grenada for burial.

Their bodies were supposed to be aboard a vessel anchored outside St. George's harbour since last week.

The rumour was spread in different ways, the numbers of dead soldiers varying from 50 to 200, and in one case, it said that they were being buried, five at a time, at night.

Major Gahagan's voice cleared it up: "I want everybody to know that I have never been to El Salvador, and that although our country is internationalist in outlook, we have never interfered in the internal problems of other states, and therefore none of our soldiers have ever been to fight in El Salvador".

The boat the rumour referred to turned out to be a Cuban vessel which had escorted the latest four fishing boats donated to Grenada by the Cuban government.

It had broken down soon after arrival, and was awaiting spare parts to return to Havana.

Major Gahagan, who spoke from the Grenadian embassy in Cuba, called on the PRG to "deal firmly" with those responsible for creating and circulating such rumours.

But it is not only Major Gahagan who wants such action. His resentment is shared by the majority of patriotic Grenadians, who have been fed an overdose of rumours since the Revolution.

These rumours circulating at home and abroad have become the reactionaries' weapon in their efforts to keep away tourists, frighten residents and destabilise the economy and the people's revolution.

Recently, one rumour was circulating in New York that a bomb had exploded at RFG, destroying the station. Another was that a bomb had exploded aboard a tourist ship in St. George's harbour, killing many tourists.

The most blatant propaganda effort, however, appeared in Aruba over the weekened, during Prime Minister Maurice Bishop's visit there to attend an international conference of the ruling party.

The same picture of a large crowd attending a flag-raising ceremony in the Dutch colony appeared in the two leading local newspapers. But while one paper acknowledged that it was the flag-raising ceremony, the other said it was a large crowd demonstrating against PM Bishop's visit.

This is all part of imperialism's plans and activities aimed at giving the Grenada Revolution a bad international image and destroying the PRG's image at home.

But, as with the Gahagan story, such rumours are doomed to failure as the people get to know the truth.

And, as a student said after hearing Major Gahagan's voice on RFG: "Imperialism attacks, not only with gunboats, but with words and lies as well."

FWI, March 28, 1981

VULGAR LIES ABOUT SOVIET PLANES, SAY PRG

A spokesman for the People's Revolutionary Government (PRG) has said that he views "with both amusement and utter contempt," a recent report appearing in the "Washington Times," which quoted extensively from the "publicity-seeking mercenary" Michael Sylvester.

In yet another ridiculous lie against the Grenada Revolution, Sylvester told the magazine that Grenada received in crates, 10 fighter planes from the Soviet Union recently, and that the Revolution was a threat to neighbouring countries.

The PRG spokesman said it is obvious that this latest attack on the Revolution is part of the general build-up to attempt to isolate the Revolution and eventually to set the basis for a mercenary or direct invasion of our land.

What is incredible, he said, is that imperialism now has to hide behind a known liar and madman, whom even corrupt Gairy had to get rid of for corruption and total loss of credibility. This, he pointed out, shows the extent to which imperialism will go. It is prepared to scrape the bottom of the barrel and literally go into the gutter to build a cage for isolating Grenada, he said.

Imperialist counter-revolutionary attempts at economic aggression and threats of direct or mercenary invasion, he noted, have not had the effect of slowing down the pace of the Revolution nor of reducing its popularity in the eyes of its neighbours.

Even more amusing, he said, the "Washington Times" went further and had the guts to report that the Grenada economy was now in shambles, despite the recent World Bank report to the contrary. . . .

Overall, the report was so positive that many who oppose the Revolution are green with envy over it, he said. "We can understand, therefore, why they must invent more lies everyday."

He said imperialism and counter-Revolution must understand that none of their crude and vulgar lies and outright slander will succeed in isolating the Grenada Revolution in the eyes of the masses in the region. The Caribbean people continue to come to Grenada to see for themselves the benefits that have come since 1979.

In fact, only last August, over 400 people from the region came to Grenada to participate in the Carnival celebration and to see the Revolution in action.

He noted that the attempts at isolating Grenada are bound to fail, pointing out that the Revolution will continue to be respected in the region and internationally, despite attempts by imperialism and their allies to make it seem like a threat to its neighbours.

FWI, October 20, 1982

28
The People's Armed Forces

Introduction

The People's Revolutionary Army (PRA) officially came into existence on March 13, 1979, when Hudson Austin (later General Austin) led his small band of fighters against Gairy's barracks. To all appearances the PRA became in time a well-armed and well-trained unit, though there were occasional mumblings about excesses on the part of individual soldiers.

In the tradition of revolutionary armies the PRA made efforts to feed itself and involve itself in various ways in the day-to-day activity of the people. Its protestations of loyalty to the people and to Commander-in-Chief Maurice Bishop (reproduced below) make poignant reading in light of the events of October 1983. The army was, as in most countries, supplemented by a militia force.

PRA TO FEED ITSELF

"Our army will move forward in 1981 with greater discipline, loyalty and dedication. As revolutionary soldiers we have a responsibility to be always on duty, on call 24 hours a day serving the interests of the masses and defending the Revolution . . . and by the end of this year the PRA will be able to feed itself, thereby easing a burden on our economy."

So pledged General Hudson Austin, commander of the nation's armed forces, at an impressive ceremony Tuesday, marking promotions in the People's Revolutionary Army.

Describing the event at Fort Rupert as historic and important, Gen. Austin said it represented the largest volume of promotions to higher ranks that they will witness for a long time. He added that the promotions will mean an increase in responsibility for our patriotic soldiers,

There were promotions from all ranks of the army and those who received promotions were acknowledged at the ceremony. Majors in the army are Brothers Ewart Layne, Tan Bartholomew, Einstein Louison and Chris DeRiggs.

Secretary for Defence and National Security, Bro. Hudson Austin has been promoted from the rank of colonel to general, and member of the PRG, Brother Liam James, is now a Lieutenant Colonel.

Stressing the urgency to increase production in this Year of Agriculture and Agro-Industry, the nation's top soldier promised that the PRA will contribute to this effort by producing enough food on its farm to feed itself "because our economy cannot continue to support us."

"Ours is not an army that can sit back and polish its boots. We must be engaged in productive work growing crops and rearing cows, sheep, goats, pigs and chickens. Furthermore, we will continue serving the masses in 1981 by stepping up our voluntary community work," he said.

Gen. Austin thanked the leaders of the New Jewel Movement for their "guidance, inspiration and commitment" and said that he and his soldiers "are always ready and willing to obey any order from our commander-in-chief, Prime Minister Maurice Bishop."

In addition to Cde Bishop, others in attendance included members of the Political Bureau, the commissioners and senior officers of the Police and Prison Services, captains of the People's Militia and the Police Band, which gave a stirring rendition of "Forward March Against Imperialism."

Congratulating those promoted Cde Bishop said the promotions "of our people in uniform" were not based on whim, on patronage or on any popularity contest. Instead, they were based on discipline, proficiency and efficiency, commitment to the people, loyalty to the Revolution, selflessness and self-sacrifice, responsibility and care for state property and fraternal spirit and attitude."

Echoing the importance Gen. Austin placed on agriculture, the PM described it as "the motor and heart of our economy," the productive sector, which provides money to pay salaries, to buy medicines, to import manufactured goods.

He applauded the army for getting more involved in agriculture and said that for the PRA, 1981 should be the year of production and defense. He also called on the nation's soldiers to increase discipline, efficiency and preparedness and to raise their political consciousness.

"As comrades on the front lines of the struggle you have a serious task," said Cde Bishop. "We are confident that you have the qualities and material to accomplish these tasks especially since you are led by Gen. Austin, an outstanding human being, a patriot and a fine revolutionary."

The programme ended with lively cultural presentations by Captain Cecil Belfon ("Flying Turkey") singing a revolutionary rockers number, "Innocent Blood Shed in Vain" and by Lieutenant Alan Lowe, offering two of his militant, anti-imperialist poems.

FWI, January 7, 1981

THE PEOPLE ARE ONE WITH THEIR ARMED FORCES

As the oath of the People's Revolutionary Armed Forces (PRAF) states, the primary duty of every soldier is to defend the Revolution, while being totally committed to the masses. He is to protect the Revolution's gains from any form of aggression, even to the extent of dying in the process.

Last year, PRAF members carried out many different activities in an effort to raise their political consciousness, increase their patriotism, and train for rigorous defensive combat. These activities were designed to make PRAF members more aware about who are the Grenadian people's real enemies, how to fight them, and when to do so, in defence of the Revolution.

A lot of time was also spent on classes geared at raising the armed forces' cultural level. "Because we don't know when the imperialist invasion will come, we have to be constantly prepared," said Deputy Secretary of Defence, Captain Chris Stroude, recently.

Also PRAF Chief of Education and Politics, Capt. Stroude said the preparations of leaders and officers at all levels in training schools went well. PRAF mobilised for many mass activities, such as rallies, conferences and seminars, among others, while doing voluntary construction work on projects such as the new international airport, feeder roads, camp buildings and St. Paul's Community Centre, along with repairing roads, cleaning drains, cutting overhangings, and painting different communities together with other villagers.

We moved from forces of divided sections to where Grenada now has a totally united, more organised and controlled armed forces," said Capt. Stroude. Army, people's militia, police, prisons, cadets, coast guard, fire service, immigration and security are now united under one banner, to move forward with one code of discipline.

"In January this year, we held our first anniversary, marking one year since all areas of the armed forces came together under a common banner." This brought a week of activities—Armed Forces Week, creating an avenue for PRAF members to display their talents in culture and sports. "All this showed we are moving from strength to strength," he said.

"Last year we were able to achieve many things while on our way to becoming self-sufficient," said Capt. Stroude. "This year we already gave ourselves the task of cultivating every square inch of land around our camps, while pushing different forms of production on our farm." Besides cash crops, PRAF will begin growing livestock on a large scale.

"In this Year of Economic Construction, with the energies, commitment, and dedication of us all, we feel confident of success in cutting waste, increasing production, and advancing the economy," he added.

Emulation programmes at all levels will begin soon, he added. The best individuals for a particular period would be selected as the most outstanding soldier, policeman, or militia member, as the case may be. This would generate greater discipline and more commitment, explained Capt. Stroude.

Meanwhile PRAF is looking at the possibility of publishing a journal which will highlight its members' creative works, along with other burning issues affecting PRAF systems and structures. Radio programmes on a consistent basis are also being considered.

Born with the March 3, 1979 Revolution, Grenada's PRAF started a new relationship between "the people in uniform" and the masses of simple, ordinary working people. Being good from the very first day, this relationship continued to blossom, "getting better and better."

"Our relations are particularly good because our armed forces are part of the masses; our armed forces and the masses are the same. We are not there to subdue, repress and oppress the people, but to assist them in building and defending the Revolution, while we march towards the new society," Capt. Stroude said.

In all the mock battles and defence trials, in all the route marches and manoeuvres, how Grenadians feel about PRAF was convincingly displayed. When the revolutionary troops were in the countryside and towns, in the bushes, and on the sea coast, the smiles on Grenadian faces, over stretching hands bearing food and drink for the hungry units, told the story of love and loyalty clearly enough for all.

The success of the two national manoeuvres held recently, consolidated PRAF's popularity. The "Heroes of the Homeland" manoeuvre was very significant in responding to the United States' hostile invasion manoeuvres last August, while mobilising thousands of Grenadians to show their willingness to fight, and die, if necessary, to defend the benefits they have won through sweat.

Grenada needs a powerful people-oriented armed forces, not one to threaten, intimidate, and make war on neighbours or peace-loving mankind, but one there to defend all Grenadian men, women and children as we build a new and just social order.

"The armed forces must come from the people themselves, and it must serve them and not harass them. All these qualities are being emulated and followed today in the PRAF."

This is very different from the past when Gairy's things, the "Green Beasts" army and Mongoose Gang secret police, got together to beat up innocent children.

FWI, **March 13, 1982**

THE ARMY AND THE ECONOMY—A SOLDIER'S VIEW

I was a delegate for the People's Revolutionary Army at the National Conference on the Economy, and a workshop leader at our local zonal council in St. David's.

At the conference the overall participation of the people was real good, with a lot of important contributions. The soldier delegates too came up with a lot of suggestions and concrete proposals as to how the economy could be developed to really meet the needs of the working people. We questioned ourselves hard on how we could cut down waste in the armed forces. For example, in our use of military vehicles and gasoline—and also the reckless driving which some young soldiers had been guilty of, resulting in a number of accidents and mashed-up vehicles. We became far more conscious of the cost of all this to the country and the people, and we were very self-critical. We also criticised ourselves for not being productive enough, and we came up with proposals to start up farms and really set about feeding ourselves seriously.

Since the budget process we have made sure that our accident rate has gone right down, and a log-book system has been implemented to keep a tight rein on the gasoline. If a driver takes unnecessary or longer routes than he should, he is now disciplined. Then in terms of the productive side we have developed plots next to our camps to grow corn, peas and cabbages, and we now have our own farm at Hopevale, near Calivigny, with sheep, goats, pigs, cows and fowl. Then at Camp Fedon we have as many as sixty beautiful pigs, and our target for the end of the year is two hundred. So the suggestions that were raised at the National Conference were taken very seriously by the PRA, and we now have a system where all the soldiers go on a once-weekly basis to work at the Hopevale farm.

Quite a number of our soldiers became leaders of parish workshops, and this helped very much to increase their confidence and ability to mix directly with the people. At St. David's Zonal Council I led the workshop with the local farmers. They didn't see it as strange that a soldier should be leading their discussion, as I know most of them and we often help local farmers in community activities and road repairs. Their main concern was with prices—not only the low prices they were getting for their nutmeg, banana and cocoa, but the high prices they were paying for their implements and fertilisers. They were also interested in finding markets for non-traditional crops like egg-plant, tomatoes and cabbages. Since March, they have certainly seen the price of fertilisers drop, so they know the government was listening to them.

In the Gairy days you would never find soldiers in activities like this, so close with people. He would never have brought the Budget to the people anyway, and his soldiers were only good for robbing and brutalising the masses and squandering their money, never working alongside them. We are trained to work with and consult the people all the time. Our army is of the people and our first duty is to the people. This is our sacred duty. So it is a natural process for us to be involved in the budget consultation, side by side with the people.

We had our own meetings too in the armed forces, and we discussed the issues of the Budget and the Economy ourselves. Each unit had its own council and we all agreed on the need to cut our food bill and eat local. What Grenada produces, we must eat! We should stop importing tinned foods when we could get the fresh thing here. It would make us more healthy too to fight imperialism!

Since the Budget process we have definitely seen a real change in our soldiers' consciousness and attitudes. They have begun to really understand what the economy is all about and how we must both cut back and produce. They now understand that they have to be actively involved in building the economy. Every now and again you would hear a comrade say, if we were dong some wastage or cooking too much food, 'You all want us to be parasites for the rest of we days?' Or you would see posters made by the soldiers saying that we must not forever live like parasites on the backs of the working people! The comrades are definitely much more economy-conscious now.

The Budget process also helped us to improve the cultural and educational level of the armed forces, and there is no doubt about that! This aspect is key for our development, and you would see its results in more of our posters in our camps, like: "The political, cultural and combative preparation is vital for defence!" Grenada has had enough of ignorant, brutal soldiers like Gairy's Green Beasts. We are a new type of soldier and our army is an army that respects as well as defends the people. One of our criteria is fraternal co-operation—how well you co-operate with your comrades and how well you relate to the people.

But looked at overall, the whole budget process clearly lifted the morale of the people. It has encouraged them to really work harder, produce more and build a people's Grenada. It did bring home the fact too that in Grenada we do have true democracy, and that our people are definitely running the country. They are the true managers of the economy.

It also had regional and wider international effects. It was certainly a booster to the other Caribbean countries to struggle harder to have people's government and build socialism in their own islands.

For me personally, it has made me a lot more conscious—even in terms of taking greater care of my uniform and boots, because they come from the people's money too! It has caused me to work harder in my community work and to struggle harder with the youth, so that we could be much more effective in building with the new society.

FWI, December 4, 1982

MILITIA PROCLAIMS LOYALTY

Militia Chiefs from the People's Revolutionary Militia of St. Andrew's were formally presented with their weapons by Commander-in-Chief of the People's Revolutionary Armed Forces (PRAF) Prime Minister Maurice Bishop, in an impressive ceremony at Seamoon, St. Andrew's, on Wednesday afternoon.

Properly uniformed militia units from throughout St. Andrew's turned out for the occasion and pledged aloud their loyalty to defend the gains of the Revolution and the Grenadian working people.

The weapons presented to the chiefs would be used solely to defend the Revolution, stressed political commissar, Francis Gill.

PM Bishop termed the occasion an "historic and momentous one," adding that "St Andrews' militia comrades have reached a high level of discipline and efficiency."

"People of St. Andrew's," he said, "can now feel a lot more confident that their Revolution is in good hands—in the hands of the militia."

He reiterated that a strong people's militia is a "bulwark and bastion for the Revolution's defence against both external and internal enemies."

According to PM Bishop, the Revolution has three main pillars that are closely inter-related: people's participation in the decision-making process, a strong national economy and national defence.

Strengthening the people's militia means building the national defence pillar, which cannot be separated from the other two, he said.

He urged the militia members to increase their level of skills and efficiency, deepen their political understanding and ensure that their structures and units are complete and consistent.

The St. Andrew's militia pledge, which he presented to PM Bishop, highlighted the danger U.S. imperialism poses to the Grenadian, Cuban and Nicaraguan revolution.

And, it pointed out, "our arms will never be used against the working people."

On Thursday in the Parish of St. Patrick's PM Bishop made a similar presentation to militia units from St. Patrick's and St. Mark's.

Also present were Minister of Agriculture, George Louison and Minister of National Mobilisation, Selwyn Strachan.

PM Bishop said that when he inspected the troops, he was pleasantly surprised to see a unit comprising several women. "It was really a heart-warming sight," he said.

"We are seeing one of three main pillars of the revolutionary process being solidified by this process," he said, adding that all three pillars needed to be standing at the same time.

"Our country, with a poor economy, can never reach the stage of having a permanent army and that is why the militia is of such importance," he explained.

Major Tan Bartholomew said that this was an extremely important day in PRAF's history. It had followed weeks and months of hard training.

"Over the past months, you have displayed your seriousness and determination to defend the Revolution at all times," he said, echoing compliments to the militia units for their training.

FWI, September 11, 1982

29
Invasion Threats

Introduction

The entire revolution was acted out against the backdrop of an overriding fear of invasion. In the early days it seemed that a mercenary force, backed by Gairy and the United States, might be the most likely scenario. As time went on, however, the possibility of a direct United States invasion seemed more and more plausible. Precedents for both were easy to come by. The mercenary Bay of Pigs invasion against Cuba in 1961 and the U.S. invasion of the Dominican Republic in 1965 were two of the more recent. Even as the PRG tried to consolidate in Grenada its Nicaraguan allies were locked in combat against the U.S. backed "contras."

And then in March of 1983 President Ronald Reagan dramatically announced to the world that Grenada was a threat to U.S. security. This came amidst a steadily escalating tempo of U.S. military manoeuvres in Caribbean waters and airspace. One of these exercises, the notorious "Amber and the Amberines" manoeuvre of 1981, was codenamed after Grenadian geographical locations. When the invasion finally did come in October 1983, it was shown to have been a rerun of well-rehearsed earlier manoeuvres.

Not insignificantly, Grenada accused some of its Caribbean neighbours of complicity in the developing invasion drama. President Reagan's visit to Barbados in April 1982 helped convince Grenada of this.

U.S. PRACTISES GRENADA INVASION

Only the force of international public opinion can stop a planned military invasion of Grenada by the United States' administration of Ronald Reagan, now that it has already been rehearsed, the People's Revolutionary Government has stated in a world-wide appeal.

The invasion rehearsal came in the Caribbean phase of the U.S. and its North Atlantic Treaty Organisation (NATO) allies' military manoeuvres, code-named Ocean Venture '81, and heralded by the U.S. Defence Department as "the largest maritime exercise" since World War II.

Over 120,000 troops, 250 ships and 1,000 aircraft from 14 nations are participating in the manoeuvres, from August 1 to October 15, stretching from the South Atlantic, through the Caribbean, to the Baltic Sea.

The Caribbean phase, co-ordinated by Rear Admiral Robert P. McKenzie, commander of the Caribbean Contingency Joint Task Force (CCJTF) at Key West, Florida, is being conducted at Vieques Island and Salinas in Puerto Rico and Guantanamo Bay in Cuba, from August 9-21.

According to the script of the first mock battle, rehearsed last week in Vieques, the target is the Eastern Caribbean country of "Amber and the Amberines," an obvious reference to Grenada and its island wards of Carriacou and Petit Martinique in the Grenadines.

"Amber" is described as being influenced by "Country Red" (obviously socialist Cuba) to "export terrorism to various countries in the Caribbean Basin" and engage in various "anti-democratic activities." These are propaganda themes used consistently by the Reagan administration against Grenada.

Amber is supposed to be supporting a guerilla movement of about 300-500 in "Country Azure," described as "a small island" with an inadequate police force.

U.S. military forces have been "invited" by Azure to neutralise the guerillas, the scenario says.

The practice invasion of Amber, "to rescue 20 U.S. citizens held hostage there after negotiations with the Amber government had broken down," began August 9, with a dawn parachute drop into Vieques of over 350 troops of the 75th Ranger Battalion, based in Fort Lewis, Washington.

The paratroopers flew during the night non-stop from Norton Air Force Base, California to Florida, covering roughly the same distance as from their Washington base to Grenada.

During the night, an unknown number of support combat troops landed in the western mountains of Vieques, to prepare for the drop.

Grenada also has mountainous terrain, the PRG noted, and the combat units used were specially trained for warfare in such rugged conditions.

The drop was followed up by the landing of 1,000 marines in amphibian units on Vieques' southeastern shore, and air assaults.

An area on Grenada's southern tip is called Amber, and is close to a security zone and the site of the international airport now being built, the PRG pointed out.

The battle supposedly lasts 17 days, while an unconventional force of Army Rangers, Navy underwater demolition teams and other special forces—"the guys that do the dirty tricks," says Navy Captain Dale Lewey—move to free the hostages on Amber Island.

After rescuing the hostages and seizing power, Rear Admiral McKenzie said the U.S. troops would stay on Amber Island until elections are called, and "install a regime favourable to the way of life we espouse" and opposed to the previous "unfriendly" Amber government.

Again, these are frequent U.S. propaganda themes against Grenada.

Justifying the need for the war games, McKenzie described Grenada, Cuba and Nicaragua as "practically one country," alleging that no passports or visas are necessary to travel among them.

"What we have here is a political-military problem," McKenzie said. "When Carter created the Task Force, he did it for political reasons. Now we see that it fulfills one of the most valid military reasons," which, he said, was the need "to respond to the activities of Cuba and Castro."

The manoeuvres, he said, would reinforce U.S. military commitment, and "give an example of one facet of U.S. capabilities to respond in the Caribbean basin."

Also taking part in the Caribbean phase, the U.S. Defense Department reported, are units from the Netherlands and the United Kingdom, both of which have colonies in the region.

"In addition to the Navy and Marine corps, U.S. participation," according to the Department, "will include Army Ranger and air assault forces, Air Force Military Airlift Command, Tactical Air Command, Strategic Air Command, and the North American Air Defense Command (NORAD), as well as elements of the Puerto Rico National Guard, along with reserve forces from all services."

Calling this development "shocking," the PRG noted that earlier intelligence reports it received, indicated that "either a mercenary invasion or direct U.S. military aggression" against Grenada, would take place before November 1981.

Noting its initiative to have the Caribbean declared a zone of peace, the PRG said these developments "pose a grave threat to our country and to the peace and security of the entire Caribbean."

"We firmly believe that the Caribbean will never be able to achieve true social justice and equality for its people in an atmosphere of tension and insecurity . It is surely the right of all peoples to develop their own processes in their own way, free from all forms of external dictation and pressure," the PRG said.

It therefore urged "all peace-loving and democratic peoples" to protest the threatening situation, and "ensure that the Reagan administration does not proceed with its monstrous plan."

FWI, August 22, 1981

GROUPS LASH U.S. MOVE

In the face of growing threat of United States' invading Grenada, a number of local and regional and international organisations have expressed strong support for the Grenada Revolution, and have condemned the current military maneouvres which are dress rehearsals for the attack.

Locally, solidarity statements have come from several mass organisations including the Media Workers Association of Free Grenada (MWAFG), the National Youth Organisation (NYO), The National Women's Organisation, the Trade Union Council, the People's Revolutionary Armed Forces and a number of New Jewel Movement support groups.

Internationally, support and solidarity have come from the Workers Party of Jamaica (WPJ), the Dominica Liberation Movement (DLM), the Canada/Grenada Friendship Society, the National Black United Front of the U.S., the United People's Movement (UPM) of St. Vincent, the People's Progressive Party of Guyana, the Grenada Revolutionary League of the U.S., the Antigua Caribbean Liberation Movement, the Trinidad and Tobago Peace Council, the February 18 Movement of Trinidad, the Council of Progressive Trade Unions of Trinidad, the Latin American and Caribbean Study Group of New York University, the Progressive Labour Party of St. Lucia, the Workers Revolutionary Movement of St. Lucia, the "Militant," organ of the Socialist Workers Party of the U.S., the NJM Support Group in the UK and the Movement for National Liberation of Barbados.

Expressing its deep concern at the threats, the MWAFG has called on all the media workers in the region "to condemn the obvious propaganda campaign directed against Grenada" and have urged all patriots to participate in the military manoeuvres at the end of this month.

NYO's firm statement of condemnation denounced the imperialist plan to invade Grenada, "two years after the new found freedom of the Grenadian people." It called on all youths to join the militia and participate in the national manoeuvre.

NYO stated it would not stand by "and" let imperialism attack the homeland. More than that, it would ensure that its entire membership would be in the forefront of the leading squads, platoons and battallions that would meet any invaders.

The Canada-Grenada Friendship Society asserted its "support for the Grenada Government, people and Revolution is based on the concrete evidence of the aspirations of this country for peace and progress, both within and without Grenada. . . . In the strongest possible language then, we condemn all attempts by the U.S. to terrify and destabilise the Grenada Government."

The DLM condemned the U.S. military manoeuvres and "denounce even more forcefully, the U.S. planned invasion of our sister island, Grenada, as a most obscene violation of the principles of international law. . . . We therefore call upon regional governments separately, and under the banner of Caricom, to bring pressure to bear on the U.S. military penetration into our region."

The UPM expressed severe concern about the U.S. military manoeuvres. "From all appearances it seems that these exercises are preparatory threats to an invasion of revolutionary Grenada. . . . The Caribbean must remain a zone of peace, and now, before it is too late, Caribbean leaders must issue a stern warning to the U.S. Government to desist from interfering in the internal affairs of Caribbean states."

The WPJ affirmed "total solidarity with the revolutionary people and government of Grenada, faced with the danger of U.S. military intervention in their internal affairs and is absolutely confident that the imperialists will pay a heavy price for such invasion. The WPJ further calls on Jamaica and other Caricom Governments to make known to the U.S. Government . . . their unqualified opposition to any further attempts to interfere in the internal affairs of the sister island of Grenada."

To celebrate the 94th birthday of one of the most popular Caribbean black heroes, Marcus Mosiah Garvey (1887–1940), the MWAFG and PRG will hold tomorrow a Block-o-Rama at the Market Square beginning at 2 p.m.

At 6 p.m. the action will be followed by a massive anti-imperialist rally which will focus on the U.S. military manoeuvres.

At the rally, former CIA officer Philip Agee will reveal how the CIA works to overthrow and/or destabilise progressive governments world-wide.

Prime Minister Maurice Bishop will give the feature address, centering around the country's preparation for the impending U.S. military invasion. In addition, leaders of Caribbean liberation movements will give solidarity messages.

Free transportation will be provided.

FWI, August 22, 1981

THE ELEPHANT VS THE ANT

We note with horror that Operation Ocean Venture '81 is the largest Western military exercise since World War II.

The Yankee imperialist plans to invade our country which have been designed by the crooked cowboys in the White House and the psychotic warlords in the State Department and the Pentagon represent the most vulgar and obscene display of brute force by a huge country against a tiny nation. It is like the elephant planning to crush the ant.

Moreover, it is yet another blatant example of imperialism's total disregard for the independence and sovereignty of other nations.

We remember the consistent pre-election campaign threats by candidate Reagan to deal with the Grenada Revolution after coming to power. We see all these threats materializing today.

We note the recent CBS television programmes in the U.S.A. which aired for five consecutive nights in the New York City area and branded Grenada as a police state. Only last week, CBS presented a new and equally damaging programme on Grenada.

We also recall the recent film, "Attack on the Americas" which was designed to tarnish the good names of the Grenadian, Nicaraguan and Cuban revolutions.

We note likewise the recent United States International Communication Agency conference attended by editors of all the national newspapers of the English-speaking Caribbean except Grenada and Guyana.

At that conference, propaganda plans against Grenada were finalized and this has led to systematic, coordinated attacks against the Grenada Revolution in recent weeks by the most reactionary newspapers in the region.

The objective of all this is undoubtedly to psychologically prepare the people of the region and the world for the impending military invasion.

Since information of Operation Ocean Venture '81 has been played down by the imperialist puppet media in the region we are calling on our fellow media workers throughout the Caribbean to fully expose the true meaning of these aggressive manoeuvres since they constitute a threat not only to the Grenada Revolution but to the peace and security of the entire Caribbean and to join the international appeal for the Caribbean to be declared a zone of peace.

We further call on our colleagues in the regional media to always seek the truth of the Grenada Revolution and not be a part of the imperialist propaganda destabilization campaign now being conducted against Grenada.

We also call on media workers in the U.S. itself to expose and condemn Reagan's military adventurism and his callous disregard for world peace.

We're living in dangerous times and therefore we must prepare ourselves for any emergency. Indeed, we need to put the country on a war footing.

Reagan and his gang may be crazy but they're not joking. They're dead serious, and those among us who don't believe this cowboy means business let them take heed. He and his administration which represent the reactionary ruling class and the military industrial complex of the U.S. are dead set on destroying all revolutionary gov'ts and movements of national liberation around the world.

Other countries have been in similar situations as ours and they have emerged victorious in the end which proves clearly that imperialism is not invincible.

FWI, August 22, 1981

U.S. INVASION THREAT GROWS

Grenada once again faces a threat of invasion from the United States. This is evident in the renewed manoeuvres codenamed "Red X 183" being carried out on Vieques, an island off Puerto Rico.

The manoeuvres, held last week, involved bombings on the island and the use of thousands of troops and dozens of U.S warships and planes.

These manoeuvres are part of the consequences of a two-day meetings of military chiefs from Latin America and the Caribbean (among them Jamaica, Barbados, Trinidad and Suriname), with top U.S. military men at the Pentagon, where they were briefed on how "to deal" with the development of popular people's movements in the region.

Since this meeting, there has been an obvious increase in the U.S.A.'s military presence in the region and also its propaganda attacks against countries which have won their liberation and those still fighting.

Since then, U.S. Secretary of State Alexander Haig has said that within a matter of days, Washington will make a "decisive move to deal with the source of the problems" in Central America and the Caribbean, and claimed that Cuba is engaged in actively destabilising Caribbean governments. It must be noted that two days after he made this statement, Seaga's government in Jamaica broke diplomatic relations with the Cuban government.

Haig's latest position on the process Nicaragua is building was manifested yesterday, in a statement he made before the U.S. House of Representatives, that he does not rule out U.S. assistance (not excluding direct invasion) for attempts to overthrow the Nicaraguan government.

This clearly reflects his support for Nicaraguan counter-revolutionaries and his willingness to turn back the Nicaraguan process. In answer to this, Nicaragua has expressed hope for support from Mexico in the event of a U.S. invasion.

During the joint sea, air and land exercises carried out in Honduras, close to Nicaragua's border, by Honduran and U.S. troops about a month ago, Haig stated that the Nicaraguan army is too large for the country's population.

The presence of one of the U.S. Navy's largest airplane carriers in Barbados waters now is a new addition to the U.S. military presence in the region, at a time of the U.S.A.'s major military exercises, and months after both countries carried out two manoeuvres on Barbados soil.

The U.S. claims that the carrier "S.S. Eisenhower" is on a goodwill visit to Barbados, but several political groups there do not share this view, as is evident from their protests. Among these groups is the People's Progressive Movement, headed by Bobby Clarke. The ship will carry out aerial displays.

These U.S. actions are not new in the region's history. These same methods of propaganda warfare and military build-ups were evident when the U.S. invaded Guatemala in 1953, and Cuba in 1961. These same tactics are now being used against Libya.

It is reported that the mood of Cubans now is similar to that in 1961, when the U.S. invaded the country—militant and fighting.

FWI, November 14, 1981

BE ALERT, PM TELLS MILITIA

The Grenada Revolution is in danger, along with other revolutions and revolutionary processes in the region, members of the region one militia were told by Prime Minister Maurice Bishop, at a meeting to issue ranks to militia members, Wednesday.

PM Bishop warned the militia members that there may soon be an invasion of El Salvador and Nicaragua at the same time, and also an attempt to invade Grenada or to step up counter-revolutionary activities here.

Now that the budget debate and the March 13 celebrations are over, he said, more attention must be given to the militia.

The next few days demand vigilance. This means militia members giving more time to training sessions to ensure that their units are ready, willing and capable to defend the country when the time comes.

PM Bishop said that a number of statements which strengthen his conclusions were made by the "Washington Post," a United States newspaper, and confirmed by Senator Barry Goldwater, an extreme rightist, and former presidential candidate.

The "Post" said that President Ronald Reagan had approved a plan by the Central Intelligence Agency (CIA) since November last year, to put aside $51 million (EC) to destabilise liberation forces in the region, and to finance a para-military force of 500 exiled elements to make sabotage against Nicaragua and other countries in the region.

PM Bishop said, however, that it would be madness for the U.S. to invade any progressive country. He quoted Voice of America radio as saying that some 87 per cent of the U.S. people are opposed to the U.S. fighting any war at present.

The U.S. economy was in shambles, he said, and although the military industrial complex thinks that a war can build it up, a war cannot sustain an economy for any length of time. Nearly all Reagan's allies are against his war policies and this is evident in the many peace marches in these countries.

Inside the progressive countries of the region, the people are willing to fight back and will not roll over and die.

The logical conclusion, PM Bishop said, is that it is irrational, illogical and insane for the U.S. to think of war, or sending troops to countries, but Reagan is behaving irrationally and desperately.

At the ceremony, PM Bishop called on the over 50 militia members given ranks to work and earn the respect of the other members because any disciplinary actions to be taken will be harder on those with stripes.

FWI, March 27, 1982

U.S. MANOEUVRES A DANGER, PM TELLS ROTARY

Prime Minister and Minister of National Security, Maurice Bishop, has described United States manoeuvres in the region last week as a total violation of the island's air space which endangered life in the region.

He made this statement on Thursday as guest speaker at a Rotarian luncheon at the St. James Hotel. He is the first Grenadian head of government to address Rotarians, who considered the occasion a red-letter day.

Speaking to the Rotarians on peace and understanding, their main focus as an international organisation this year, PM Bishop said the violation of the air space was "a classic example of the arrogance, contempt and insensitivity of the United States administration of Ronald Reagan."

Explaining how the manoeuvres began, he said that last Sunday night a message was received at Piarco airport in Trinidad, from the Washington Federal Aviation Administration Air Traffic Control System Command

Centre, telling Piarco air space controllers to advise all the countries in the region to which they were responsible that as from 3 a.m. the next day, only three hours notice, military manoeuvres will start in the region.

He said Grenada received the message, after 6 a.m. Monday, saying: "Danger area exists in Piarco, surface to flight 29,000 feet from 3.31 a.m. April 26 to 5 a.m. April 29. Instrument flight rules not permitted within 50 miles bounded by the following coordinates. . . ."

The area marked out, PM Bishop said, defined an irregular area in the Caribbean Sea to the west of Dominica in the north, Montserrat, St. Lucia, St. Vincent, Grenada and the Grenadines to the south. This area, he said, is approximately 100 miles north of Venezuela and 40–50 miles northwest of Grenada and 25 miles west of St. Lucia at its closest points.

It meant that Piarco suddenly had no control of the air lanes which the U.S. planes were going to use and that it would be unsafe for them to control flying in the region.

He continued that the move had serious implications for commercial and air traffic in the region because pilots had to use visual means in taking-off and landing.

It also meant that some pilots had to postpone flights until April 29 and that Piarco was no longer able to give technical coverage for a number of flights operating in the LIAT system.

PM Bishop said that when the Grenada authorities checked on the issue the next day "because we have no international airport to monitor the control tower at nights," they discovered that LIAT did not know officially until late on Monday.

The PM recognised the Rotarians' work over the 12 years of their existence in providing scholarships for students and equipments for the hospital among other things.

He told Rotarians that the world is threatened with war by the warmongering U.S. administration of Reagan, and at the same time, noted the growing peace movement internationally even right within the U.S.

Observing that the Rotarians can play a significant role in supporting world peace he urged them to struggle for peace, independence and development, and to invite their counterparts, especially those in the U.S., to come to see the realities of Grenada and eventually prevent the U.S. from invading with their mercenaries.

PM Bishop emphasised the importance of peace for development, saying that the two concepts are inseparable.

FWI, May 1982

PM CALLS PEOPLE TO ARMS

Making a final call to the United States for sanity, Prime Minister Maurice Bishop on Wednesday night warned Grenadians of an "imminent invasion" by U.S.-backed counter-revolutionaries, and urged them to prepare to defend their homeland and their birthright.

On a national address over Radio Free Grenada (RFG), the PM presented dramatic, new information, the most specific and detailed ever collected on any plot, which he said confirms the view that the Revolution faces its gravest danger yet of military aggression, backed by the U.S. administration of Ronald Reagan.

"The continuing economic crisis in the U.S. and its effects, the increasing successes of the popular liberation movements particularly in El Salvador, the continued deepening and strengthening of the revolutionary processes in Cuba, Nicaragua and Grenada, the total collapse of Reagan's so-called Caribbean Basin Initiative, and the growing popular opposition to his mad nuclear policy, have made imperialism more desperate and determined to halt revolutionary processes in this region," PM Bishop said.

And even as he talked, Reagan was on nation-wide radio and television, showing an aerial "spy plane" photograph of the international airport at Point Salines, claiming it was evidence of a "military airfield" in Grenada.

PM Bishop said the intelligence services have been gathering information on counter-revolutionary groups who have publicly declared their intention to overthrow revolutionary governments in the region, and have discovered that the key figures have been meeting more frequently recently, and have begun to resolve their leadership differences with the aim of creating a more united front.

Their co-ordination with the U.S. Central Intelligence Agency (CIA) has stepped up, he said, and they have got money, arms and training from the CIA, offers of transportation, logistical support and supplies, and a promise of recognition for their counter-revolutionary governments, as soon as they attack Grenada.

PM Bishop said the PRG knows the name and full background of the main CIA case officer co-ordinating the plot and the other revolutionary processes he has tried to subvert, as well as that another CIA case officer involved was also the director and mastermind of the bomb-blast attempt to assassinate the PRG in June 19, 1980.

The couner-revolutionaries have established links with the Cuban exile group responsible for the Air Cubana sabotage off Barbados in 1976, and with supporters of the late Nicaraguan dictator Anastasio Somoza.

With CIA help, they have been able to get criminals trained in Miami, in the same camps that have trained various mercenaries and the Somocistas now involved in the invasion of Nicaragua, he said.

The CIA, he added, allocated different groups for the invasion of Nicaragua and Grenada, and planned several weeks ago to attack during this period, to coincide with the massive U.S. military manoeuvres taking place in the region.

PM Bishop said the main base of operations is in a neighbouring territory, a few miles away.

The PRG knows, he said, not only of the actual plan to overthrow it, but also of the actual period in the near future they are hoping to use.

It also knew the approximate number of men to be used, the number and type of arms they have, the kind of logistical support they expect, the targets they intend to destroy, the persons they plan to arrest, those they plan to kill and "and how they plan to strike terror and fear among the broad masses," he added.

Noting that the U.S. has intervened militarily in this region well over 100 times in the past 100 years, the PM said that when Reagan, commander-in-chief of one of the largest and most advanced armies in the world, classifies a tiny island as a threat to U.S. national security, "this must be cause for serious concern."

Therefore, he called the people to arms, saying "we have to shoulder our fundamental responsibility to defend what we fought for and won after many years of bitter struggle."

The fundamental duty is to be prepared for attack in whatever form or at whatever time it comes, he said, urging people to join or reactivate themselves in the People's Militia.

He stressed that there was a role for everyone—even the elderly and the young, to play in time of war, since invaders do not choose who to kill.

"There are trenches to be dug, vehicles to be driven, food to be cooked and distributed, first-aid assistance to be organised, the care of the young and elderly to be guaranteed, and many more specific tasks."

PM Bishop also announced that there will be recruitment into some sections of the People's Revolutionary Army and the Police Service, and there will be a massive military manoeuvre, the "Jeremiah Richardson Defence of the Homeland Manoeuvre" from April 21–24.

However, he added, "even at this late hour, we want to repeat that our preference is for peace and normal relations with the U.S. administration.

"We do not want war," he said, noting that only an environment of peace would allow Grenada and Grenadians to develop.

Nevertheless, he added, "we are not prepared to give up our birthright or to allow others—no matter how big and powerful they are—to shape our destiny for us, or to tell us what we can do, when we can do it, and how we must do it."

FWI, March 26, 1983

GEN. AUSTIN—IT'S THE PEOPLE THAT WIN WARS

Ordinary Grenadians are the country's defence and are armed to defend every aspect of the Revolution, General of the Armed Forces and Minister of Construction and Public Utilities, Hudson Austin, said Thursday.

In a special session of the radio and television programme "Perspective '83," he said that members of the Grand Mal militia had intercepted a boat without lights with five men approaching shore near the Emulsion plant and fuel storage tanks.

The Coast Guard also intercepted a Venezuelan ship with South Korean and Venezuelan crew, fishing in our waters last Sunday. Militia members guarding Pearl's Airport apprehended a foreigner walking around the airport at 2 a.m. on Thursday, and have turned him over to the security forces for questioning.

He commented that the militia was the "eyes and ears" of the Revolution. "Imperialism," he said, was always afraid of a country's militia, because they are not easily identified and are everywhere. Armies, he said, can't win wars, only a people knowing what they're fighting for.

The defence plans for key economic installations are in the militia's hands, Austin said.

This latest invasion threat to the Revolution is the most serious so far, he said, because it is the first time that a United States president has attacked the country twice within days.

U.S. President Ronald Reagan's national broadcast on U.S. radio and television Wednesday night, when he showed a photo of the international airport at Point Salines, saying it was a military base, has reaffirmed the seriousness of his threats.

In response to this claim, Gen. Austin said that U.S. medical students at the St. George's University School of Medicine, know that Reagan's claims are false, since they are located at the end of the runway, and run in the vicinity daily.

The PRG, through its ambassadors in the U.S., has been mobilising international condemnations of plans to invade the country, and has scored some success. Groups and organisations, such as the Black Caucus of the

U.S. Congress, have been sending the PRG letters protesting Reagan's claims that Genada is a threat to U.S. national security.

Minister of Foreign Affairs Unison Whiteman is now in the United States, and with ambassadors Dessima Williams and Caldwell Taylor, is mobilising Grenadians to protest the planned invasion.

Here in Grenada, General Austin urged the people to join the militia and receive military training, to get together and do whatever is necessary to secure food, young children and old people, and to begin digging trenches.

To the "doubting Thomases" who believe that Grenada wouldn't be attacked while there were U.S. citizens here, Gen. Austin pointed out that when Cuba and the Dominican Republic were attacked, there were U.S. citizens there.

Asked if the PRG had notified the neighbouring country where it had identified local counter revolutionaries gathering to invade Grenada, Gen. Austin said, it wasn't always necessary to notify a government of these things, particularly when the government knows of them.

The PRG was waiting, he said, to see what that government had to say.

The Jeremiah Richardson Defence of the Homeland Manoeuvre, planned for April 22 and 23, has nothing to do with the expected invasion, which may come in a few days, Gen. Austin said. It is to commemorate the martyrdom of Richardson, shot in April 1973 by a policeman of the Gairy regime.

He compared the upcoming manoeuvre with the ones the U.S. is conducting in Caribbean water and airspace. Grenada's manoeuvre was to practise how to defend the country from invasion, while the U.S. one is to prepare to land troops to invade other countries.

Gen. Austin, reiterated that Grenada's relations with the Soviet Union and Cuba were purely economic, and that Grenada had the right to choose its own friends.

FWI, March, 1983

PRG ON DIPLOMATIC OFFENSIVE

Putting confidence in world public opinion, the People's Revolutionary Government (PRG) has launched a diplomatic offensive to alert the world of the danger it faces from an invasion backed by the United States administration of Ronald Reagan.

This has become increasingly clear through frequent verbal attacks made in the past few weeks by Reagan and other top U.S. administration officials, speaking of a massive military build-up in Grenada, and characterising Grenada as a threat to U.S. national security.

The most recent attack came Wednesday night from Reagan himself in a national radio and television broadcast, beamed by satellite throughout the world.

Speaking of a "Soviet military build-up" in the Caribbean region, Reagan showed three aerial spy-plane photographs: two of Cuba, one of Nicaragua and one of the international airport at Point Salines in Grenada, all obviously taken in violation of the countries' national air space.

The Point Salines airport he cited as an example of "the rapid build-up of Grenada's military potential."

This and a similar statement from Reagan on March 10, follows the invasion of Nicaragua by well-armed counter-revolutionaries last week, and ongoing U.S. military manoeuvres in the region.

The success of Reagan's attempts to arouse U.S. public interest in Grenada is indicated by two visits from U.S. television companies.

An NBC-TV news crew came last week, and on Thursday, following Reagan's last speech, an ABC-TV crew came to interview Prime Minister Maurice Bishop.

The ABC crew hoped to fly out on Thursday night, to put the PM's interview on TV immediately. However, because there are not night-landing facilities at Pearl's Airport, they were unable to leave, demonstrating to them the necessity of the international airport.

Before they left Friday, the ABC crew toured the international airport site.

Foreign Affairs Minister Unison Whiteman, who is now in New York at the United Nations, said that the focus on Grenada is so deep, that every few minutes on TV there is something about Grenada.

The PRG has made an official response to the U.S. Embassy in Barbados, again pointing out the civilian nature of the airport, as confirmed in a hearing of the U.S. House of Representatives' Subcommittee on Inter-American Affairs of the Committee on Foreign Affairs, on June 15 last year.

A copy of this letter to the U.S. Embassy has been sent to the Caribbean Community Secretariat in Guyana.

Ambassador Dessima Williams, delivered a similar letter to OAS secretary-general Alejandro Orfila.

Congressman Ron Dellums of California, a member of the Armed Forces Committee, said that before visiting Grenada, he had visited the headquarters of both the Atlantic Fleet and the Air Defense Command

and on both occasions was assured that the international airport "is of no consequence" to the U.S. and "further, it has not now or ever presented a threat to the security of the U.S."

The PRG expects that once the world is aware of the threat tiny Grenada faces from the mighty U.S.A. the shock and indignation that will follow will force the U.S., to hold back its hand, as it was forced to do after the 1981 practice invasion of "Amber and the Amberines."

It has also written to the President of France, the Prime Ministers of Spain, Sweden, and Greece, the Chancellor of Austria, the secretary general of the Commonwealth of Nations and Jamaica's Opposition leader, Michael Manley, who is also a vice president of Socialist International.

All the letters underscore Grenada's repeated attempts to establish good relations with the U.S.

The diplomatic staff in the U.S. are also mobilising support among U.S. Senators, Congressmen and university people.

In addition, the PRG has written its case to the U.S. Senate Foreign Relations Committee, the House Foreign Affairs Committee, the Inter-American Sub-Committee and the Congressional Black Caucus.

On Thursday, as the UN Security Council debated Nicaragua's complaint of aggression backed by the U.S., Grenada was given the floor as an "interested party."

Grenada's Ambassador to the UN, Caldwell Taylor, underscored Grenada's support for Nicaragua's charges and also spoke for seven minutes on the threat facing Grenada.

FWI, March 26, 1983

SOLIDARITY COMING FROM ALL QUARTERS

In wake of the invasion threat against Grenada and the current United States-backed invasion of Nicaragua, solidarity messages expressing support for the Grenadian people and Revolution have been coming from various quarters, regionally and internationally.

The Libyan government, in a statement issued by its foreign liaison bureau, reaffirmed "the Libyan people's support and solidarity with the Grenadian people and other friendly Latin American peoples."

It noted that Foreign Minister Unison Whiteman, at a meeting of all ambassadors accredited to Grenada, including Libya's, informed them of hostile U.S. threats against the country.

These threats started last year December when U.S. vice-president George Bush attacked Grenada at a press conference in Miami, and escalated recently when U.S. President Ronald Reagan alleged that Grenada poses a threat to U.S. national security.

The military threat against Grenada, was real, particularly in light of the invasion of Nicaragua and naval manoeuvres now being carried out by U.S. battleships in the Caribbean Sea.

"All these hostile U.S. acts," the statement ended, "deserve strict condemnation by the world community and the unification of the world's progressive forces to deter U.S. aggression.

In Canada, Dan Heap, Member of Parliament of the New Democratic Party (NDP), condemned the Reagan administration's campaign of blackmail and threats against Grenada, and its using the international airport as an artificial pretext to justify such attacks.

Speaking in the House of Commons, Heap emphasized that the airport is being built to attract foreign tourists, adding that the British firm of Plessey Airports Ltd., and Finland, France and Venezuela are also involved in construction efforts.

On Monday, a demonstration to protest U.S. interference in the affairs of Central American and Caribbean peoples and to denounce its imperialism's subversive activity against revolutionary Grenada and Suriname was held in Guyana's capital, Georgetown.

The demonstrators called on all Latin American states to raise their voice in defence of Caribbean peoples, especially through the Organisation of American States (OAS), from Reagan's aggressive plans.

In condemning the counter-revolutionary invasion of Nicaragua, the Dominica Liberation Movement (DLM) said: "We regard this latest act as a U.S.-organised attempt to turn back not only the Nicaraguan Revolution, but also the revolutionary processes in Cuba, Grenada and Suriname, the liberation movement in El Salvador and the anti-imperialist movement in the region."

Meanwhile, right wing Jamaican political scientist and commentator, Prof. Carl Stone on Monday called on Caribbean peoples to reject attempts by the U.S. to provoke militarism in the region and suggested to the Edward Seaga Government that it "whisper" to Reagan that his approach will produce more enemies than friends for Washington.

Sone, a supporter of Seaga and his Jamaican Labour Party (JLP), made this point in an article in the reactionary Jamaican "Daily Gleaner" newspaper.

Criticising Reagan's aggressive approach to Caribbean and Central American problems, Stone added: "The idea that tiny states like Nicaragua and Grenada represent threats to U.S. security is a simple-minded and ludicrous distortion of regional power realities that insults the leaders of the region who are asked to believe this nonsense."

He said Reagan's allegations that Grenada was not tied to the so-called Soviet military axis placed it in "pretty much the same target for aggression as had earlier U.S. pronoucements on Nicaragua.

"The political conflicts in Nicaragua, Stone stressed, "have a basis that is quite independent of either the United States [or] the Soviet Union. Clearly their outcome so far has not comforted the States, and the same can be said for Grenada."

According to Stone, the interest of Caribbean people would never be served "by giving our support and endorsement to this U.S. effort to provoke militarism.

"The countries of the region have a responsibility to mobilise regional support for peace initiatives and de-escalation of military aggression through the OAS, the United Nations and other regional and international bodies which can help defuse what is building up as a serious threat to regional security."

FWI, April 1, 1983

GUNBOAT SIGHTED OFF PT. SALINES

A foreign gunboat was sighted some three to five miles off Point Salines, near the almost completed international airport, on Monday night.

Coast Guard patrol boats saw the boat at around 11:15 p.m. while patrolling Grenada waters. The gunboat remained in the Point Salines area for about three hours, and then moved slowly up the north coast, according to a Ministry of Interior spokesman, "well within our territorial waters." It then disappeared.

The Coast Guard approached the gunboat and tried to establish contact through radio, but received no response. They came close enough to it, however, to note some numbers written on its stern. They saw no name.

The grey gunboat was reported to have shone a powerful light on the Coast Guard vessel, "blinding" its crew, when it approached.

On Monday morning, the vigilant Coast Guard crew rounded up three United States trawlers, but soon let them go after checking them.

FWI, April 1, 1983

THIRD U.S. MANOEUVRE IN 18 MONTHS

The United States military manoeuvre now being held in the Caribbean Sea, is the third in 18 months, to be held in the region.

The manoeuvre, code-named "Readex," was preceded in May 1982 by "Ocean Venture '82" and in August 1981 by "Ocean Venture '81."

"Readex," which began in January in the Caribbean Sea near the Honduran border with Nicaragua, has, according to U.S. Navy Secretary Lehman, 77 ships, six of which are British warships, and one Dutch vessel.

The manoeuvre, he said, was designed to "reflect the lessons learned from the Falklands war between Argentina and Britain. We are applying the kind of tactics and lessons learned in the Falklands," he said.

Commercial flying in various parts of the Caribbean, and just north of Grenada, has become dangerous for pilots and passengers because of 300 aircraft in the manoeuvre.

Between March 23 and 27, pilots were forced to use their eyes only, rather than instruments, to check for air traffic on routes.

A message from Piarco Airport in Trinidad to Pearl's control tower here stated that "due to intensive military operations, military hazards to aircraft and missile firing, San Juan Centre (Puerto Rico control tower) will not accept instrumental flight ruled aircraft" within 50 nautical miles of some areas listed.

The manoeuvres, which mainly affect an area east of San Juan, and countries further north in the Caribbean, are close enough to Grenada to cause concern.

Grenadians leaving here for Puerto Rico or Anguilla, or Trinidadians leaving for the Dominican Republic, will get no guidance from the San Juan control tower, since it considers the area dangerous, and has thus restricted commercial traffic.

Pearl's control tower has not yet received any surety that the area is now safe. The warning is active from the surface up to 41,000 feet.

Meanwhile, the Puerto Rican based Caribbean Project for Justice and Peace (CPJP) has expressed concern for what it calls the "increased participation of the Puerto Rican National Guard (PRNG) in the Central-American Caribbean Region."

It claims that PRNG has had units participating in both Ocean Venture '81 and '82 manoeuvres, as well as in the Honduran-United States war manoeuvres which began on January 20.

The manoeuvres later grew, with forces from the North Atlantic Organisation (NATO) joining. Over the past weeks, the U.S. has had battleships in a number of Caribbean ports.

The CPJP fears that the U.S. will eventually use the PRNG to repress activities within Honduras and in military operations against the Salvadorean freedom fighters and Nicaraguan Revolution.

FWI, April 1, 1983

N.W. ST. GEORGE'S CALLS FOR MORE MILITIA TRAINING

Expanded militia training and more shooting practice for old militia members, as well as immediate training for new recruits, were called for by residents of northwest St. George's on Monday.

At a zonal council meeting held at the Bernadette Bailey Secondary School to discuss their role in defence, the residents called for duty time for militia members guarding intallations to be so organised as not to wear them out.

They called for training for volunteer drivers to learn to use army transport, and have advised that medical supplies be stockpiled.

A security committee was formed at the meeting to lead security work in the area. Places were identified for child-care and first-aid training.

Addressing the meeting, Deputy Minister of Defence and Interior Liam James said that within the past few weeks, counter-revolutionaries in the United States have been meeting in Venezuela and Miami, with Cuban exiles responsible for the 1976 Air Cubana bombing, as well as with Nicaraguan counter revolutionaries.

The counter-revolutionaries have a three-man leadership, and are being directed by a U.S. diplomat in a neighbouring country.

FWI, April 1, 1983

U.S. MANOEUVRE ON VIEQUES

The United States Pentagon has announced that another military manoeuvre is taking place in the Caribbean, in the island of Vieques, east of Puerto Rico.

The manoeuvre, code-named "Universal Trek," began on May 31 and will go on for a month, it said. About 5,000 U.S. troops and fighter planes are taking part.

U.S. Naval officials told the Voice of America on Thursday night that the manoeuvre is "to show how U.S. forces could land in a small Caribbean nation where a civil war is taking place."

Vieques Island was the scene in August 1981, of another U.S. military manoeuvre, part of the North Atlantic Treaty Organisation (NATΘ) exercise code-named "Ocean Venture '81."

In that exercise, U.S. forces practised an invasion of "Amber and the Amberines," an obvious reference to Grenada and its Grenadines island wards of Carriacou and Petit Martinique.

The U.S. Navy's latest destroyer, the "U.S.S. Hayler", arrived in Bridgetown, Barbados, last Friday for a five-day visit.

The U.S. Information Service there said the ship has 280 men. It is also reportedly equipped with guided missiles and sophisticated electronic gear.

Last week also, two other NATO warships were in Bridgetown harbour. They were the British ships, "HMS Olna" and "HMS Penelope", on their way back to England from the Malvinas (Falkland) Islands off Argentina, in the South Atlantic.

FWI, June 11, 1983

Militia women. *Free West Indian*